Great Risks Had to be Taken

Great Risks Had to be Taken

The Jesuit Response to the Second Vatican Council, 1958–2018

PATRICK J. HOWELL, SJ

 CASCADE *Books* • Eugene, Oregon

GREAT RISKS HAD TO BE TAKEN
The Jesuit Response to the Second Vatican Council, 1958–2018

Cascade Books
An Imprint of Wipf and Stock Publishers
199 W. 8th Ave., Suite 3
Eugene, OR 97401

www.wipfandstock.com

PAPERBACK ISBN: 978-1-5326-6179-2
HARDCOVER ISBN: 978-1-5326-6180-8
EBOOK ISBN: 978-1-5326-6181-5

Cataloguing-in-Publication data:

Names: Howell, Patrick J. |

Title: Great risks had to be taken : the Jesuit response to the Second Vatican Council, 1958–2018 / Patrick J, Howell

Description: Eugene, OR: Cascade Books, 2019 | Includes bibliographical references and index.

Identifiers: ISBN 978-1-5326-6179-2 (paperback) | ISBN 978-1-5326-6180-8 (hardcover) | ISBN 978-1-5326-6181-5 (ebook)

Subjects: LCSH: Jesuits History. | Jesuits. | Religion Institutions and Organizations. | Autobiography. | Vatican II.

Classification: BX3706. H45 2019 (print) | CALL NUMBER (ebook)

Manufactured in the U.S.A.   FEBRUARY 12, 2019
I'm grateful for these permissions:

America Media, Inc. for cover photo of Pope Francis; Gonzaga University Archives for photo of Jack Kennedy and students; Seattle University Archives for several photos; Oregon Province Archives for material related to Jesuits and mental illness

Dedication

To all young Jesuits in their stages of formation
that you might enjoy the graces and blessings
for the next fifty years, as I have for the last fifty.

"Great risks have to be taken in many places," Arrupe stated. And then he explained: We made a communal discernment and set out in a certain direction. No discernment gives us 100 percent certitude. We make mistakes, we move on. "The elasticity of this experimentation and risk-taking should be all in one direction—the direction pointed out by the Holy Spirit." — Pedro Arrupe (August 6, 1981)

Acknowledgements

A GREAT CLOUD OF witnesses, including Jesuit mentors like Joe Conwell, Jack Leary, Dan Shine, Frank Furlong, Ed McDermott, Mike McHugh, and Jim McDonough, who have gone on before us, have been an inspirational presence that pervades whatever I have recorded here. Other Jesuits steeped in the traditions of the Society have also been my companions for the book, as will be evident from the frequency with which I quote some of them: Howard Gray, John W. O'Malley, Pat O'Leary, Pat Lee, Steve Sundborg, Bob Grimm, Paul Fitterer, John Fuchs, and Michael Buckley. And I am grateful for Dr. Bill Zieverink, companion of my interior life and of the mental health of the Society of Jesus. My colleagues, friends, and students at the School of Theology and Ministry have helped me realize the fullness of grace unleashed by the Second Vatican Council. Seattle University Fr. David Leigh, SJ and Fr. James Eblen, a priest of the Archdiocese of Seattle, were immensely helpful in raising questions and proofing my text. My long-time friend Charlie Allen provided key insights on the upheaval in Jesuit high schools, and Jerry McKevitt was my boon companion in all the trials and triumphs of writing.

Catherine Punsalan Manlimos, director of the Institute for Catholic Thought and Culture, has been a crucial support for finishing the manuscript. And I am grateful to Wipf & Stock for their innovative publishing process and for the assistance of their editors throughout the production. My dear friends Terri and Joe Gaffney have shared this journey with me, and my Jesuit brothers at the Arrupe Jesuit Community at Seattle University supported me day in, day out for all the thirty-three years I have lived there. My parents, my brothers and sisters, my twenty-three nieces and nephews, our expanded family have been my lifetime companions and support in this journey for which I am forever grateful.

Patrick J. Howell, SJ
Seattle University
Pentecost, 2018

Table of Contents

1

A Lifetime of Discernment

THIS IS THE STORY of the transformation of the Jesuits from 1958 to 2018. Inspired by the Second Vatican Council, 1962 to 1965, which had been convoked by Pope John XXIII in January 1959, the Society of Jesus largely refounded itself during these sixty years. It responded to the mandates of the Council with courage, obedience, integrity, and fidelity. Its efforts were sometimes marked by mistakes and missteps, but it sought to discern the dynamic, surprising action of the Holy Spirit. I first wrote a short piece with this theme for *Conversations* magazine.[1] At that time, as I scanned the web and consulted a few Jesuit experts, I was surprised to discover that no one had yet attempted this project. So I felt impelled to take it on. I have lived in the midst of all these changes since I was fortunate to have entered the Society of Jesus in 1961 just as the Council was about to get underway. It has been a terrific time to be a Jesuit, a priest, and a Catholic.

My primary focus will be the Society of Jesus' response to the Council's mandate to all religious orders to return to the sources of all Christian life, to retrieve the inspiration of its founder, and to adapt to the changing times.[2] The Jesuits began the process immediately, but it took decades before the main features of the modern Society were in place.

---

1. Patrick J. Howell, SJ, "The 'New' Jesuits."
2. Pope Paul VI, "The Up-to-Date Renewal of Religious Life."

We Jesuits are neither the ideals described in our founding *Constitutions* nor the sinister papal army described by our detractors. We are like the rest of society, a combination of strength and weakness, grace and sinfulness, energy and apathy. Our charism is a hard-earned realism inspired by the beauty of God who graces all things. Our General Congregation 32 in 1974 to 1975 gives an accurate account of what it is to be a Jesuit today. "It is to know that one is a sinner, yet called to be a companion of Jesus, as Ignatius was."[3] Our sinfulness and weakness teach us about God just as much, perhaps more, than our talents and strengths. We learn over many painful mishaps, we integrate that darker side into our spiritual autobiographies, and this unexpected grace becomes self-liberating.

I relate the story from my own limited, but engaged perspective as a Jesuit who has lived through all the changes. And so woven through the mega story of these last sixty years, beginning with the election of Angelo Roncalli as Pope John XXIII in the fall of 1958, is my own small part in it. The strength of my perspective is that I had a glimpse of what the old society was like and the riches it had to offer, and I played a role within the unfolding of the sixty-year discernment of wherever we were headed. My focus is necessarily that of an American Jesuit since I'm not equipped to handle the much broader, worldwide changes. However, some of these global changes directly affected the Society in the United States, so I will describe some of their impact on the attitude and lives of American Jesuits.

The year 2016 marked the fiftieth anniversary of the close of the Jesuits' General Congregation 31 in 1966, which inaugurated the updating of all dimensions of our religious life and apostolic work. The year closed with GC 36, which elected a new Superior General Arturo Sosa from Venezuela to replace Father Adolfo Nicolás. Sosa is the first general of the Society born outside of Europe. So the span of sixty years is a particularly appropriate bracketing of time to discern how God has worked in and through the joys and sorrows, hopes and fears of the Jesuits in the midst of this transformation. I will track some of the significant turning points in this journey and delve into key factors and world events which impacted the long-term outcome of the Second Vatican Council.

When Pope John XXIII convoked an ecumenical council on the feast of St. Paul on January 25, 1959—just three months after his election

3. "Jesuits Today," Decree 2, no. 1.

as pope, I was a freshman at Gonzaga University and only vaguely aware of what was occurring. I had no idea of the revolution about to begin. I was more interested in the fact that the new pope a year unexpectedly elevated the bishop of Fargo, my home diocese, as one of the new cardinals.[4] When Roncalli, the seventy-seven-year-old patriarch of Venice, was elected pope, most had expected a transitional papacy, which would continue in the same vein as the previous pope Pius XII—a cautious steadying of the ship and a continuance of the church's wary stance towards cultural innovations. Even the cardinals to whom Pope John announced his intentions about convoking an ecumenical council were taken by surprise.[5]

Multiple events hovered over the beginnings of Vatican II. The world, especially Europe, had suffered two devastating world wars, and the Great Depression. Throughout the 1950s and 1960s developing countries were seeking the overthrow of exploitative colonial powers. And, as many have observed, after the Holocaust of World War II and the horrible tragedies of the Nazi concentration camps, Catholic theology could never be the same again—Jewish-Christian relationships had to be radically reconceived. Europe had witnessed the bombing and devastation of its cities, the massive displacement of peoples, and the reality of the Soviet gulags. And on the consciousness of all thoughtful religious leaders was the unleashing of the atomic bomb, the development of the hydrogen bomb, and the accelerating arms race by the United States, the USSR, and their surrogates. After having borne the brunt of all these changes and often devastating events, my parents and grandparents were cautious about success and frugal with their resources. During the Korean War, for instance, we kept a fifty-pound bag of sugar in the closet—against the day when sugar might be rationed again.

In grade school we had gone through the drill of what to do in case of a bomb by crawling under our wooden desks. Even as a ten year old, I found these exercises rather silly. What I do recall though, from when

4. Aloisius J. Muench had simultaneously been Bishop of Fargo and Papal Nuncio to Germany in the years following World War II. John XXIII, who had been papal nuncio to France during some of the same time, 1945–1953, would undoubtedly have known him well. My mother dated Bishop Muench's nephew when she lived in Fargo around 1936.

5. The eight French cardinals were vigorous supporters of Roncalli in the conclave for the election of the pope during the eleven ballots of voting. Because of their experience of him as nuncio to France, they may have had an inkling of how strong, pastoral, and forthright he would be. See Hebblethwaite, *Pope John XXIII*.

I was about eight years old, was my horror at seeing magazine photos of the cadaverous bodies of those who had been gassed or died in the Nazi concentration camps.

Up through the 1950s the church itself was still in a highly defensive posture—over and against Protestantism and modern philosophy. It maintained a fortress mentality stretching back to the bloody, political overthrow of the *ancien regime* in France in 1789, which began the dismantling of the political and economic power of the church itself, especially the Papal States. Likewise, the Enlightenment had, in the terms of the philosophies of the day, attacked the superstitions and perceived manacles of religion.

However, the battle cry of freedom—"Liberté, Égalité, Fraternité ou la Mort," liberty, equality, fraternity or death—was viewed with a great deal less enthusiasm by the church than it was by liberated, freedom-loving peoples. All the understandable, defensive reactions by the Catholic Church led to what the eminent church historian John O'Malley, SJ, called "the long 19th century for the Church," a defending of the ramparts—lasting in effect from 1789 to 1965, that is, from the beginning of the French Revolution until the close of the Second Vatican Council.[6]

In considering this epoch prior to the Council, I will highlight a sample of the Jesuit contributions or resistances, and I will identify a few of the many spiritual and ecclesial forces at work in the years prior to the Council. My goal is not a detailed history, but to give a living sense of all the pent up energies unleashed by the Council.

What seems indisputable is how the Fathers of the Council brought front and center initiatives by theologians previously suppressed either by Pope Pius XII or by his inquisitional watchdog Cardinal Alfredo Ottaviani in the Holy Office.[7] The Council Fathers also vigorously affirmed the role of the laity by reason of their baptism. The bishops, gathered from all over the world,[8] deemed the scholarship and well-honed insights of theologians engaging the ancient sources and the modern world as

6. John W. O'Malley, SJ, *What Happened at Vatican II?* This masterpiece is essential reading for anyone reviewing the history, the meaning, and the enduring importance of the Second Vatican Council.

7. The previously suspect *nouvelle theologie* of Henri de Lubac, SJ, Jean Danielou, SJ, Yves Congar, OP, and others would be prime examples.

8. Though the statistics vary, 2,860 bishops participated in one or more sessions. While Europeans still tipped the balance with over 1,000 bishops attending, Vatican II was the first time a council counted 489 bishops from South America, 404 from North America, 374 from Asia, 84 from Central America, and 75 from Oceania.

positive, even central, to the renewed life of the church. What had been suspect in Rome up until 1962 was now officially embraced for the life of the church.

A guiding principle throughout the book will be my argument that the church and the Society of Jesus were engaged in an ongoing communal discernment under the guidance of the Holy Spirit. Certainly the participants of the Second Vatican Council had a palpable sense—in so many subtle and obvious ways—that the dynamics and results of the Council far exceeded their own personal expectations. Even during the Council, the American bishops set up twelve commissions to help them implement all the various dimensions of their conciliar decisions once they returned home. Bishop Bernard Topel of Spokane, for instance, took the inspirations of the council about simple lifestyle radically to heart by selling the bishop's mansion, buying a cottage house, and dedicating every morning to tending an extensive garden, much like a monk who took a vow of poverty. When I was principal of Gonzaga Prep in Spokane, I knew the genial bishop, but I also witnessed the priests grousing about how difficult it was to see the bishop for decisions that needed to be made. In any case, during this extraordinary period in the church, bishops became not just *ecclesia docens*, but *ecclesia discens*—not just a teaching community, but a learning community.

The Council's call to religious orders to undertake an in-depth updating and renewal called for a profound discernment. For us Jesuits, this practice of discernment came naturally, but it needed a great deal of rethinking and renewal because Jesuit spirituality had become rationalistic, pedantic, removed from daily experience, and overladen with monastic habits. The dynamic character of the daily examen, the annual retreat, and especially the Spiritual Exercises needed revitalization. Fortunately, the scholarship for such a renewal had been underway already for several decades, and, as usual, the example of holy men—both Jesuit priests and brothers—offered the most obvious pathway into this renewal. As early as 1957 my own mentor at Gonzaga, Father Joe Conwell, had made a pioneering contribution to this reexamination of the foundations for Jesuit spirituality in his breakthrough book *Contemplation in Action: a Study in Ignatian Prayer.*[9]

9. Joseph F. Conwell, SJ, *Contemplation in Action*. French Jesuits, inspired by Maurice Giuliani, SJ, who founded the *Christus Revue* in 1954, had also undertaken the necessary scholarship for reviving a more personal, more dynamic Jesuit spirituality.

With the prodding of the Council, Jesuit spirituality rapidly became revitalized at a much deeper level, which allowed the Society to discover once again its charism at the heart of the church. It became what Pedro Arrupe, the charismatic Jesuit general, 1965 to 1983, called, "our way of proceeding." The discernment appropriate to the 36,000 Jesuits spread throughout the world was vastly different from the much simpler, though challenging communal discernment of the first ten Jesuit companions in 1539 gathered to consider how they could continue as "Friends in the Lord," even as the pope and bishops were calling them to urgent pastoral needs in distant places. Now it was not a "founding" but a refounding, that is, a purgation, a renewal, and ultimately a revolutionary transformation from what had been into what we became from 1966 onward. But at the time it was murky, messy, and often ambiguous.

Hegel's dictum that the "Owl of Minerva flies only a dusk" certainly holds true for this sixty-year period. Hegel explained that only in the light of historical consciousness, symbolized by the wise old owl of the goddess of Wisdom, can the patterns of history be discerned. For those of us going through this period, day by day, month by month, the patterns were so variegated that their trajectory was necessarily multiple or even muddled. So the reader of this tract may sense that my narrative is just "one darn thing after another." Where are we headed? Why should I read this? What difference does it make?

My effort is to try to describe it—as we went through it—not to impose some pattern or cookie cutter to these tumultuous years, for which we still need a great deal more distillation in order to determine their long-range effect. What I offer, rather, is a patch quilt: several swaths of my experience, which I hope when stitched together will enlighten those searching for whatever happened during these years.

One thing is clear: Now for the first time the Society of Jesus is truly part and parcel of a world church, not just a Society with Europeans and North and South Americans scattered and active throughout the world, but Jesuits native to every culture in every local church. Jesuits have grown up and shaped their local habitat, taking on the flesh and blood of whatever culture they inhabit, and simultaneously the Jesuit DNA has integrally structured whatever ministry is undertaken.

The first point of the Examen, practiced each day by Jesuits, is "to give thanks to God our Lord for the favors received." In my fifty-eight years as a Jesuit, I have experienced a wonderful lifetime of grace and joy in being a participant to this challenging renewal of the church and of the

Society of Jesus. For all this, I give thanks. And now I would like to share our journey and my journey with you.

2

My Early Journey

THE SIXTIES WERE A record-breaking turbulent time for American society and for the Catholic Church. But either by choice or by location, I
was amazingly impervious to it all. Of course, the assassinations of John
F. Kennedy, Martin Luther King, and Robert Kennedy deeply affected
me, and I would have had to have been religiously hermetic to ignore
the breakout of the civil rights movement and the stirring, sometimes
violent, Vietnam war protests, and the riots in the cities in 1968. But I
was a remote spectator. What impacted me most were all the changes
in the Catholic Church and in the Society of Jesus, which immediately
followed the closing of the Second Vatican Council in December 1965.
Only in the decade that followed did I become cognizant of how so many
assumptions about American life had come tumbling down. Of course,
my focus for this book is on the Catholic Church and the Jesuits, and it
would be easy to stray off into all the social upheaval that occurred during this time. I'll treat some of this unrest, but mainly to indicate how it
affected the American Jesuits and me.

Since the age of seven, I had felt called to be a priest, but it wasn't until I met the Jesuits that the nature and form of my vocation took shape. I
had grown up in Lisbon, North Dakota, in a Catholic family with devoted
parents and eight brothers and sisters. Our town of 2,000 was nestled in
the lovely, wandering Sheyenne River Valley, so we escaped Arctic winds
and summer dust storms. It was green, tranquil, and "a great place to

raise kids," as all the parents affirmed. We lived on Main Street, where the high school kids cruised up and down every Saturday night looking for whatever activity they could rustle up. It wasn't much. There was only one stoplight at the intersection of the two county highways to slow them down. My dad owned the Rexall Drugstore, and we kids learned the trade by washing windows, dusting shelves, and shoveling the snow off the walk in the winter.

Our little town had fourteen churches, ranging from Seventh Day Adventist to Methodist, from Episcopal to Catholic. All assumed, however, that you "went to church." Lutherans were dominant—with both Norwegian and German congregations. In these pre-Vatican II days, we were ecumenical by location, but not by choice. Ancient suspicions and barriers lingered on. During the 1920s the Ku Klux Klan had surged throughout the US and was active in North Dakota as well. Certainly in North Dakota, Catholics were more the target than Negroes and Jews. Years later a Protestant pastor in Tacoma told me that his first assignment was the Presbyterian Church in Grand Forks. He said he was shocked to discover, during a remodel of the church, major documents of the Klan in a sealed off stairwell. By the 1950s the Klan had died out, but suspicions still lingered. No Catholic in my hometown, for instance, was ever elected to the local school board until the 1960s. My experience of the Catholic Church within a Protestant culture seems typical of the American church during that era. As an eighteen-year-old, my views were local, parochial, and confined to family boundaries.[1] I think that everyone breathed a sigh of neighborly relief when the Vatican Council warmly acknowledged the truth and salvific value of the churches of our "separated brethren."

I recall one Sunday evening coming back from Benediction in our Catholic parish and passing by the Gospel Tabernacle Church. The piano was roaring and congregants were singing full throttle. My mother wistfully said, "I wish we could sing like that." Every Catholic knew "Holy God, We Praise Thy Name," which was about as close as we came to an American Catholic fight song. We also had the Marian standards of which the saccharine "Bring Flowers of the Fairest, Bring Flowers of the Rarest" was the hymn of choice for every celebration of Mary in May.

I learned all the Latin responses for Mass when I was nine and was one of the lead altar servers. My mother was a strong Catholic—in a good sense—active, cleaning the church, singing in the choir, and serving as

---

1. I related the story of my early years in my book *Reducing the Storm to a Whisper*, so I won't repeat it here.

president of the Altar Society, which, among many other things, meant putting on an annual chicken dinner as a fundraiser. I remember how steaming mad she was, along with all the other hardworking women, when the Irish pastor complained from the pulpit how the dinner had had a few scrawny chickens running through it.

In our little world, Catholicism was traditional, community-centered, and devotional. Lots of saints: we featured the Blessed Virgin Mary, St. Patrick, St. Thérèse de Lisieux, St. Aloysius, and, of course, St. Anthony (for lost articles). Sunday Mass was a given, mandated under pain of sin. Daily Mass was encouraged. And we marked the year with the holy days of obligation, the Ember Day fasts, and the great feasts of Christmas and Easter. Even the phrase "holy days of obligation" gave us a sense of the rigor of the faith but also of being special. For the Catholic grade school holy days were holidays. And so we were briefly the envy of our public school friends who were dutifully trooping off to what must have been an inferior school since they needed all that extra time in class.

We had a felt sense of the international dimension of Catholicism. Presentation Sisters, originally from France, taught us—eighty-five students of eight grades clustered into three classrooms. The sisters had been founded in Brittany right after the French Revolution. Almost a century later during the period from 1901–1904, the Third French Republic expelled all religious congregations. Close to 60,000 priests and nuns were exiled during a time of intense persecution. Many went to Ireland, Britain, Italy, Spain, and Canada. The rest of Europe was appalled at what it saw as French extremism. However, our beloved Presentation sisters arrived as exiles in North Dakota and Illinois to found a whole string of grade schools. We were the beneficiaries of the French persecutions.

Our Irish pastor Father O'Donoghue—straight from the "auld sod"—was our pastor for forty years. From his experience of the British oppression of Ireland, we gained an insight different from the benign American view of the British imperial empire. It wasn't all good. Father O'Donoghue offered a pungent, contrarian view to our otherwise favorable bias towards the British and, for that matter, towards Protestantism. He had a genial twinkle in his eye. Every Lent he would "give up drinking alone." So after Sunday evening Benediction, he would stand on his rectory porch and wave my dad or some of the other men into the rectory for a licit Lenten drink. My dad happily obliged.

From the Baltimore Catechism we memorized the description of the three dimensions of the church: The Church Militant, here on Earth; the

Church Suffering, in Purgatory; and the Church Triumphant, in Heaven. All one church—but at various stages of beatitude and union with God. The element of the Church Militant that prevailed in our education might be best captured in the Catholic Action Hymn that Daniel Lord, SJ, composed in 1932:

> An army of youth
> flying the standards of truth,
> we're fighting for Christ, the Lord.

The battlefield imagery was set to the rhythm of a rousing march. As the hymn suggests, we were "dauntlessly" on the move as the Catholic Church of the future:

> Heads lifted high,
> Catholic Action our cry,
> and the Cross our only sword.
> On earth's battlefield
> never a vantage we'll yield,
> as dauntlessly on we swing
> Comrades true, dare and do
> 'Neath the Queen's white and blue,
> for our flag, for our faith,
> for Christ the King.

Similarly, we were constantly praying for the "poor souls" in Purgatory. In the last pages of our missals for Mass were a host of prayers we could recite to earn indulgences of thirty days or even a full year. I, of course, drifted towards the better bargains. And then we could apply them to friends, relatives, or anyone "most in need of our prayers."

The Presentation Sisters were excellent teachers—some of the best I ever had. By the time Sister Germaine Marie had drilled us in grammar and sentence construction in the seventh grade, I could breeze through whatever exams in English we had throughout high school. My third grade teacher was Sister Margaret Rose. She captivated our hearts. After lunch each day she read a story to us. We could put our heads down on the desk and rest awhile as her enchanting voice unfolded the plot. We had a little science reader, and I remember my wonder that the planet Pluto had been discovered just a few years before (1930). Sister Margaret Rose was probably only twenty-two or so. She played softball with the boys. She was good. I was playing second base one day, when she rapped a solid hit. The ball was relayed to me at second, and I'm not certain what happened next. I think I realized I couldn't tag her, so I reached out and grabbed her veil flying in the wind. Imagine my horror when the whole veil and starched coif came off in my hands, and revealed her cropped hair. She quickly grabbed the veil and ran back into the school. I was left aghast.

Sister Margaret Rose lived until the summer of 2017. A few years ago I gave a retreat to her and the Presentation Sisters at their mother-house in Valley City, North Dakota. It was a joy to know her as an adult and how she had played a major role in the North Dakota health care system throughout her life. A certain sadness also hit me when I saw how aged and diminished the community of sisters was.

In the fall of 1958 I set out by train for college at Gonzaga University in Spokane, Washington, 1,150 miles from home. It was a long trek and marked the beginnings of a whole new life. Though I did not realize it at the time, the Gonzaga student body numbered only 1,600, of which 1,200 were undergraduates. Our graduation class at Lisbon High School had been forty-nine, so Gonzaga's numbers seemed immensely larger. Spokane, in fact, was an overgrown small town, so it provided an excellent fit for me as I migrated from Lisbon, population 2,000. I look back now on that leap from Lisbon to Gonzaga as the most significant turn of my life. That choice was more challenging than it was for me to enter the Society of Jesus three years later. After my time at Gonzaga, entering the Jesuits was largely a seamless journey into the novitiate at Sheridan, Oregon.

Those first days at the university were a swirl of greetings, welcomes, and orientation. I surprisingly found my way into the first honors program. Someone mentioned that there was going to be a meeting for anyone interested in signing up for the new honors program, so out of curiosity I went along. Three days later I was accepted, registered, and practically joined at the hip with my intelligent, lively classmates—twenty other young men and women—all of whom seemed brighter, better prepared, and more confident than I. Initially, I was too numbed by excitement for it to matter. My first semester veered towards disaster a couple of times. My first composition received a C-, and I nearly failed the first physical chemistry exam. I met with Father Lou St. Marie, the comp teacher. After getting acquainted more directly with him, I aced all the papers. I got better, but he lightened up. I find as a teacher myself I am always pulling for a student whom I have gotten to know personally. Chemistry was a bigger challenge. Fr. Leary, my honors advisor, suggested I get to know

Ed Haasl, who was also in the class. Ed was bright, grossly humorous, and quick to help.

In those years the heart of a Jesuit education was its heavy commitment to philosophy, in which I eventually had a total of twenty-one semester hours. I can't say that I retained much from all these courses. Thomistic philosophy seemed rationalistic, remote from life, and a game of demolishing adversaries. Social ethics class, however, has stayed with me all these years. Theology was just emerging from the catacombs of a strictly apologetic approach. Up until the mid-1950s, the Jesuits assumed that any Jesuit could teach theology because he had had "the course," that is, the three years of philosophy and four years of theology that were requisites for every Jesuit.

I was fortunate to have several inspirational Jesuit teachers. In our bull sessions in the dormitories—having surreptitiously secured a few beers—we often commented on how happy they seemed. I was impressed with their practical prayerfulness, though I could not fathom how they fit all the required prayers into their ultra-busy lives. A few could speed through the Latin Mass, which normally took a half hour, in record time. I clocked Fr. Bill Costello, whose Mass I occasionally served, at eighteen minutes flat.

All of the Jesuits wore the traditional cassock, often spattered with chalk dust. Occasionally, we would see them dressed in their "civvies," as when four of the priests sang a stunning barbershop quartet during the talent show for Founder's Day. I will dwell on the two of them who had the biggest personal impact: Fr. Jack Leary, the academic vice president and founder of the Honors program, and Fr. Joe Conwell, chair of the theology department.

Amiable, second-generation Irish, Father Leary was our honors advisor and taught our general ethics class. He managed multiple engagements in the midst of his duties as academic vice president, dean of the College of Arts and Science, and graduate school dean. Leary's lectures in ethics were a tour de force, replete with references to contemporary songs, literature, and foreign films. He managed to weave Bergman's *Wild Strawberries* and Fellini's *La Dolce Vita* into his lectures—films which were just on the verge of becoming the rage among academics and whose significance I would finally grasp only when I was studying philosophy in Boston a few years later. Leary coupled solemn ideas with surprising images. He might take the pop song "A Rainbow is a Many Colored Thing" as the launching point for the richness of the philosophical tradition. His classes brought laughter, misted up a few eyes, and raised our spirits. His Irish heritage of wit, charm, poetry, and spiritualism was magical.[2] We dubbed him the "preacher of prudence," since he so often waxed eloquently on its importance.

Drawing from Father Leary's six-page reading list, some of us read *The Intellectual Life* by the A. G. Sertillanges, a Dominican philosopher and spiritual writer. It was a practical guide for how to structure one's life so as to make progress as a scholar. In Sertillanges's world, you would have had to be a monk to be a scholar. My friend Ed Haasl and I agreed it was balderdash to us nineteen-year-olds. It certainly was not practical.

A few years later, Leary became president of the university. His acceptance speech at his inauguration typified his mesmerizing effect on his audience: "God is wont to energize frailty, and He can lace even inconclusive substance with such cords of vigor and compassion, and even at times with vision that the perceptive will know to whom the glory redounds." Those of us who knew and loved Father Leary well were shocked when about a decade later the dark side of his sexual misconduct with young men emerged.

When the Jesuit scholar John Courtney Murray made the cover of *Time* magazine in 1960 for his theological theories on the relationship of church and state, Father Leary proudly displayed the magazine cover of his fellow Jesuit in our social ethics class. Murray had been silenced by the Vatican for his writings, which praised the advantages of democracy, freedom of speech, and freedom of conscience and how these contributed to the liberation and advancement of religion. But within the Vatican's monarchical stronghold, the princes of the church were less than enthusiastic about the virtues of democracy, which Murray extolled. That moment in class was my first inkling of the monumental times about to unfold in the Catholic Church.

Given the destructive zeitgeist of the French Revolution from 1789 to 1795 and how it had laid waste to churches and prescribed the wholesale slaughter of priests and bishops, it was not hard to understand why the Roman Church had had such an unrelenting, defensive stance towards anything positive that might have come out of the Enlightenment period. Despite the Catholic Church's aversion to the Enlightenment, we American Catholics took for granted democracy, freedom of the press,

---

2. See Monda Van Hollebeke, *Jebbie*, 34.

freedom of religion, and a greater sense of the role of conscience over against the law than our traditional European Catholic counterparts did.

My other mentor, Fr. Joe Conwell, taught a course in Sacred History, a study of Old Testament texts in their context. He was wiry, intense, and had a Mediterranean look to him so that he was able to pass as a Greek, a Jew, or a Spaniard in his travels. He taught Hebrew Scriptures through the standard Catholic lens of seeing all the Old Testament as a preparation and prototype of Christ. A reading of the Hebrew Scriptures in their own right—without seeing them simply as the overture to the New Testament—was still a few decades away. He creatively compared King David to the Maverick brothers, the protagonists in the popular TV Western by the same name. I guess the point was that Maverick was constantly getting into life-threatening trouble, usually involving money, women, or both. I missed the question when it came up on a multiple choice exam, and so I remember it well. Conwell was inspirational and his commitment was transparent. I found it intriguing to actually study the Old Testament and gain a sense of the purpose, intent, and inspiration of the prophets, such as Jeremiah and Isaiah. Earlier I had simply followed along in my missal while the priest read the readings in Latin.

Conwell was one of the Jesuit moderators, living on the third floor of De Smet Hall. Within the first few weeks of my freshman year, a major water fight broke out between the freshmen in De Smet and the sophomore men in Walsh Hall across the way. The battle quickly escalated until the veteran sophomores pulled out the fire hoses and were about to launch the final campaign. Just at the moment Conwell appeared exactly in the middle of the quad between the combatants, and in a loud, stentorian voice commanded us to cease and desist. The scene was a marvel to behold. Suddenly, all these enthusiastic aquatic warriors disappeared back into the dorms. I ducked for cover into my own room. From that moment on Father Conwell carried the image for me of an Old Testament prophet—much like Jeremiah shaking the Israelites to their core.

Perhaps the most challenging teacher we had was Dr. Franz Schneider, a young German-born scholar of comparative lit, who, in a course on The Epic, raced us through *The Iliad*, *The Odyssey*, *The Aeneid*, Dante's *Divine Comedy*, and Goethe's *Faustus*. To this day I remain good friends with him (now ninety) and his wife Ann.

In Doc Schneider's course, I began to grasp the great vision about the human journey that he was proposing. But all these years later, only a few scenes and insights remain. One is certainly the touching rescue of

Anchises in *The Aeneid* by his son Aeneas, who bears him on his shoulders and simultaneously takes his own son Ascanius by the hand—as their native Troy is going up in flames all around them. Vergil describes Aeneas, the legendary founder of Rome, as *Pius Aeneas,* as if it were part of his name, certainly of his identity. Schneider explained in his rich German tones, *pius* doesn't translate as pious, rather it means dutiful, conscious of one's heavy destiny, religiously observant, and fittingly humble.

And, of course, the separation of Dido and Aeneas after their love affair in Carthage stands out. Dido's heartwrenching farewell to Aeneas memorably lingers on. Aeneas's destiny as the future founder of Rome overrules his passion for Dido, and in spite of his longing, he coolly bids farewell. At one point after multiple trials and shipwreck, Aeneas proclaims to his battered men: *Forsan et haec olim meminisse iuvabit.* (At some future time we shall remember with fondness these times past). Meanwhile, in terrible anguish Dido invokes vengeance on the Trojans (the future Romans) and commits suicide.

But what I remember most about that course in the epic from Franz Schneider was his account of his narrow encounter with death as a sixteen-year-old German soldier when Hitler was madly scrambling to fill the ranks of his decimated armies with teenagers. Franz described how a "G.I. bullet went whizzing by my head and narrowly grazed my helmet."

Another notable faculty member was Archbishop Thomas Roberts, the retired Jesuit archbishop of Bombay, India. The only concession Roberts made for his episcopal rank was to consistently wear bright red socks. "I keep my episcopal ring in my back pocket," he said. Thoroughly British, outspoken, and notably liberal for his day, Roberts taught us a course in the Epistles of St. Paul. Almost every lecture, however, was on the nonviolent movement of Mahatma Gandhi to bring down British rule in India. Roberts, of course, had personally known Gandhi during his thirteen years as archbishop, 1937–1950. Roberts emphasized with us the parallel nonviolent movement of Martin Luther King to address segregation and oppression of the Negro in the United States. We didn't get much on St. Paul, but we admired Roberts's memorable wit and keen commitment to justice.

Once the Second Vatican Council opened in 1962, the archbishop left Gonzaga and was present at all four sessions of the Council. After the Third Session of the Council, when the guilt of the Jews over the death of Christ was debated, Roberts remarked sarcastically, "I never could understand what the fuss was about. It is so plain that the guilt lay not with the Jewish people, but with the Jewish priestly establishment, that it seems legitimate to wonder whether the refusal to face up to this may not have been a subconscious reluctance to face up to the analogy in the Church today."[3] He also argued that the church's teaching on birth control should be reversed, and he advocated a strong leadership role for the laity.

Our Jesuit education at Gonzaga gave us a jump-start on how to speak and write correctly and a philosophy of life so that we could think through ethical standards and apply them in concrete situations. Whether we knew it or not, we were introduced into the oldest themes in Western humanism. We cultivated the power with words, along with moral virtue—which found its roots in fourth-century-BC Greece.

Traditional Jesuit education grounded in the humanities had two great purposes: the development of critical thinking and the development of character. In those formative years from 1958 to 1961 at Gonzaga, I experienced stirrings in my heart that I could not exactly explain, but wished to act on. The simple refrain from Psalm 42 probably captured it best: *A thirst is my soul for the living God.* Many of us regularly attended daily Mass at noon in the university chapel, and that was consoling, doubly so because we were given a chance for our interior lives to unfold in communion with everyone else.

In the summer of 1960 I landed a summer office job in Walla Walla, Washington, at the Libby, McNeil, and Libby packing plant, which was processing and canning the pea harvest. My brother Mike and I found a traditional boarding house with the Walmsley's—much like our Grandma Mikkelson had run in her home in North Dakota. We had a single room upstairs and then three meals a day, which included a packed lunch. I recall watching the Democratic convention with Mr. and Mrs. Walmsley, at which Jack Kennedy was nominated on a nail-biting first ballot. Wyoming put him over the top. The Walmsley's said they were lifetime Republicans ever since "we first voted for Roosevelt," by which they meant Teddy Roosevelt! "But this time we're going to vote for Kennedy to show Ethel (their Seventh-Day Adventist friend) that a Catholic can be president." During that election Catholics kept a low profile—recalling perhaps the searing defeat of Al Smith in 1928—but when they went into the voting booth, they pulled the lever with unrestrained resolve for Kennedy.

3. Frederick Franck, *Exploding Church*, 230.

That same summer I decided to enter the Society of Jesus. I wrote a letter to my folks. They were surprised. I was surprised that they were surprised. Later my brother Mike wrote to them in which he generously said, "The Jesuits are getting a good man." My decision was not filled with angst or unresolve. It simply flowed out of the life choices I had already been making. I realized years later that my biggest leap of faith out into an unknown was my decision to go to Gonzaga, 1,150 miles away where I didn't know a single soul. That leap was bigger than entering the Society of Jesus. For some years I had a strong sense that I was called to be a priest, but being a diocesan priest was not appealing. So when I encountered the Jesuits, everything fell into place. Any doubts dissolved. And I have been remarkably blessed ever since. Through all these years, I have had no doubts whatsoever that I was called to be a priest and that by temperament, talent, and grace, it was the best decision I could ever have made.

My final year at Gonzaga was chock full of activities—with considerable success. I received a Ford Foundation scholarship (one of six) for future university teachers of science or math and collaborated with the chair of the math department on a research project. I was also elected class treasurer of the junior class with a corny slogan: "Principles and interest to give you dividends." My friend Ed Haasl ghosted my campaign speech: "I make no pie-in-the-sky promises." As a result I was in the thick of a lot of social activities my third and last year.

To prepare to enter the Jesuits, I sought out Fr. Conwell for spiritual direction—he was already my academic advisor, so the two roles merged into one. One of my stumbling blocks about the Jesuits was the expectation of Ignatian "indifference." Jesuits were supposed to be available to be sent anywhere in the world, and the Jesuits had a mission in Alaska, where forty-two Jesuits were stationed. Having grown up in the harsh winters of North Dakota, I was quite averse to going to Alaska. Conwell did not let me off the hook. He could easily have said, "It's usually only someone who has volunteered that goes to the missions." But, of course, that would have diminished the spirit of the Society to go anywhere in the world for the sake of the Gospel and the mission of the church. I had to pray through my turmoil. Eventually peace descended. I realized whatever happened would happen.

3

My Jesuit Formation During the Council

BY NARRATING THESE EARLY years of my life, I hope to adumbrate what it was like to grow up Catholic prior to the Second Vatican Council. The Catholic Church was vibrant and successful. High percentages of Catholics attended Mass every Sunday; seminaries were full of dedicated young men; the nuns were the backbone of Catholic education and of passing on the faith. Notre Dame football, Father Peyton's Rosary Crusade, and Bishop Fulton Sheen's weekly TV program *Life is Worth Living* were rallying points for Catholics in the fifties. More devotional Catholics fasted during the seasonal Ember Days, attended Benediction on Sunday evenings, and even attended Daily Mass during Lent. Priests were revered; the Sisters were loved. Of course, every once in a while you ran across a sour nun or a cantankerous pastor. And American Catholics no longer comprised an immigrant Church; they were coming into the ascendancy in politics, finance, business, and education. And even movies like *Going My Way, The Song of Bernadette,* and *The Bells of St. Mary's* portrayed an attractive, compassionate Church.

During my college years, I had caught a glimmer of the Church emerging from the past into a promising future. The move from North Dakota to Gonzaga was already a big leap for me. The Jesuits were liberal, intellectually vibrant, mildly skeptical of directives from Rome, but also deeply spiritual. I soon found that we Catholics, no matter what our origins, were only just beginning a journey of renewal, which was both exhilarating and confusing.

From my early days as a Jesuit, I have experienced constant change. One of my wise-beyond-his-years Jesuit classmates said to me, "Pat, the only thing we can prepare for is change." The Jesuits have responded to the Second Vatican Council with courage and integrity, as well as with several mistakes and some self-inflicted wounds. Most evident, on the positive side, is how we have become habituated to discerning the action of the Spirit prodding us towards reconciliation, justice, and becoming peacemakers. Discernment of spirits is a key defining characteristic of Jesuit spirituality. Of course, in the beginnings I had only a glimmer of this spiritual depth to our vocation.

This fifty-to-sixty–year discernment, on which I am focusing, occurred at every level, but it was most manifest during the General Congregations.[1] These were international meetings of the appointed leadership (provincials and assistants to the General) and elected delegates who met in Rome to update all the aspects of Jesuit life and apostolic ministry. In all we have had six congregations since the Vatican Council. GC 31 in two sessions 1965 and 1966 and the most recent GC 36 in 2016. I was an elected delegate to GC 34 in 1995, which I consider my "fifteen minutes on the world stage." More on this later.

After his election as Superior General at GC 31 in 1965, Pedro Arrupe led the reform of the Society of Jesus by prudent commitment to experimentation. The new times demanded a venturesome spirit and several risks. Reflecting on the founding of the Jesuit Relief Services program in 1977 to attend to the dire needs of refugees, Arrupe suggested, "Great risks have to be taken in many places."[2] The times involved trial and error, he added. Mistakes certainly occurred. That's the nature of discernment: you go forward with the best human response available at the time. The poet Maya Angelou puts well the challenge we faced in those early days: "I did then what I knew how to do. Now that I know better, I do better."

Arrupe embarked upon his role with enthusiasm for the new directions called for by Vatican II. He advocated greater individual responsibility and, at the Synod of Bishops in 1971, warned against "authoritarian

---

1. A General Congregation is regularly abbreviated as GC. It meets to elect a new general or to consider matters of greater moment. See John W. Padberg, SJ, Martin D. O'Keefe, SJ, and John L. McCarthy, SJ, eds., *For Matters of Greater Moment*.

2. Pedro Arrupe, SJ, Letter to Jesuits in Jesuit Relief Services (August 6, 1981), as quoted by Peter Balleis, SJ, *In the Footsteps of Pedro Arrupe*, 11, on the occasion of the 100th birthday of Arrupe.

or paternalistic attitudes" in the church. Most importantly, he strove to reform the Jesuit order by having it identify more strongly with the poor rather than with the power elite.[3] His reflections were repeatedly informed by the dynamics of the Ignatian Spiritual Exercises, the need for metanoia or change of heart for the whole church, and ongoing, continuous discernment in order to "see what to do," as he would say. In a world marked by the grave sin of injustice, he said, "It will become the duty of whoever claims to be a Christian to speak out and take action against injustice."[4]

Some Jesuits resisted these calls for change. Some felt a sense of betrayal or were shaken in their religious foundations so severely that they became embittered and never recovered from the upheaval. But most emerged from these turbulent times all the better for it. The great majority of those who remained felt a tremendous surge of the Holy Spirit recreating the church. A fresh vibrancy revitalized all the multiple Jesuit ministries.

Ironically, the most prolific writers of what happened during this era were those who left the Society. A whole library of literature could be collected from their perspective. Two examples suffice, both of them by former Jesuits.[5] Garry Wills, a former Missouri Province Jesuit scholastic, became a prolific writer on several aspects of Jesuit life, and another significant book was by the layman Peter McDonough and former California Jesuit priest Eugene Bianchi. Someone else may profitably want to sift through the mix of turbulence, the prayerful discernment, the prideful egotism, the self-justification, and the call by God to a more authentic way of life that inevitably characterized those who departed.

On September 7, 1961, I entered the Jesuit novitiate at Sheridan, Oregon. "The farm," as some older Jesuits referred to the 891 acres of the novitiate, was fifty-two miles southwest of Portland. The land rose 400 feet above the Yamhill Valley to give a panoramic view of the valley with the Cascade Range to the east and the Coastal Range to the west. The

3. Pedro Arrupe, SJ, "World Justice," *A Planet to Heal*, 33–73. The Pontifical Council of Peace and Justice in 1972 was the first to publish his address to the Synod of Bishops (1971).

4. Ibid., 43.

5. Garry Wills, *Bare Ruined Choirs*, offers a highly literate, richly detailed description of the times. After Wills graduated from Campion High School, Prairie du Chien, Wisconsin, in 1951, he was in the Society in the 1950s. See also Peter McDonough and Eugene C. Bianchi, *Passionate Uncertainty*.

Jesuits had bought the farm from a retired Portland brewer, but there was no evidence of anything brewing on the property.[6] Even so, one of the enterprising novices cooked up a batch of sour beer, which we immensely enjoyed at villa one summer until one of the "scroops," an overly scrupulous novice, piously informed the Superior, and the brew was all dumped out on the ground. Great joy gave way to great sadness.

In those years mother houses and novitiates of religious orders were frequently outside the city in some beautiful rural setting, often on a prominent ridge or hilltop. My mother once observed, "The sisters and priests knew how to pick the most scenic locations." After the restoration of the Jesuits by the pope in 1814, Jesuit life had devolved to a monastic style rather than the contemplative-in-action charism, which Ignatius had envisioned. This monastic default accounted for these beautiful, bucolic settings.

Lack of water was a major concern from the very beginning. Despite many attempts over twenty-five years, the water issue was not finally resolved until the rector (the religious superior) hired a "water-witcher." When the witcher's hazel stick twitched in an unlikely spot and said, "Drill here," they did. Water spouted up, yielding 150 gallons per minute. A special shrine to St. Joseph was built in thanksgiving—baptizing what might have otherwise appeared as an unseemly pagan incantation.

Six years before I arrived at the novitiate, it had had a truly sinister look—worthy of a Sherlock Holmes scene wreathed in mystery and shocking skullduggery. In the early 1950s the raw concrete had started to corrode because of the constant winter rains, and the plaster on the interior was starting to peel. So the Jesuits hired a company to seal the building in black tar to prevent further erosion. The ominous, black, three-story building looked like a medieval fortress dominating the valley. Finally, by 1956 an attractive veneer bricking sheathed the building. In addition, two wings and a gracious refectory were added to accommodate the increasing number of novices. The construction was financed by harvesting majestic, old-growth forest timber at the ocean villa and on the farm.

In his short history, Fr. Wilfred Schonberg ("Schonie") summed up the novitiate building history. "It had taken five generations to produce it, but it is there for at least ten more." Schonie was extremely optimistic about it lasting for another ten generations. In fact, in a short twenty years

6. For some of the early history of Sheridan I have summarized material from Wilfrid P. Schonberg, SJ, "Jesuits in Oregon."

"all was changed, utterly changed," as Yeats would have put it. By then the number of novices had plummeted, the monastic style of novitiate was abandoned when the Society restored the original charism of Ignatius. Whoever was left rattled around in a near-empty shell. Put up for sale, the State of Oregon briefly considered it for a minimum-security prison. Seeing the interminably long hallways, state prison authorities exclaimed, "It has perfect sight lines." Eventually, it was sold to the Scientologists.

Almost every Jesuit province in the United States could report similar, optimistic expansions in the fifties and then a rapid decline in the number of novice entrantants and the closing of buildings that had taken millions of dollars to build. An abbreviated list would include: St. Bonifacius, the Wisconsin novitiate outside Minneapolis; the second California novitiate at Santa Barbara; the New England novitiate at Shadowbrook, rebuilt after a devastating fire destroyed the original Carnegie mansion in the Berkshires; Shrub Oak, the philosophate for the New York province; and Colombiere, the novitiate-juniorate for the Detroit province.

We had an extraordinarily large number of Jesuits in those years. The Oregon Province peaked in 1962 at 701 when a class of forty entered the novitiate the year after me. The total in the United States was over 8,000 and two of the ten American provinces were on the verge of splitting because they had so many promising young Jesuits in formation. The Buffalo Province, comprising Upstate New York, was spun off from the New York Province, and the California Province started a second novitiate in Santa Barbara, anticipating an eventual split into two provinces, which never occurred. A crucial factor in the years immediately after the Vatican Council was the vast number of Jesuits, especially scholastics, who left the Society. They left a void. Like a weathered Greek temple, I felt: "We are columns left alone of a temple once complete."

When I entered the Society, Jesuit training still clung to a severe monastic withdrawal from the world. Only after seven years of seclusion, asceticism, and study did the young Jesuit scholastics venture back "into the world" to teach high school boys during a three-year regency period. Just before I entered in 1961, the provincial appointed Fr. Frank Mueller, thirty-nine, to tighten the screws because too many scholastics were leaving the Society shortly after first vows. The new Father Master tightened the reins—less free time, fewer options to choose from, and a stricter code of behavior were the prescriptions. Levity or frivolity was unbecoming of religious men. The decision-makers had identified the problem, but their solution was disastrous. Our generation was decidedly different from those entering after World War II. A more moderate, more personal, more adaptable novitiate might have made some difference. With all the social, ecclesial, political, and personal upheavals coming just around the corner, probably no novitiate in the traditional sense was going to be adequate to ensure retention.

On the eighth day of entrance to the novitiate, we all received a hand-me-down cassock, the standard dress for Jesuits for almost 400 years. We wore these cassocks throughout the day with the exception of times for cleaning up after meals or other work orders, such as gardening, picking prunes, cleaning toilets, and, of course, during any sporting activity.

My mother and brother Tom, thirteen, visited the novitiate my second year. Afterwards—at least four different times—Mom sent a care package from the Howell Rexall drugstore, usually toiletries, such as toothpaste. Each time she included a can of Right Guard deodorant. I had enough Right Guard to supply the whole novitiate! Finally, I wrote to her, saying "enough." She confessed that when they had visited the novitiate, the odor from our cassocks, even though we took a shower every day, was horribly rank! That's about as subtle as Mom ever got. She was usually much more direct.

The daily order of our novitiate had been the same for decades, even centuries. One can easily surmise that Jesuit superiors had arrived at the unchanging, perfect routine for the formation of novices. The Ignatian dynamic of "experiments," such as a pilgrimage, teaching youth, a hospital aide, and so forth, when the novice would shed the safe cocoon of the novitiate, had been lost.

Our day started at 5 a.m. with a deafening bell. Before breakfast, we had an hour's meditation and Mass and Communion. The rest of the morning was devoted to spiritual reading, studies of Latin, and the rules and history of the Jesuit order. Three or four days a week the novice master gave us an instruction. There were chores to be done. The entire day was all neatly divided up into periods from a quarter of an hour up to an hour. *The Common Rules of the Society of Jesus* attended to every particular in one's life. Here are a few examples:

- No one should have books without permission, and in those allowed to him he should not write anything or make any mark. (#8)

- No one should leave his room without being properly clad. (#12)

- Those who have permission to visit the sick should speak not only in a low tone of voice, but with such calmness as not to annoy them. They should speak of such topics as are likely to comfort the sick and have some spiritual profit for others who may happen to be present. (#27)

- For the purpose of safeguarding the dignity and reserve proper to religious men, no one should touch another, even in jest. An exception may be made for the embrace of charity, when one returns from a journey or sets out on one. (#32)

- No one should leave the house or return except by the ordinary door. (#43)

- Everyone must have a copy of these Rules and those of his office and understand them. (#47)

An earlier rule book for the Sacred Heart Novitiate at Cataldo, Idaho, in the frontier era of 1890 had a unique combination of an Emily Post-style manners coupled with religious asceticism. It admonished the Jesuits: "No one should expectorate (spit) on the floor during meals." The world of rules could descend to the bizarre. For several years, Fr. Zack Meagher, the former California provincial, was the American Assistant or the right-hand man for the General regarding the American Jesuits. Meagher made a famous visitation of the American Assistancy in 1938 and afterwards composed a comprehensive *Memoriale* mandating corrections in every dimension of Jesuit life. In his admonita (warnings) to the Jesuit high school principals, he told them to take diligent oversight of the school yearbook. No young women should be pictured, only mature, married women. Special care should be taken, he said, about photos of swimming or wrestling teams, lest there be an "unseemly display of animal muscle and brawn."

Living in close quarters some of the brothers could grate on others. For instance, we had the fresh air freaks, who wanted the windows wide open in the middle of the night, even in winter. Often we worked in companies of three and had to finish a task in a timely fashion. One of the three might be a slacker, forcing the others do double time. Small things became overblown.

The only time anyone got off the hill was for a dental appointment or for the local doctor—Doc Wilbur, who would have been more adept as a vet for horses. In fact, one day Wilbur was examining one of the novices and tellingly declared, "You're really sick. You need to see a doctor!" For something genuinely serious, we went into Portland. Poison oak was abundant and occasionally someone would have such a severe reaction, gaining twenty to thirty pounds of liquid and being so totally miserable, that they had to be hospitalized.

The most important part of the novitiate was the long retreat, the thirty-day spiritual exercises of St. Ignatius. Under the direction of the novice master, we meditated on God and his creation; the rebellion of sin and God's compassionate response, the incarnation; the life of Christ and the Gospels, the passion of Christ, and finally his resurrection and ascension. The exercises concluded with the *Contemplatio ad Amorem* or the contemplation for experiencing God's love. In this final section St. Ignatius invites the retreatant to gaze on God's goodness as evidenced in Christ, in all of history, and in the beauty of creation, in order to have some palpable experience of God's love. The retreat was foundational for our lives as Jesuits.

But our day-to-day novitiate experience did not reflect the spiritual freedom which the Spiritual Exercises envisioned. Rather, our regimented days left little room for personal initiative. The tiniest minutiae could become a cause célèbre. For instance, one early, wintry morning at breakfast, one of the novices was warming his hands on a cup of coffee. A little later he was summoned into the Master's office with the dreaded note from the beadle, the novice coordinator: *Pater Magister vult videre te.* "Father Master wishes to see you." The Master began by asking, "Brother Christiansen, do you have something to tell me." Poor old Christiansen. Before he knew it he was confessing to every possible infraction he thought he might have committed—quite an outpouring. Finally, the Master interrupted, "Brother, don't you think the sensuous warming of your hands on the coffee cup is a lack of Christian mortification"? (!)

Another event captures some of the starkness of the training. During my second year, the table reading was from the Jesuit John Clifford's account of his three years of confinement and brainwashing by the Chinese Communists in a Shanghai prison.[7] Clifford had incredible interior resolve in the face of his enemies. He described the bleak daily order and living in exceedingly small quarters with another prisoner. In fact, some of his descriptions were so similar to our own experience in the novitiate that we started laughing. This outburst during the meal impelled

---

7. John W. Clifford, SJ, *In the Presence of My Enemies.*

the Novice Master to give us an exhortation two days later in which he explained in great detail the difference between a Jesuit novitiate and a Chinese prison! It came down to a matter of intention: unlike Clifford in prison, we freely chose to be here. Later I met Clifford when he was in studies at the University of Washington. He was a tough, hardened individual whom you had to admire for his endurance and fidelity.

High up on the hill, only fifty miles from the Pacific Ocean, we could be subject to some mighty storms, including an occasional silver thaw when layers of ice formed on trees and bushes, and heavily laden fir trees split or came crashing done. The most spectacular storm was Columbus Day, 1962, my second year when the novitiate was in the middle of the Thirty-Day Long Retreat. Hurricane-level winds whipped through the mountains and valleys. The wind gauge on Mount Hebo, thirty miles away, blew out at 160 miles per hour. Trees were strewn like toothpicks; all the electrical lines were downed. To continue the retreat, we gathered at night by candlelight to hear the points for prayer the next day. Candlelight heightened the gothic shadows of the Novice Master's face, as we sat in the flickering, dancing light. The setting had all the mysterious, even sinister, elements of Umberto Eco's story of murder in the monastery in *The Name of the Rose*. During those darkened days, my good friend Joe Hauer had a catastrophic mental breakdown, which I will explain in Chapter 13, "Jesuits and Mental Health."

Jesuits from these eras tell novitiate stories over and over again. I have run into men who left the Jesuits years ago, and they still harken back to those novitiate days as their most memorable, formative experiences.

THE CHANGES BEGIN

When I entered in 1961, Pope John XXIII had already announced the convening of an ecumenical council and had set in motion study commissions to prepare for its opening. Jesuit formation was about to change so drastically that even traditional, centuries-old processes would be shaken with incredible rapidity.

The abrupt drop-off in Jesuit vocations cannot solely be traced to the Council's injunctions to religious orders to return to their sources and update their formation. It's true that traditional, ascetical features were suddenly overturned. Freedom reigned. But the social, cultural, and political upheavals in the sixties and seventies were an even greater influence. Perhaps the Great Depression, World War II, the Holocaust, and the devastation of vast sections of Europe had also artificially contributed to the huge surge of men entering the Society in the thirty years before 1966.

After the long cautious reign of Pius XII (1939 to 1958), most had expected a transitional papacy without a whole lot of change. A short papacy would give the church a chance to regroup and presumably go forward, much as it always had. But the seventy-seven-year-old Pope John XXIII surprised everyone. He called for opening the windows and letting a fresh breeze blow through the church—namely, the unpredictable winds of the Holy Spirit.

The Second Vatican Council began in October 1962 while we were still sequestered. Newspapers, radio, television—anything that might have given us an inkling of the drama about to unfold—were all embargoed.[8] Perhaps twice during our whole two-year novitiate, the Novice Master gave us a news briefing. One of these was in October 1962 during the Cuban Missile Crisis. I guess he thought we should know that a catastrophic end was potentially near. Nothing on the opening of the Council during that same month! His only other news release was the brief outbreak of war between India and China over a boundary dispute.

By 1963, however, we did have a reading at table of the juicy account of the proceedings and arguments among the bishops as the Council unfolded. Written by Xavier Rynne (a pseudonym)[9] and serialized in *The New Yorker*, it was a wonderfully written insider's account of what was actually happening. Rynne served up a shrewd, candid account of the struggles by the progressives to inaugurate genuine reforms of the Church, rather than business as usual. Those shaking up the foreordained script were pastoral, intellectually sharp, European bishops responsive to the modern world, more open, more inclusive, and less defensive. In the silence of the novitiate dining room, the readings from *The New Yorker* brought hope, frequent smiles, and often laughter, even from the "dads," as we called the priests.

A typical Xavier Rynne "Letter from Vatican City" described the struggle between the bishops and the powerful Roman Curia. Cardinal

---

8. The prohibition on having a private radio was still on the books, but rarely observed, except in the novitiate. Father General Ledóchowski in 1931 allowed for one radio in each Jesuit community. "An Instruction on the Use of the Radio," 432–34.

9. Fr. Francis X. Murphy, a Redemptorist priest, eventually acknowledged his authorship. His middle name was Xavier and his mother's maiden name was Rynne.

Frings of Cologne, West Germany, said, "The [Curia] Theological Commission is a source of harm to the faithful and a cause of scandal to the world." He added, "It is not necessary to be a bishop, or even a priest, in order to serve in the Roman Curia." And then he observed, far in advance of his time, that "many of the functions could perfectly well be carried out by laymen."[10]

And, though we had no newspapers, we did participate in our own workshop on the Council in the summer of 1963. One of the striking features was that we took a survey among ourselves of certain key reform questions. One of them was: *Should the vernacular replace Latin in the celebration of the Mass? Yes* or *No.* Seventy-five per cent of the fifty novices said, "No!" I was in the minority, not because of any prescience on my part, but more likely because I had such a minimal background in Latin—having had only one year, poorly taught, in a public high school. Perhaps the result should not have been surprising. Most of the men had gone to a Jesuit high school where they had taken four years of Latin, and many were perfectly at home in it. In addition, we were all preparing "to go onto the altar of God," *ad altare Dei,* expecting to celebrate Mass in Latin as had been done for centuries. Even today, Jesuits have a few favorite Latin chestnuts, pithy phrases for choice occasions. Mine are "solvitur ambulando," "it will be solved by walking around," which has some of the same nonchalance as, "it'll all work out." The other is "quidquid recipitur ad modum recipientis recipitur," "whatever is received is received in the manner of the recipient." It's an excellent reminder for teachers of sophomore boys—"what they learn will be determined by their own (limited) capacity." These Latin jelly beans got many a scholastic through the gauntlet of philosophy oral exams taken in Latin. But by the time I arrived at Weston for philosophy in 1964, all these time-honored customs had vanished. We still had a few philosophy manuals in Latin because a couple professors were slow to modernize.

In the 1964 presidential election, my novice classmates favored Goldwater over Johnson. By then, I was gone to studies in philosophy at Weston, so I missed out on these undoubtedly hot discussions. But as American society dramatically shifted, most of these Goldwater supporters became passionate liberals and active in the civil rights campaigns for the next decade.

10. Xavier Rynne, "Letter from the Vatican."

Naturally, there was no attempt during these years to provide a venue for discussion of sexual and emotional issues or to discuss sexual orientation and related challenges. The Novice Master did have a medical doctor, the genial Dr. Jim Layman from Seattle, give us a lecture on the biology of sex, but that was rather bland—just the mechanics of it all. An early motto of Ignatius was taken as the standard: "We should have the purity of angels and there was no need to talk about it."[11] This glaring absence later had major repercussions throughout the Catholic Church when the sexual abuse scandal broke publicly, beginning about 1985. But the real explosion occurred when the *Boston Globe* on January 6, 2002, extensively reported on the major abuses and cover ups that had occurred under Cardinal Bernard Law and his auxiliary bishops. Indicative of the times, the *Globe* itself had had all the tips and information they needed to have broken the story in 1987, but only after a new editor who was Jewish took charge did the *Globe* dig in for its Pulitzer prize-winning series.

By the spring of 1964 my college friend Ed Haasl was studying for the diocesan priesthood at Mount Angel, a Benedictine seminary, which was celebrating its seventy-fifth anniversary. Ed invited me over for the festivities—about fifty miles away. Surprisingly, I was given permission. More surprising, I witnessed the kind of contentious dispute that would be normal fare in the church for the next couple of decades. The occasional preacher for the day was the famous American church historian Monsignor John Tracy Ellis. In the course of a very long sermon, Ellis outlined the future of the church and the major role the Benedictines had played historically around liturgical renewal. He was forceful, powerful, and electric.

But then at the dinner following, Cardinal James McIntyre of Los Angeles, one of the last of the truly curmudgeonly American cardinals, already fighting a rearguard action, was invited to give a few remarks. Instead, he launched into a tirade refuting Monsignor Ellis point by point. That same year at the Council, McIntyre was famous for one of his few interventions when he gave a discourse in butchered Latin on the importance of maintaining Latin in the liturgy and in seminary training. His Latin was so atrocious that his intervention was a telling example of precisely why the opposite of what he was arguing for needed to occur.

11. Ignatius, "What pertains to the vow of chastity requires no interpretation, since it is evident how perfectly it should be preserved, by endeavoring therein to imitate the purity of the angels in cleanness of body and mind." For a limpid, contemporary explanation see: Joseph F. Conwell, SJ, *Impelling Spirit*, 386–87.

After taking first vows of chastity, poverty, and obedience in September 1963 and after enduring another year of classical, humanistic studies at Sheridan, I was sent to Weston College, the Jesuit affiliate of Boston College, in the summer of 1964 to do my studies in philosophy, as well as a Masters in mathematics. Flying for my first time in transit to Boston, I landed in Fargo to visit my family in North Dakota—my parents and eight brothers and sisters. Except for visits by my brother Mike and later by my mother and brother Tom, I had not seen any family members for three years. Travel for Jesuits was still strictly regimented: I had one day to arrive, three days for the visit, and one day to depart. I accepted it all as normal, but it had to be challenging for my parents, especially my mother. Fr. Joe Conwell recounted similar restrictions when he was studying philosophy at Mount St. Michael's in Spokane in the 1940s: scholastics could not visit their parents in their own homes. One Sunday Joe and some of his Jesuit friends visited his mother. His Jesuit friends could go inside, but Joe had to visit his mother outside on the porch.

Originally, I was supposed to have gone to St. Louis University for my philosophy studies, but by the time the dean at Sheridan sent notice, the St. Louis philosophate was already filled to capacity at 162 scholastics. I was relieved. St. Louis had a notorious reputation for being unlivable— hot, humid, no air conditioning, and as a Jesuit house already coming unhinged. Nationwide the total number of scholastics for the three years of philosophy studies about that time numbered about 780.[12] By way of comparison, in 2016 the total number of scholastics in the collegiate program or first studies (the successor to the philosophies) in *all* of the United States was sixty-six.[13]

At Weston, under a single roof, we had ninety scholastics in philosophy, another 120 men in theology, a faculty of thirty or so, and lay brothers who ran an infirmary and oversaw the grounds. Perhaps 260 Jesuits at any one time—with a single rector. These large numbers led our psychology professor John McColl, SJ, to say, "Huge numbers of Jesuits stacked up in one place are like fifty Good Humor men trying to sell ice cream to the Eskimos at the North Pole."

Our protected religious life began to change rapidly even during the Council. When the Second Vatican Council closed on December 8, 1965,

12. This represents the accumulated numbers from the individual catalogues for 1966–1967 from the provinces that hosted a philosophate: Oregon, Missouri, Chicago/Detroit, New York, New Orleans, and New England.

13. *USA 2017: Catalog of the Provinces of the United States.*

it was eminently clear that all was changed. The original inspiration of our founder St. Ignatius was rediscovered and proved to be revolutionary.

Already the previous May, Jesuits delegates had gathered in Rome from all over the world to replace John-Baptiste Janssens, superior general from 1946 to 1964. Even before Janssens died, the Society had been on automatic pilot for a long time since he was subject to severe asthma attacks and was allergic to people. There's no good way to say this: his allergies kicked up whenever he was around people.

The GC 31 delegates elected Fr. Pedro Arrupe, the provincial of Japan, on the third ballot—opting, for the first time, to elect someone who had spent the major part of his life outside of Europe. My mentor/friend Father Jack Leary, by now president of Gonzaga and an elected delegate to GC 31, returned to the USA from Rome and stopped at Weston to give a briefing on the General Congregation, just as many of the other American delegates did—to the delight of all of us. Leary was upbeat: "We didn't get much done, but we elected the most promising leader." The Congregation adjourned, appointed numerous commissions to study the necessary changes, and set a date for the following year to reconvene after the ecumenical council would be completed.

Those were heady years for us younger Jesuits in studies. Within a short time some of the outstanding *peritii,* or Council experts, made their appearance. We flocked to the downtown center in Boston to hear firsthand Fr. Bernard Häring, the Redemptorist theologian who used the law of love as his ethical framework. Häring was one of my many heroes as I grew to know more about the Council's implications. From his experience as a chaplain and confessor during World War II, Häring developed a deep commitment to changing moral theology from its legalistic approach to a biblically based, dynamic understanding of the Christian moral life.[14]

Soon after Fr. Karl Rahner, the great German Jesuit theologian and arguably the most outstanding Catholic theologian of the modern era, spoke to all of us at Weston—in Latin! After his lecture he took questions in either Latin or German. If someone spoke in English, he seemed to understand the question, but a young Jesuit who had studied under him in Germany did all the translation. While respecting traditions, Rahner preached a new philosophical language for understanding the foundations of faith. He saw a world church emerging that would be less

14. Bernard Häring, CSSR, *The Law of Christ,* 3 vols. His autobiography is *My Witness for the Church.*

defensive, less Eurocentric, and more engaged with all peoples of faith. Rahner's contributions during the Council had been prodigious. Rahner's grounding as a Jesuit in the Spiritual Exercises is imminently obvious. The purpose of the Exercises, according to the shorthand of Ignatius, is to realize sufficient spiritual freedom to make choices, which reflect God's very self.

The tragedy and mayhem of war had shaped both Häring and Rahner. They witnessed firsthand "man's inhumanity to man," and nothing could ever be the same again. After the Holocaust, all Christian theology was changed—had to change. Biblical scholars reclaimed the obvious fact that Jesus was a Jew. The first message of Jesus, the deepest desire of his heart, was to minister to his own people, and biblical exegetes identified passages in the Gospels that apparently condemned the Jews as a people, when, in fact, the critique was of Jewish leaders who had collaborated with the Romans. Other passages, such as those from John's Gospel, which described apparent conflicts with the Jews, were, in fact, portraying the arguments between synagogue Jews and Christian Jews, the latter recently expelled from the synagogue. Another problem among Jewish Christians was discerning which elements of traditional Judaism should be retained along with the new way of Christianity.

The Council released a pent-up theological reservoir, which poured out upon the church. These few vignettes are but a brief sample of some of the influences—philosophical and theological and cultural—which were coursing through our young Jesuit lives at that time.

The Second Vatican Council, yes, was going on, but the bigger impact on me was living in close quarters with ninety other young Jesuits with similar interests, but very diverse personalities. A fringe group was intimately involved with the civil rights movement, and some few obtained permission to participate in the marches in the South, which I'm sorry to say I wasn't part of. I probably avoided them because they seemed rebellious against most anything that had to do with authority. Because of my cautious assessment of the protesters, I was blind to some of the injustice at our doorsteps in the United States.

In the winter and spring of 1965 some of the civil rights marches came to a culmination and finally motivated President Johnson and the Congress to act. An Alabama state trooper shot Jimmie Lee Jackson, a twenty-six-year-old church deacon from Marion, Alabama, as he attempted to protect his mother from the trooper's nightstick. Jackson died eight days later in a Selma hospital. In response to Jackson's death, activists in Selma and Marion set out on March 7 to march from Selma to the state capitol in Montgomery. Led by John Lewis, the marchers made their way through Selma across the Edmund Pettus Bridge, where they faced a blockade of state troopers and local lawmen commanded by Sheriff Clark and Major John Cloud, who ordered the marchers to disperse. When they did not, Major Cloud ordered his men to advance. Cheered on by rabid white onlookers, the troopers attacked the crowd with clubs and tear gas. Mounted police chased retreating marchers and continued to beat them. Television coverage of "Bloody Sunday," as the event became known, triggered national outrage. Lewis, who was severely beaten on the head, said: "I don't see how President Johnson can send troops to Vietnam—I don't see how he can send troops to the Congo—I don't see how he can send troops to Africa and can't send troops to Selma."[15]

On March 15 President Lyndon Johnson, in a ground-breaking televised address to Congress, movingly identified himself with the demonstrators in Selma: "Their cause must be our cause too. Because it is not just Negroes, but really it is all of us, who must overcome the crippling legacy of bigotry and injustice. And we shall overcome."[16] On August 6, in the presence of Martin Luther King, Jr. and other civil rights leaders, President Johnson signed the Voting Rights Act of 1965. Up until then, only 2 percent of the black voters had been able to register and to vote. Johnson also knew it would mean the loss of the South to the Democratic Party. What he could not see was how subsequent Republican candidates—Nixon, Reagan, Trump and such—would covertly and then overtly exploit the white racist vote. On a day-to-day basis I was immersed in my studies—rather immune to the momentous events swirling around the country and me.

I did become involved in this larger story in the summer of 1964, however, when, along with five other scholastics, I was conducting a door-to-door census of a Catholic parish in Roxbury—the heart of the inner city—what we called the ghetto in those days. A couple of the scholastics were attuned to the prevalence of racism and acute poverty right there in Boston. I was surprised to be invited by George Murphy and eager to join them. Dressed in our clerics, we were cordially and warmly received. Many were not Catholic, but were eager to share their lives with someone who would listen. Several were recent immigrants

15. Roy Reed, "Alabama Police Use Gas and Clubs to Rout Negroes."
16. Lyndon B. Johnson, "Voting Rights Act Address."

from the Caribbean. The level of poverty in the projects was shocking. Single moms especially were concerned about their kids—the violence and the gangs. One incident in particular was horrifying: the night before an aborted human fetus had been discovered in the community garbage bin. The mayhem seemed symptomatic of the cyclic malaise in which so many felt entrapped. What I remember most was the gratitude people had for the conversations.

Most of my formative experiences at Weston occurred right there in our huge community of 260 Jesuits in the scenic New England country-side. Among the more instructive events was my exposure to a wide variety of foreign films, followed by in-depth discussions among ourselves. These included Fellini (*La Strada; La Dolce Vita*); Antonioni (*La Notte*); Ingmar Bergman (*Wild Strawberries* and *Seventh Seal*); François Truffaut (*Jules et Jim* and *400 Blows);* and Jean-Luc Godard (*Breathless)*—mostly French and Italian—except for the Swedish outlier Ingmar Bergman. Many of these reflected the bleak existentialist philosophy that flourished in the aftermath of World War II.

We were good at entertaining ourselves. Every Saturday night we gathered for a social, songs, and banter. It was the one night when beer flowed freely. We had some superb musical talent among us and we would pick off popular folk songs to sing from Harry Belafonte ("The Banana Boat Song"), Joan Baez ("All My Trials, Lord"), Petula Clark ("Downtown"), and Kingston Trio's "This Land is Your Land" and the absurd tale of "Charlie on the MTA": "He may ride forever 'neath the streets of Boston. And his fate is still unknown. He's a man who never returned." A few scholastics were even writing original liturgical music. Only later did the music take a turn towards protest and political commentary. Bob Dylan would capture the white-hot moment with lyrical intensity. Joan Baez seized the times with softer tones, but just as radical. She was one of the first musicians to use her popularity as a vehicle for social protest, singing and marching for human rights and peace. This era was the only time in my life when I paid attention to popular folk music.

In the classroom I was absorbing what I could of philosophy from Plato to Kant, from Aquinas to Heidegger. Later on Charlie Allen, a classmate and good friend, who had barely survived philosophy studies, said to me as he was about to depart for Rome for theology: "If at the end of theology, I feel the same way about God, as I did about *being* at the end of philosophy, I may as well pack my bags to leave and get out right now."

During these years I was ordained to all the minor orders that existed in the church at that time: porter, lector, exorcist, acolyte, and received tonsure—a little snip of the hair, not the real monastic cut that left a big bald spot. Most all of these were suppressed, with the exception of lector and acolyte, when the Council inaugurated the reform of all the sacraments.

But all this was later. In the summer of 1966 I returned to the province to begin high school regency, a three-year period when Jesuits teach high school students (at that time all boys), prior to going on for theology and ordination. After a torturous first year of teaching when my control of a classroom of twenty-eight boys was sorely lacking, I managed to acquire and somehow embody an inner authority so that I could interact strongly, humorously, and effectively. Pedro Ribadeneyra, a young Jesuit in the time of Ignatius, had given three reasons for why Jesuits should not be involved in the education of boys. I could resonant with what he said: "It is a most tedious, troublesome, and anxious task to drive, teach, and control a mob of boys, who by nature are giddy, restless, garrulous, and lazy creatures, so that not even their parents can restrain them at home. The consequence is that our young men, in instructing them, lead a very hard life, fritter away their strength and lose their health."[17] I said years later, "If you can keep the interest of twenty-eight sophomore boys for fifty minutes, you can give a homily, you can give a major lecture, you can manage practically any public speaking engagement." It's called survival!

In those years I was also the adviser for the school newspaper and the yearbook. And I took advantage of a terrific, all-expenses-paid summer program sponsored by the *Wall Street Journal* for high school teachers assigned to moderate the school newspaper, who had not had training in journalism. So I benefited from an intensive six-week editing and writing course at the University of Minnesota. Afterwards, back in Portland, I volunteered to work at the local Catholic newspaper *The Catholic Sentinel.* I was on staff when Pope Paul VI issued his long-awaited encyclical on birth control *Humanae Vitae* in August 1968. The pope reaffirmed traditional Catholic teaching—going against the recommendation of the decisive majority of pastors, theologians, and lay people whom he himself had appointed to the study commission. I witnessed firsthand how the Catholic editors scrambled to tell the story and to provide a moderate, pastoral context, even some critique. They drew heavily on statements

17. As quoted by Thomas H. Clancy, SJ, *An Introduction to Jesuit Life,* 129.

from the German and Canadian bishop conferences, which offered some astute pastoral guidance to Catholics, emphasizing the importance of freedom of conscience, as well as respectful attention to the teaching of the Magisterium. The dissident voices in the United States were moral theologians, mostly priests, led by Father Charlie Curran at the Catholic University of America. The American bishops largely fell into line, loyally supporting the pope's teaching without much care for how it affected the faithful. The year 1968 with the publication of *Humanae Vitae* was the demarcation for a break in the church. Several markers characterized the divisions in the church which followed: theologians publicly, mostly prudently, dissented from papal and episcopal teaching; many laity questioned papal authority, in a way they never had before; married couples more confidently followed their own conscience about methods of birth control, and so forth. Nineteen-sixty-eight was clearly the turning point, and a few years later when the new Roman Rite liturgy was implemented, change, dissent, and individual assertion of conscience accelerated.

On the secular front, as the sixties became more and more politicized, upheaval was the order of the day. The ultimate symbol of this was Woodstock 1968, which some organizers, with self-absorbed superiority, characterized as: "We are trying to do what no one else has done before: to find a new way for humanity." An idyllic sense of freedom, of sexual promiscuity, and experimentation in drugs shrouded the movement.

1968 also saw terrible public tragedies. After the assassination of Martin Luther King and Robert Kennedy in the spring of '68, violence in the streets accelerated. The killing of King ignited a conflagration. Outrage could not be contained. Someone commented, "OK, you killed the dream, this is what the nightmare looks like." One hundred cities had major riots; over 20,000 were arrested. The revolutions of the 1960s became the cornerstones for the issues in our society today and constructed the ongoing political, social, and economic divides. They began with the civil rights movement against segregation and white supremacy. They accelerated with the feminist movement and protests against ecological degradation. And they culminated with the gay revolution, beginning with the Stonewall riots in June 1969. The key issue was: who has authority? Who has power? And what are the limits? Identity politics and the balkanization of the country took root. In reaction to these unaccustomed ways, the silent majority paved the way not for the liberating utopia but for the likes of Richard Nixon, who mustered an unlikely comeback in 1968 after major defeats.

From that point onward for the next decade, so much happened all at once that it's a blur and the proper sequence of events is lost to me. Ironically, as I noted before, those who left the Society of Jesus have written more on this period than those of us who remained—perhaps because their experience of the Society became frozen in time. Their time as a Jesuit had a clear beginning and a definitive ending.

Changes began in small steps. Up until 1966, every large Jesuit community had separate recreation rooms for the scholastics and the priests. Now, without any more preparation than a sign on the bulletin board, we were integrated into a single group. But the day that I walked into the Fathers' Recreation Room as a "mere scholastic," one of the older Jesuit priests stalked out. Table reading at dinner was abbreviated and then abandoned all together. Instead of having to ask the assistant superior for permission each time we needed some toiletries or a couple of bucks for a movie, we had access to a cash box. You can see what a stark contrast there was between what we considered important, and what was happening on the streets of America. All these changes seemed significant, but compared to what was coming next, they were minor and cosmetic.

4

Jesuit Pioneers Before
and During the Council

As I DELVED INTO these fifty-plus years of the transformation of the Society of Jesus, I knew I had to go back in history to understand the amazing whirlwind that the Council created and why the Jesuits, in my view at least, were able to respond so positively and creatively. In fact, the stirrings of change had come long before the Council opened in 1962. The breakthrough work of the Council would not have been possible without the dedicated labors, theological insights, and fidelity of outstanding theologians—almost all of them drawn from religious orders, largely the Dominicans and Jesuits, such as Yves Congar and Karl Rahner.[1] Likewise, in the liturgical world, the Benedictines had made major contributions through the Solesmes Benedictine monks in France and Virgil Michel at St. John's Abbey, Minnesota, who founded the liturgical journal *Worship*. The German Jesuit Josef Jungmann also did pioneering research on the liturgy.

Pope Pius XII (1939 to 1958) had opened the doors to contemporary and scientific studies of Scripture with his breakthrough encyclical *Divino Afflante Spiritu* (1943), drafted almost entirely by Augustin Bea,

---

1. The Dominican theologians included Yves Congar, Marie-Dominique Chenu, and Edward Schillebeeckx. Leading Jesuits were John Courtney Murray, Karl Rahner, Henri de Lubac, Jean Danielou, and Scripture scholars, such as Stanislaus Lyonnet, Maximilian Zerwick, and others.

SJ, the rector of the Pontifical Biblical Institute and later a major player in the Council. The progressive encyclical called for new translations of the Bible from the original languages, instead of reproducing the venerable, but antiquated Latin Vulgate of St. Jerome. It advocated the study of textual criticism and how the Bible was transmitted, and it encouraged the use of the latest research in historical circumstances and archaeology. It allowed for hypothesizing about matters such as authorship, dating, and similar concerns. It entirely reversed the repressive measures instituted by Pope St. Pius X (1903 to 1914), a very devout man, but weak intellectually. In fact, Pius X seemed typical of the former age of the church—remote, exceedingly devotional, judgmental, and rigid. In 1907 he inaugurated a series of repressive measures against scholars who were steeped in the new exegesis, in archaeological discoveries, and in attempting to engage with modern scientific endeavors. It's no wonder that the eminent Catholic Scripture scholar Raymond Brown called the encyclical *Divino Afflante Spiritu* "the Magna Carta for biblical progress."[2] It was the liberation from a repressive regime dating back even earlier to the papacy of Gregory XVI (1831 to 1846). In 1907 to repress the new approaches to theology and scripture, Pius X had imposed on all priests and bishops the obligation to take an oath against Modernism. When I attended the Gregorian University in Rome, this oath was still required for the degree. With considerable trepidation, I declined to take it because it was totally contrary to gospel freedom and to the very theology we were being taught. No oaths. An oath was not going to make me any more faithful to the teaching of Jesus Christ, to the church, or to my vocation as a Jesuit. It fact it would undermine it.

The breakthroughs in Scripture study prior to the Council did not immediately affect the average Catholic. Local pastors and the nuns in the schools, who were still the major transmitters of the faith, cautioned against reading the Old Testament, and they regularly invoked the canard that the God of the Old Testament was the God of judgment and the God of the New Testament was the God of love. It would take another fifty years to lay this false dichotomy to rest.

These twentieth-century, more-liberal trends among the Jesuits were starkly different from the Jesuit order's orientation during the nineteenth century. After the Restoration of the Society of Jesus in 1814, the Society's focus was missionary. It resumed its apostolic activity of preaching and

2. See the historical significance in John Donahue, SJ, "Biblical Scholarship 50 Years after *Divino Afflante Spiritu*."

teaching, spiritual ministries, scientific research, and social action, the missions and care for the poor, the suffering, and the marginalized. But having been suppressed by the pope for forty-one years (1773 to 1814), the Jesuits took a much more conservative, cautionary bent. They became strong supporters of papal authority and papal prerogatives. Jesuit theologians were instrumental in drafting the reactionary documents of Pope Pius IX (1846 to 1878).

Much of the energy of the papacy and the church was expended in maneuvering to protect the Papal States in Italy and to shoring up papal authority. The culmination of these efforts came with the approval of the Dogmatic Constitution *Pastor Aeternus* at the First Vatican Council, 1869 to 1870, which proclaimed papal infallibility whenever the pope pronounced *ex cathedra* a doctrine of belief or morals. As the theologian Paul Lakeland observed of this era, "From the French Revolution in 1789 through the First Vatican Council some eighty years later, to the modernist crisis that marked the early years of the twentieth century, the Roman Catholic Church at the highest levels conducted a systematic campaign against the 'evils' of freedom of speech, freedom of religion, the separation of church and state, and many other so-called social ills that at Vatican II the same church would so heartily embrace."[3] The Church drifted deeper into isolationism, encouraged Catholics to avoid the evils of the world, and in its leadership became more and more monarchical and triumphalist.

Jesuits, of course, were not immune to these nineteenth-century currents and often provided the intellectual leadership for advancing the repressive papal agenda. Simultaneously they were suspect in many countries because of their sympathy and alignment with the monarchist papacy. A partial list of their expulsion from diverse countries includes: Russia (1820), Portugal (suppression of all religious order, 1834), Switzerland (1847), Austria (1848), Italy-Piedmont (1862), Rome (1873), France (1901–1904), and Spain (1931).

So we can see competing trends during the 100 years preceding the Second Vatican Council, but it's clear that the Catholic Church, as an institution, was maintaining a fortress mentality over and against an increasingly secular culture. And it sought to snuff out scholarly attempts to go deeper, to go wider, and to engage the culture in creative dialogue. It thwarted engagement with scientific and social advances, which were

3. Paul Lakeland, *The Liberation of the Laity*, 17–18.

rapidly increasing throughout the century. As usual, Jesuits, on both sides of the spectrum from progressive to ultra-conservative, were in the thick of it all.

By the 1950s currents of change were already coursing more deeply through the People of God. A surprising reform in 1951, when I was eleven, was the restoration of the Easter Vigil by Pius XII. Until then Holy Saturday liturgy was celebrated in the morning with a handful of the faithful and two altar boys. I was one of them for the long tedious ceremony—all in Latin, of course. In fact, our Irish pastor announced on Palm Sunday that he and the sisters and the altar boys would start at 8 a.m. And he recommended that the others arrive at 9 a.m. for the important part of the Mass. The reform of the Easter Vigil signaled that the unchangeable was changing.

Even in those early days, the *sensus fidelium,* the people's felt sense of faith, what I like to call grandmother certitudes, was emerging in contradiction to what was preached from the pulpit. Older women, who had raised five or six children, knew that you had to bend with the wind and that any law or norm could not possibly apply equally to all of your children. Another major factor was that Catholic lay movements were increasingly strong in the United States, paving the way for a genuine theology of the laity at the Council.

Most of my examples of the stirrings in the Church prior to the Council are necessarily drawn from the Church I grew up with. The situation of the church in Eastern Europe and China—because of severe persecution—was obviously very different. In places like India, Rhodesia, and Indonesia the native peoples were just throwing off the debilitating manacles of colonialism. A native clergy and native lay leadership would take several more years to emerge. By the time of the Second Vatican Council many of the bishops from the historic colonial lands were still Europeans or North Americans.

From the 1930s to the 1960s an otherwise conservative Catholic Church paid strong attention to the plight of workers and to the injustices of a profit-driven industrialized economy. The roots of the church's labor activism include papal encyclicals like *Rerum Novarum* (1891), the progressive US bishops' Program of Social Reconstruction (1919), and the pioneering work of Monsignor John A. Ryan on the living wage in the early twentieth century. Ryan was known later during the Franklin Roosevelt years as "Monsignor New Dealer."

The New York Jesuit Phil Carey founded the Xavier Labor School (1936 to 1988) and taught how family, faith, and union are connected in Catholic social teaching. The otherwise conservative archbishop of New York Cardinal Patrick Hayes, 1919 to 1938, had approved Carey's school because it could combat Communism by explaining Catholic social principles. As Carey told his charges, "Look, we don't save our souls in church or on our knees; we save our souls by prayer and work with others. The ideal of the mystical body of Christ gives the worker something to live for and something to work for."[4] Carey's associate John M. Corridan, SJ, (dramatically depicted by Karl Malden in the film *On the Waterfront*) also saw Christ in the workers. "You are the flock of Christ," Corridan told the dockworkers and other laborers, "and the church of Christ is strong or weak as you are strong or weak."

I came across the remarkable Phil Carey, quite by accident. In 1973 when I was academic vice principal at Jesuit High in Portland, I flew to New York to talk to Jesuit leaders at Regis and Xavier high schools, which enjoyed premier reputations. Manhattan was bleak, cold, garbage strewn, and a threatening place. I felt like a country bumpkin in the big city. The subways were a confusing mishmash of competing lines. Subway cars were layered with graffiti. It all seemed oppressive and threatening. And frankly, the head masters and presidents at the two prestigious high schools were flummoxed as well. They were grasping for direction, just as we were. Xavier High School still had ROTC and the lads wore military uniforms on drill days, which certainly was not a helpful model for us in the midst of all the anti-war rhetoric.

But on my way out of Xavier as I was heading to the airport, a kindly priest asked me whether I knew the way to the subway. Then he spontaneously took me all the way down into the subway, paid my fare, and sent me on my way. Along the way people on the streets and in the station were greeting him, "Morning, Father." "How ya doin', Father Carey?" And so forth. The dark cloud lifted and a ray of hope returned to me.

By 1962 when the Council opened, lay leadership for the sake of the gospel was not something entirely new, sprung from nowhere. Rather the Council approved, advanced, and gave theological depth to these lay movements. Ratification of lay leadership contradicted the sometimes jaundiced, suspicious view of labor movements that had prevailed among some clergy. Lay people were not just ancillary to the clergy. Through

4. Joseph J. Fahey, "The Making of a Catholic Labor Leader," 18.

their baptism, they had their own profound, God-given mandate to integrate faith and justice, to incarnate the gospel, within their workplaces.

Not all movements, however, were future-oriented. In the early part of the nineteenth century, some lay movements in Europe had tended towards reactionary political engagement. For example, *Action Française*, founded in France in 1899, advocated a monarchist, counter-revolutionary movement that objected to the legacy of the French Revolution. It was anti-democratic, tinged with anti-Semitism, and supported the re-establishment of Catholicism as the state religion. A big supporter of the movement was the Jesuit cardinal Louis Billot, who ran into a conflict over it with Pope Pius XI and resigned the cardinalate in 1927; he was the only cardinal in the twentieth century to resign. Some years later several members of *Action Française* worked hand in glove with the Vichy Regime under the Nazis during World War II.

By 1937 Pope Pius XI was increasingly concerned with Fascism at home in Italy, but even more so with the virulence of Nazism in Germany. He issued an encyclical in German, not in the customary Latin, *Mit Brenneder Sorge* (With Burning Concern),[5] which was smuggled into Germany and read from every pulpit on Passion Sunday, 1937. Among other abuses, it condemned the neo-paganism propagated by the Nazi regime—"the so-called myth of race and blood"—and the idolizing of the state.

But at the same time, some notable Jesuits continued to support Mussolini and Fascism in Italy. The Jesuit superior general Vladimir Ledóchowski, originally from Poland, emerges from history as notoriously anti-Semitic and so vigilant against Communism that he overcompensated by his unqualified support of Italian Fascism. In the fall of 1938 Pope Pius XI secretly commissioned the American Jesuit Fr. John LaFarge, SJ, well-known for his book *Interracial Justice*, to draft an encyclical for him to condemn Nazism and its racist policies.[6] "The Pope is mad," Ledóchowski remarked in English, after meeting with the pope that Sunday and learning of the task he had given the American Jesuit. Ledóchowski suggested to the pope that he assign two "more experienced" Jesuits to help LaFarge and, of course, to make certain that they reined him in. Ledóchowski viewed the Jews as enemies of the church and of European civilization, the historian David Kertzer asserts.

5. Available at http://w2.vatican.va/content/pius-xi/en/encyclicals/documents/hf_p-xi_enc_14031937_mit-brennender-sorge.html.

6. David I. Kertzer, *The Pope and Mussolini*, 320.

Ledóchowski would do all he could to prevent the pope from slowing the anti-Semitism wave that was sweeping Europe. The three Jesuits finished their draft and sent it to Ledóchowski. Meanwhile *La Civiltá Cattolica,* edited by the Jesuits and vetted by the Vatican Secretary of State, had been publishing screed after screed against the Jews in articles such as "*The Jewish Question and Zionism.*" The editors declared, "It is an evident fact that the Jews are a disruptive element due to their spirit of domination and their preponderance in revolutionary movements."[7] Ledóchowski and the Jesuit editor of *La Civiltá Cattolica* successfully kept the LaFarge draft from being forwarded to the Vatican for several months. Eventually, it was sent to the pope but when he died, it expired on the pope's desk.[8]

Fast forward a little more than twenty-five years: all the principal characters in this plot have died. And in another of the great reversals of previous policy in the Church, the Second Vatican Council approves *Nostra Aetate* ("In Our Day," 1965), which opens the hearts of Catholics to the Jews, "our elder brothers in religion." In fact, right after World War II, the successor to Ledóchowski as Jesuit Superior General, Jean-Baptiste Janssens (1946–1964) was extraordinarily different from his severe predecessor. In 1945 as provincial of Northern Belgium, Janssens had kept in hiding a large group of Jewish children in his own provincial's residence of Brussels, which earned him the title of "Righteous among the nations."

Jesuits had a major hand in advancing the breakthrough in Catholic-Jewish relations that occurred with *Nostra Aetate.* Prior to the opening of Vatican II, Pope John XXIII had appointed the German Jesuit Augustin Bea in 1960 as the first president of the newly formed Secretariat for Promoting Christian Unity, charged with ecumenical relationships. Because of his biblical scholarship and Jesuit spirituality, Bea was highly influential at the Vatican II Council. He was a principal drafter, along with Rahner and Josef Ratzinger, of the document "On Revelation," *Dei Verbum.* And he was a decisive force in the drafting of *Nostra Aetate,* which repudiated anti-Semitism and put to rest centuries of church prejudice and even persecution of the Jews. John Borelli, a Vatican II historian, has observed that, "It took the will of John XXIII and the perseverance of Cardinal Bea to impose the declaration on the Council."[9]

---

7. As cited by Kertzer, *The Pope and Mussolini,* 290.

8. See the extended account of these political maneuvers in ibid., 354–69.

9. *Tracing the Contemporary Roots of Interreligious Dialogue,* Archived June 9, 2007 at the Wayback Machine.

Nostra Aetate, I believe, constitutes a miniature version of all the major debates of the Council. All the resources of the Church—scriptural and liturgical studies, ecclesiology and church history—were brought to bear on and tested by this remarkable distillation of scholarship and pastoral sensitivity. The debates were contentious. Some anti-Semitic literature was floated around even during the Council. The enormous shift in the Catholic world in relationship to the Jews arose out of the reality of the horrors of the Holocaust, but also because priests and rabbis and lay people throughout the world had begun to form friendships and dialogues to better appreciate and welcome each other's traditions.

My interest here is to note the seismic shift which occurred within the Jesuit order in its relationships with the Jewish people over twenty-five-year period. It was another tectonic upheaval from what had gone before. As far back as the Fifth General Congregation in 1593, the Society had declared, "Those who are of the Hebrew or Saracen races are not to be admitted into the Society." Although the decree was modified over the course of the years, only in 1946 did GC 29 formally rescind it.[10] This barrier to the Jews clearly contradicted the practice of St. Ignatius and the earlier Society. In fact, the second general of the Society Lainez was a *conversos,* a descendant of Spanish Jews.

Even after the Council's affirmation of the Jews in the history of salvation, not all was smooth because by then the State of Israel had been established, and Jesuits, especially in the Middle East, were working side by side with Arab Christians, many of whom had been violently displaced by the Israeli takeover of their lands.

In my view *Nostra Aetate* remains as one of the principal litmus tests for the implementation of the Council's revised Catholic vision of other religions and of the world itself. It marks the beginning of a new age of positive dialogue and relationships between the two ancient communities—Jews and Christians.[11] Many of my Jewish friends are much more cognizant and appreciative of *Nostra Aetate* than Catholics are—most of whom have not read it. Even so, Catholics have welcomed the new atmosphere of openness and acceptance, even if they are not aware of the massive struggle it took to bring it about.

10. John W. O'Malley, SJ, *The Jesuits & the Popes,* 52.

11. *Nostra Aetate: Transforming the Catholic-Jewish Relationship* on the 40th anniversary of *Nostra Aetate.* http://archive.adl.org/nr/exeres.

REFORMS BEGIN

In the early stages of responding to the mandates of the Second Vatican Council, Jesuits made multiple decisions all at once—some minor, many major. The accumulated changes were monumental. Many Jesuits embraced them with enthusiasm, while others strongly resisted, vehemently declaring, "This is not the Society that I entered!" Conflicts developed, and the turmoil within the Society collided with and was inflated by the corresponding upheaval in civil society. My friend George Murphy told me recently that when he did theology in Cambridge, Massachusetts, in the early 1970s, "It was hard to tell the sane from the crazies. Everything was up for grabs."

Even so, for me it was a great time to be a Jesuit. I had the advantage of the old, revered traditions, and I welcomed the lively opportunity of helping to create a fresh, new Society, anchored in the tradition and yet dynamically serving people and the church in the modern era. After the Council opened, the restrictive rules cracked and fell apart. Experimentation was the order of the day. Jesuit superiors were responsive to fresh suggestions, especially when they were well argued and tailored to correspond to their own best instincts.

The transition to Weston from a restrictive, highly controlled novitiate and juniorate to the more casual philosophate took a significant adjustment. I was also shocked my first few months. For instance, after major feasts or just casual gatherings around the swimming pool, the Jesuit minister (the superior second in command) would break out cigars and cigarettes for whoever wished a smoke. Our novice master had made such a big deal of the ban on smoking, couching it as a mortal sin against the vow of obedience, that it took an emotional realignment for me to cast the whole sorry history of the prohibition against smoking in a more benign light. That experience also relativized my earlier novitiate training and softened the stigma of shame, sinfulness, and apparent lack of obedience. I realized that these ironclad laws had more than one valid interpretation.

As I mentioned earlier, liturgical practice was also up for grabs. The Council had announced in its very first document, *Sacrosanctum Concilium*, "Mother Church earnestly desires that all the faithful should be led to take that fully conscious, and active part in liturgical celebrations which is demanded by the very nature of the liturgy."[12] The new Roman

12. *The Constitution on the Sacred Liturgy*, no. 14, 124.

missal for the Mass would not be available for another three or four-years. That didn't stop us, however, from leaping in to the quicksand of experimentation. Initially, we had Mass in a large classroom, seated in a circle, all facing each other, rather than aligned in rows facing east. Folk songs, guitars, and tambourines were the order of the day. We borrowed apt tunes or adapted them to new lyrics. "Kum Ba Ya, My Lord," for instance, had been a standard campfire song; but in our heady, enthusiastic remake, it took off as a spiritual folk song.

> Hear me crying, my Lord, kum ba ya;
> Hear me crying, my Lord, kum ba ya;
> Hear me crying, my Lord, kum ba ya,
> O Lord, kum ba ya.

Another was "Rise and Shine, and Give God that Glory, Glory." This one had an ironic twist to it in our early morning liturgical trysts since the celebrant at Mass was our superior Father *Shine.*

Within a few years we had the war of petitions during Mass. These prayers were customarily for peace, healing, justice, and invocations for the well-being of the church and the world. But during the Vietnam war, protests burst out into the liturgical arena. Sample prayers included:

"That the United States might see the error of its ways, repent, and immediately withdraw its troops from Vietnam. We pray to the Lord."

A prayerful warrior might immediately counter with:

"That we might support our troops and bring about a lasting freedom among all the people of Vietnam. We pray to the Lord."

And these were tame examples.

One Jesuit wag, weary of the free-flowing guitar Masses, quipped, "Which would you rather be stuck in: a 1966 guitar Mass or a sixteenth-century Mass with polyphonic Gregorian chant?" Another humorous, probably apocryphal story, circulated that a bishop was presiding at the dedication of a parish church, and the liturgy was folksy and elaborate with a woman dancing up the aisle and around the altar with incense wafting from a bowl. As she danced, the bishop leaned over to the pastor and quipped, "If she asks for your head upon a platter, she's got it!"

THE GREAT EXODUS, THE PANICKED RESPONSE, AND CREATIVE INITIATIVES

On the institutional front, the hierarchy of the Church made several precipitous decisions, often without consultation. The resulting turbulence was caused not only by the abruptness of the change, but because we had no adequate paradigms for revolutionary changes in the Church. There was one exception. The Jesuit historian John O'Malley in a groundbreaking article in 1971 helped me understand and negotiate the upheavals that tossed us to and fro. O'Malley explained that an almost "despairing confusion" hallmarked Catholicism since the *aggiornamento* of Vatican got underway. "Religious life, for instance, seemed to explode in our faces as religious orders attempted to fulfill the Council's directive to update the authentic spirit of their founders."[13] The Council, O'Malley noted, failed to tell religious *how* the authentic spirit was to be discovered, verified, brought up to date and applied to the times.

O'Malley's pivotal article delineated five models of change which had predominated at ecumenical councils throughout the history of the church. For the first time in history, he explained, the whole sweep of 2,000 years of church history, theology, liturgy, and politics was available. Because of historical consciousness, change was transformative. Drawing on Hegel, we could now say, "the owl of Minerva [goddess of wisdom] flies only at dusk," only at the end of the day does the wisdom of ages become distinct and clear. The "long 19th century," which O'Malley extensively explored later,[14] was over. And rather than returning to a romanticized, pristine past or merely touching up the errors and scraping off the accretions of the passage of time, as the Church had attempted in past councils, Vatican II set about to enliven the gospel, the life and teaching of Jesus, in a fresh, accessible way for the new times for the People of God on pilgrimage through time and space. The Council used the twofold principles of *ressourcement*, going back to the original sources, (all previous history now being accessible) and of *aggiornamento* (reading the signs of the times and bringing the church up to date). Contemporary language made the documents easily accessible, even to the average reader. In addition to these two principles, Jesuits urged the vital need for

13. John W. O'Malley, SJ, "Reform, Historical Consciousness, and Vatican II *Aggiornamento.*"

14. O'Malley, SJ, *What Happened at Vatican II?*

communal discernment—tracking the movements of the Holy Spirit to "discern the signs of the times."

As the years went by, as tempers subsided, as opposing belligerents came to peace, and with the ongoing inspiration of the Holy Spirit, the Church began to embody the foundational texts and the enlivening spirit of Vatican II. As O'Malley pointed out later, the very *style* of the Council conveyed a new time, a transformative moment: a pastoral, rather than a defensive, condemnatory spirit. Even so, two successive popes, John Paul II and Benedict XVI, cast a darkening pall over the church as they sought to stem the tide of change. In a sense they walked facing backward, concerned to conserve what had been gained and unwilling to risk what might still come to light. By their vigilance to make sure nothing was lost, they stunted our future.

But in 1971 all this was ahead of us. The confusing turbulence in the church held sway for those first fifteen years after the Council. So it's worth highlighting some of the positives and negatives that occurred immediately after the Council.

5

Arrupe—Called to Set Out on Paths Unknown

ANY ACCOUNT OF THE response of the Jesuits to the Second Vatican Council needs to begin with Pedro Arrupe. Just as the life story of St. Ignatius was crucial for the founding of the Jesuits, so too Arrupe's life story became foundational for revitalizing Jesuit spirituality and for implementing the reforms mandated by the Council. Through his eighteen years as Superior General, I had the great privilege of encountering him several times, especially during the three years I lived in Rome.

The story picks up with the delegates to the Thirty-First General Congregation when they convened in Rome in May 1965 to elect a new Superior General to succeed Father Jean-Baptiste Janssens. They arrived after the Council had completed the first three sessions and was on the verge of mandating sweeping changes for the whole Church. In that springtime the Society of Jesus began with alacrity to respond to the inspirations, changes, and mandates of the Second Vatican Council. It began a collaborative dialogue and discernment that has lasted fifty years.

The American delegates were much younger than might normally have been expected. At that time the structure for electing delegates to go to Rome was a geriarchy. Provincial congregations, where Jesuit delegates convened locally, were weighted down with age because the forty oldest Jesuits, professed with four vows, automatically made up 80 percent of those attending. The other ten were significantly younger because they were the Jesuit superiors appointed by the Superior General. Clearly, the elders intuited that great changes were in the offing. In each of the eleven American provinces, they almost always elected younger men as their delegates to the forthcoming General Congregation. The delegates from my own province were John Kelley, forty-nine, the provincial; John P. Leary, forty-six, the president/rector of Gonzaga; and Albert "Arby" Lemieux, fifty-eight, the president of Seattle University. They were our best known, most talented men. The needs of the Society outweighed any consideration that the university presidents might need to remain at home to run a major institution.

When the 224 delegates met in Rome, they began with a week of prayer and "murmuratio," as preparation for the election of the new general. This murmuring is a time-honored custom of conversation and consultation among the delegates to inform themselves about the strengths and backgrounds of likely candidates—something crucial to the discernment. They elected Pedro Arrupe, the provincial of Japan, on the third ballot. Reportedly, a couple other choices were considered, such as Paolo Dezza of Italy and the Vicar General John Swain of Canada. They were viewed as worthy but offering "more of the same." Most delegates wanted a fresh start. Many anticipated that momentous changes were ahead because of the far-reaching reforms already promulgated by the Council. Jack Leary said to me afterwards, "We didn't get much done that first session, but we did elect a promising new general, and we set up commissions to make recommendations for our second session. We'll be back again next year after the Council is over."

In fact, Pedro Arrupe, the first Basque elected since Ignatius himself, was a most providential and enlightened choice. He had broad, international experience. Almost all his Jesuit life had been spent outside of Europe, so he was the first Jesuit general to have a truly worldwide, cosmopolitan perspective. In addition, Arrupe's early life mirrored much of what had happened to both civil and ecclesial societies during the tumultuous, violent years of the 1930s and 1940s. Arrupe's leadership was vital for the church, which was on the verge of becoming a world church for the first time in its history.[1]

Pedro's mother died when he was only ten years old. At the age of fifteen, he began medical studies at the University of Madrid. Three years later, after his father died, Pedro and his sisters made a pilgrimage to Lourdes where he offered his services to the Medical Verification Bureau.

1. I am greatly indebted for the material that follows to Kevin Burke, SJ's masterful introduction and collection of Arrupe's writing. See Kevin Burke, SJ, ed., *Pedro Arrupe.*

In that capacity, he witnessed several miracles, which changed his life forever. In later life he would identify three profound, transformative moments in his life. The first was at Lourdes. The second was the bombing and aftermath of Hiroshima, and the third was his election as general of the Society of Jesus.

He recounted his experience at Lourdes this way: "One day I was on the esplanade with my sisters a little before the procession with the Blessed Sacrament. A woman of middle age was pushing a cart with a young man of 20, all twisted and contorted by polio. The woman sighed, 'Maria Santissima, help us.' She placed him in the row where the bishop was to pass by with the Blessed Sacrament. When the bishop blessed the young man with the host, he looked at the monstrance with the same faith with which the paralytic mentioned in the Gospel must have looked at Jesus. After the bishop made the sign of the cross, the young man rose cured from the cart. After this experience, I could not return to my medical studies in Madrid in the same way. My companions said that I looked stunned." The next year in 1927 Pedro Arrupe entered the Jesuits in the province of Loyola, Spain.

Five years later, in 1932, the new Spanish government expelled all the Jesuits from Spain. Pedro was allowed to take one book from the novitiate library, and significantly he chose the leather-bound volume of 1,282 pages of the critical edition of the *Spiritual Exercises*. From then on Arrupe was in exile, completing studies in Belgium, the Netherlands, and after ordination, he spent several months studying psychiatry in Washington, DC before completing his fourth year of theology at St. Mary's in Kansas. He also did tertianship in the United States. Finally his persistent request paid off, and he was missioned to Japan.

His years in Japan were ones of suffering as well as mystical consolation. Not long after his arrival in Japan, Arrupe celebrated Mass at sunrise on Mt. Fujiyama. He treasured this moment of ecstatic joy. Strangely enough, he experienced a similar overwhelming joy in an entirely different context during the spiritual suffering he endured from being without Eucharist for thirty-three days while he was imprisoned by the Japanese as a suspected enemy agent, just after their attack on Pearl Harbor. On Christmas Eve, Arrupe heard people gathering outside his cell window and presumed that the time for his execution had arrived. However, to his utter surprise, he discovered that some fellow Catholics, ignoring all danger, had come to sing Christmas carols for him. Arrupe burst into tears of joy and gratitude. In addition, his obvious prayerfulness and his lack of offensive behavior gained him the respect of his judges, and he was set free within a month.

In 1942 Superiors sent Arrupe to Nagatsuka, on the outer edge of Hiroshima, to become the master of novices. He was in the novitiate on August 6, 1945, when the first atomic bomb obliterated Hiroshima. A magnesium flash burned the sky, followed by a cataract roar, which shook the novitiate. A monstrous mushroom cloud mounted to the heavens. The cataclysmic destruction was all around him. Drawing on his medical background, he turned the novitiate into a makeshift hospital and enlisted all the novices as medical personnel.

Fifty thousand people died immediately from the blast, and another 200,000 died in a few weeks from wounds, radiation, and from the results of the burning inferno. "Most heartbreaking," he recollected, "were the cries of the children calling for their parents. We were witness to more horrible scenes that night. As we approached the river, the spectacle was awful beyond words. Fleeing the flames and availing themselves of the low tide, the people lay across both shores, but in the middle of the night the tide began to rise, and the wounded, exhausted and now half buried in mud, could not move. The cries of those drowning are something I will never forget." Arrupe and the novices were able to treat 150 wounded in their frantic quarters. Not one of them died, except for a boy who contracted meningitis. Day and night, Arrupe said, they were removing glass (as many as fifty shards from the back of one man) without any anesthesia, and treating the burns. Fortunately, someone had found a stash of boric acid with which they were able to prevent sepsis in the open wounds, which often covered over one-third of a person's body.

In the midst of their urgent work, they always celebrated the Eucharist. "Assuredly, it was in such moments of tragedy," Arrupe reported later, "that we felt God most near to us. In turning around to say, 'Dominus Vobiscum,' I saw before my eyes many wounded, suffering terribly." Years later, he said the apocalypse at Hiroshima transformed his life. It deepened his dependence on God, and it opened his eyes to what is "deadly and truly terrible about force and violence."

In 1954 Arrupe became vice-provincial of the 200 Jesuits in Japan, and in 1958, he became the first provincial of the new province. Then on May 22, 1965, the delegates elected him Superior General—which marked the third major change in his life, and ultimately the one which most generously affected the lives of so many Jesuits and the renewal of the Church itself.

When the second session of GC 31 convened the next year, momentous changes were indeed afoot. The Jesuit delegates had a massive job before them. Every dimension of the Society was under reconsideration. Accumulated accretions had grown like barnacles on the stately ship of the Society. It was as if the delegates had to bring the Society into fresh water and dry dock and completely update and refurbish the vision and mission of the Society.

The Congregation revamped the whole process by which Jesuits were trained so that they could be more responsive to modern needs. It urged the Society to devote its efforts to those parts of the world struggling with "hunger and other miseries of every sort." This directive led to the establishment of "the social [justice] apostolate." A dozen years later in 1977 Arrupe, distressed by the plight of the Vietnamese boat people escaping their homeland in risky sea voyages, established the Jesuit Refugee Service (JRS) as an official ministry of the Society. Operative now in fifty countries, the JRS mission is "to accompany, serve, and defend the rights of refugees and forcibly displaced persons." Over seventy-five Jesuits with over 1,000 fellow workers provide education, emergency relief, and pastoral services each year to over half a million refugees. It is one of Arrupe's greatest legacies.

Another breakthrough in 1966 was that for the first time in Jesuit history the Congregation, following the lead of the Vatican Council, warmly embraced ecumenism and interfaith dialogue, and it urged Jesuits to promote understanding among all religious traditions—a remarkable shift for a group of men formerly known as sworn enemies of the Reformation. I was only dimly aware of these two decrees at the time, but they were a harbinger of what was to become a major part of my apostolic life. My ecumenical engagements have led to many wonderful friendships from diverse Christian and other faith traditions. God's grace doesn't respect our narrowed or prejudicial boundaries! These ecumenical partnerships led to my becoming an active member of the international Congress of Jesuits in Ecumenism, inaugurated in Dublin in 1965 by Michael Hurley, SJ, founder and director of the Irish School of Ecumenics.

In the early years the eyes of the Jesuits were on Don Pedro, as he was affectionately known, rather than on the decrees of the Congregation. He was the one who embodied the spirit of the new Society, and he had a profound sense of what Jesuits came to know as "our way of proceeding," our method of discernment. "What to do? What to do?" he would practically chant, as he delved into the challenges of discernment.

Although they lived 450 years apart, Arrupe and Ignatius of Loyola had much in common. Arrupe underwent an exile during the Spanish Civil War. Similarly Ignatius left home after his conversion and returned only once. Arrupe led the implementation of the Second Vatican Council among the Jesuits; Ignatius sent Jesuit theologians to the Council of Trent and sought the reform of the Church. Both suffered calumnies and unfounded accusations from inside and outside the Church. Most importantly, the interior life and mystical experiences of Arrupe and Ignatius became gifts for the whole Society of Jesus. What Jerónimo Nadal, an early Jesuit, said of Ignatius could also be said of Arrupe: "The same privilege [in prayer that] . . . was granted to Father Ignatius we believe has been conceded to the whole Society, and we are confident that the grace of that prayer and contemplation has been prepared in the Society for all of us."

And just as Ignatius had depended heavily on Nadal and Polanco to build the institutional structures of the early Society, Arrupe depended on trusted consultors. The American Vincent O'Keefe, former president of Fordham, became a long-term, trusted advisor. The initial general consultors elected by the General Congregation were Paolo Dezza, John Swain, Vincent O'Keefe, and Andrew Vargas. The vital role of O'Keefe is well known, and we will see much more of him in 1981 when the Society faced its darkest moment of this fifty-year span. Later the French intellectual Jean-Yves Calvez, former provincial of France, who replaced Vargas in 1971 and then was elected as a general consultor at GC 32, had a significant impact on Arrupe for articulating the mission of the Society today. Shortly after Jean-Yves was ordained a priest in 1957, the young scholar published *La pensée de Karl Marx*, which provided a clear and objective treatment of the German philosopher. His treatise was as much studied in Communist cells as it was in Catholic circles. After General Congregation 32, which had so strongly emphasized the preferential option for the poor, Jean Calvez toured through several provinces in 1975 explaining the gospel origins and philosophical underpinnings of the faith that does justice. In fact, he spoke to our Jesuit community in Portland, Oregon, where I was a young priest. Calvez was undoubtedly the theoretician on whom the Society's leadership leaned to map its way forward.

Twelve years after his election as general on the occasion of his fiftieth year as a Jesuit, Arrupe reflected on the call of Abraham and how he left everything to follow the promise of the Lord. Like Abraham, he said, "This last experience [as General] was an exodus, much more radical, amid extreme uncertainty." Arrupe described how the world of the Jesuits was turned upside down. We had to take leave of habits, practices, ideas, former choices, he explained, in order to face up to a whole set of challenges—some of them murky and lacking clarity. It was a genuine exodus from the old ways "in order to set out on paths that would bring [us] into a world that was still 'in the making.'"

His chapel next to his room was his little cathedral, as he called it, which, according to Kevin Burke, "would be the fountain of incalculable power and dynamism for the whole Society, a place of intimacy, consolation and strength." Certainly, the center of Pedro Arrupe's life was Jesus Christ. As Burke comments, "This personal devotion to Jesus Christ supplied energy to his words and deeds . . . it shaped his faith journey, lending unity to his countless everyday decisions."

Under Arrupe several small modifications took place in the Curia to make it more livable. Built in 1927, the Curia building, just to the left of the Bernini colonnade of St. Peter's Square, had the daunting exterior of a fortress. Under the watchful guardianship of previous generals Ledóchowski and Janssens, Jesuits had had to have special permission even to travel to Rome, let alone to visit the Curia. But after 1965 the atmosphere changed; Arrupe and his advisers warmly welcomed guests.

The long, monastic-style tables in the refectory were replaced with small tables, which facilitated conversation. A language laboratory, card tables, an aquarium, and a library were installed. Institutional browns and grays gave way to brighter colors. A couple of Americans made sure that peanut butter and Post Toasties cereal were available. And a Pepsi-Cola dispenser and an espresso machine were introduced. All of these little changes broke from the oppressive, defended air that had greeted earlier visitors.

I first met Arrupe in 1969 when I arrived in Rome to study theology. Fr. Harold Small, the American assistant to Arrupe, who was also from the Oregon province, arranged for me and my fellow Oregonian Jim Sinnerud, to share pranzo, the noon-time meal, with the General. Pedro radiated his legendary joy. Our table that day included a Spaniard from Japan, an Italian Jesuit, and us two American scholastics. Don Pedro flowed in and out of Spanish, Italian, English, with a touch of Japanese. The scramble of languages didn't matter. He communicated his passion and love. The words of Jesuit Pierre Teilhard de Chardin came alive in

Arrupe: "Joy is the infallible sign of the presence of God." All of us felt his contagious enthusiasm.

I was privy during my first year in Rome to a highly humorous encounter that Father Arrupe had with the eccentric American playwright Tennessee Williams. Another Oregon province Jesuit Fr. John Navone orchestrated the event and relayed the encounter to me a few days later in breathless, quasi-conspiratorial tones. The event also illustrates some of the craziness that Arrupe had to deal with in those early years. Months earlier, Navone reported, the playwright had converted to Catholicism and had come to Rome, oddly enough, to seek a personal blessing from the pope. Navone, who regularly cultivated friendships with celebrities, took the initiative to call on Williams and later set up the encounter with Father Arrupe. The only title by which Williams knew the Jesuit General was "the Black Pope."

The little gathering at the Jesuit headquarters that welcomed Tennessee Williams included Father Harold Small, the American assistant to the General, Father Navone, Williams himself, and Wayne, a young man with kinky hair who attended on Williams. Navone had arranged the meeting through the rubric that Tennessee Williams was a descendant of the brother of the famous Jesuit missionary to the Japanese, Francis Xavier. While they waited for the General to appear, Williams became agitated. Beads of sweat coalesced on his forehead. He twitched and asked, "When is the Black Pope going to appear?"

When Arrupe arrived, he asked the disoriented visitor if he had ever visited Japan.

"I've just come from there," the visitor answered nervously as if he were facing a modern-day Inquisition.

"It's a country one never really leaves," said Arrupe graciously.

Tennessee elaborately narrated his conversion to Catholicism. And Arrupe acclaimed, "You've been favored by a great grace, Mr. Tennessee."

"I know, Black Pope, I know," the visiting playwright gasped. "Ever since that grace I have felt enveloped by a strange and mysterious luminosity." Then rolling his eyes, he added, "I feel the presence of Mary Immaculate."

In the palpable silence that followed, Father Small acquired an intense interest in the painting of St. Ignatius, which hung on the wall. Even the loquacious Navone was at a loss for words. But then he blurted out, "Is it a warm presence, Mr. Williams?"

An index finger pointed upward, his voice in a reverent hush: "There is no temperature."

Arrupe was delighted the man had such a Marian devotion and rescued the moment: "If you are devoted to Mary Immaculate," he said, "You'll have to go to Lourdes."

"Where's that?" asked Williams suspiciously.

"Just on the other side of the Pyrenees from where I was born."

"Wayne, get that down," said Williams over his shoulder to the young man. The Jesuits were letting him in on their secrets.

"You know, Black Pope, every day I memorize a few prayers and doctrines, just a little at a time. I keep the Haily (sic) Mary written out on my bedside table."

As Navone was recounting all these conversations—seemingly verbatim—I was rolling with laughter. He described some more exchanges in this vein, but then finished with one final curtain call.

Williams suddenly said, "I have a special favor to ask. Today I finished a new play, and I would like you to bless it."

Arrupe, according to Navone, shot a silent appeal for help to Small and then to him.

"It's a comedy," the playwright advised. And Arrupe shrewdly suggested, "Would you like to bless it, Father Navone, as you're more familiar with Mr. Tennessee's comedies?"

In a moment of dramatic inspiration Navone took the play, raised it on high and dramatically intoned, "O God, you whose creative spirit brought forth the grape to bring the joy of wine to your thirsty people in the desert, grant that your spirit descend on this play bringing laughter to all who watch it."

Relieved, Arrupe bade Mr. Tennessee farewell and disappeared into the folds of the Curia headquarters.

Navone opened a few other doors for me while I was in Rome. He inveigled a dinner party invitation from the British novelist Muriel Spark. The two of us arrived early at her apartment in Travestere and were greeted by the maid. Soon Muriel arrived, decked out in an elegant black sheath dress with subtle turtle design in the cloth. John had brought some reviews of her latest book, and he gushed over these with her for a spell and then introduced me as Deacon Howell. That was my moniker for the evening: "Deacon Howell." It lent a certain cachet to the conversation. Soon the British ambassador to the Holy See and his wife and niece arrived. They were the only sane, grounded element to the whole party.

Then Baron Brian Debrevny arrived. John whispered that he claimed to be an Irish baron, but was actually born in Wyoming of hardworking miners. He was recently divorced from his wife, an Indian princess, and was lamenting that now he could rarely see his five-year-old daughter. Then there was a gay couple—a photographer for *National Geographic* and the other an interior designer. The conversation was robust, witty, sharp, cosmopolitan, but also banal. One had the sense that Muriel arranged these little soirées as warm ups for her next novel. In fact, a priest bearing a remarkable likeness to Navone had appeared in one of her earlier novels.

Much of Arrupe's work in those years was behind the scenes. As the Jesuits took up the mandates of Vatican II, especially those relating to the preferential option for the poor and becoming a poor church for the poor, they upset a good many of the ruling elite, among them influential bishops and cardinals. Inevitably some of the hierarchy complained to the pope, who in turn brought their complaints to Arrupe's attention.

Arrupe also had to make some strong, controversial decisions regarding formation programs throughout the world. By the early 1970s it was clear that the United States could no longer sustain five theologates, the centers for the theological and pastoral formation of young Jesuits. The number of Jesuits was rapidly falling off and expenses were mounting. I will delve into the outcome of these discussions in the next chapter.

Throughout these upheavals, Arrupe maintained a solid, steady course of renewal and renovation. He was in the vanguard; it took the rest of us another fifteen years to catch up with him. Arrupe traveled widely. More Jesuits met him personally and heard him speak than was true of any previous general. He was much loved and widely admired, but he had severe critics, not just among bishops, but also among a few recalcitrant Jesuits, especially in Rome at the Gregorian University and in Spain.

In fact, the Spanish Jesuits, facing multiple pressures all at once, were in danger of a schism. The lingering aftermath of the bloody Spanish Civil War and the dictatorship of Franco heightened the divisions already occurring over the renovations mandated by the Council. Franco had staged a coup in 1936 and received support from Fascist, monarchist, and right-wing groups, as well as from most of the Catholic clergy over and against the Republicans and Communists. Hitler's Nazi Germany and Mussolini's Fascist Italy also stepped into the Civil War on the side of Franco. Over a three-year period, leaving half a million dead, the war was eventually won by Franco in 1939. He established an autocratic dictatorship, which endured until his death in 1975. Communists had killed scores of Catholic priests, but when Franco restored the privileges of the Catholic Church, most Jesuits were relieved and grateful.

Shortly after Vatican II ended, the divisions in the Church in Spain became even more pronounced. Much of the divide for the Jesuits broke out along the lines of younger Jesuits, who had entered the Society after the Second World War, and older traditional Jesuits, who had suffered through the great trials of civil war and World War II. The traditionalists were upset with Arrupe's leadership, and they were balking at all the changes of the Council. Because of Arrupe's unwavering commitment to social justice, they thought he was opening the doors to dreaded Communism. They urgently proposed that a new, separate Spanish province be organized, which would be directly under the General of the Society— which, in fact, meant that they would have great autonomy because as general, Arrupe could not possibly provide regular governance.

During this same time the American Cardinal John Wright, head of the Congregation for Clergy, had come out publicly in favor of this division of the Jesuits. I gained entrance into the inner sanctum of these Spanish battlefields because one Sunday afternoon Cardinal Wright and his entourage were guests of our rector Father Furlong at the Gesù. In the recreation room after pranzo, everyone was crowded around the rotund Cardinal. I noticed a young priest, good looking with immaculate clerics and French cuffs, off in the corner by himself. I introduced myself.

He said, "I'm Father Donald Wuerl, the cardinal's secretary."

Little did I know that I would encounter him later in the much more ominous role as the auxiliary bishop of Seattle, with undisclosed powers to correct perceived aberrations in our archdiocese. After some innocuous conversation, I tested the waters: "I suppose you and the Cardinal have been to Spain recently." And Wuerl surprisingly said, "Oh no, we've never been to Spain, although I'd like to go there." I kept this little revelation to myself, but I was certainly surprised that Cardinal Wright, who had publicly come out in favor of the Jesuit split in Spain, had not personally investigated the local situation. I was also distressed that such an apparently talented young priest should be harnessed as secretary for the cardinal's every beck and call.

Soon after, I read in *Il Messaggero* that Cardinal Vicente Tarancón, the archbishop of Toledo and primate of all Spain, had suddenly flown to Rome to consult with Pope Paul VI about the Jesuits. A close ally of the pope, Tarancón was seen as an enemy by the far right, Fascist elements.

Arriving in Rome, he explained as urgently as he could that the split in the Jesuits not be allowed to go forward because if it did, it would split the entire Church in Spain. The pope acceded and quelled the potential schism.

These kinds of complaints against the Society were probably weekly occurrences for Arrupe and the Curia staff. In 1970, Boston College law school dean Robert Drinan, SJ, was elected to the US House of Representatives from a liberal, largely Jewish, district on an anti-Vietnam war platform. He was reelected four times, serving from 1971 until 1981. He was the first member of congress to recommend impeachment for Richard Nixon because of the 1970 secret bombing of Cambodia, which Drinan considered illegal and meriting an article of impeachment for "high crimes and misdemeanors." Drinan's overt political support for legalized abortion rights drew vehement opposition from Church leaders, who repeatedly requested his resignation from Congress or his removal by superiors. Drinan claimed to reconcile his position with official Church doctrine by stating that while he was personally opposed to abortion, its legality was a separate issue. This argument failed to satisfy.

In 1980, Pope John Paul II unequivocally demanded that all priests withdraw from electoral politics. Drinan complied and did not seek reelection. "It is just unthinkable," he said of the idea of renouncing the priesthood to stay in office. "I am proud and honored to be a priest and a Jesuit. As a person of faith I must believe that there is work for me to do which somehow will be more important than the work I am required to leave."

The New York Jesuit and poet Daniel Berrigan meanwhile was dramatically protesting the war through civil disobedience. In May 1968, he manufactured homemade napalm and, with eight other Catholic protesters, used it to destroy draft board files in Catonsville, Maryland. The group became known as the Catonsville Nine. "Our apologies, good friends, for the fracture of good order, the burning of paper instead of children," Berrigan announced at the time of the destruction of the draft files. "How many must die before our voices are heard, how many must be tortured, dislocated, starved, maddened? When, at what point, will you say no to this war?" Berrigan was arrested and imprisoned in the Danbury, Connecticut federal prison. When Arrupe visited the United States, he made an unannounced trip from New York up to the Danbury prison to personally visit and encourage Berrigan. Berrigan believed, as did Martin Luther King, Jr., that "the evils of capitalism are as real as the evils of militarism and the evils of racism." And he dedicated his life to fighting them.

The Second Vatican Council had set in motion all these diverse movements. Most Jesuits had responded with joy, alacrity, and perseverance—the three hallmarks that Ignatius had laid down as signs of a genuine vocation. Arrupe, in particular, exuded this joy, and he responded with great energy, fueled by his profound mystical prayer life. But, from the beginning, there was also considerable resistance and opposition to the changes. Some tried to stem the tide of changes engulfing the Church and the Society of Jesus. Disagreements and divisions cut across the whole Society.

Like Ignatius himself, Arrupe was a practical mystic. His encounters with the poor and his witnessing the catastrophic destruction at Hiroshima transformed his spirituality. Nothing could ever be the same again. Just as the theology of Vatican II was implicitly shaped—at least in part—by the European horror at the Holocaust and violence of two World Wars, so too Arrupe's awakening experience at Lourdes, his grasp of the destruction of the Spanish Civil War, his arbitrary imprisonment by the Japanese at the outbreak of WWII, and especially his witnessing the holocaust of Hiroshima, coupled with his compassionate medical response in the midst of the subsequent mayhem—all carved out an interior receptivity for the mystical graces granted to him by God. "When will we discover," Arrupe reflected in his later years, "that in the core of our person there lives that divine reality? For this we will need a flash of light far more powerful than that which blinded us at Hiroshima: the light of faith which illumines without blinding because it is both powerful and gentle."

In some ways Arrupe was a traditionalist. He revived the devotion to the Sacred Heart and gave it a strong theological and scriptural foundation. In fact, I was there on June 9, 1972 (my birthday) at the Church of the Gesú in Rome when Arrupe rededicated the Society of Jesus to the Sacred Heart, on the one-hundredth anniversary of its original dedication in 1872. I was an altar server because our American rector wanted all English-speakers in the altar area so that no confusion in communications could take place. In his homily Arrupe exclaimed, "It could be said that every line of the gospel, every word of it is throbbing with the boundless love of Christ." When he celebrated Mass, Arrupe was serene, more subdued, intent on the mystery within the Eucharist.

Burke comments again, "Arrupe's prayers, letters, and spiritual writings continually echo the mysticism and holiness of his 'father in faith,' St. Ignatius Loyola." Burke adds that Arrupe did not merely replicate Ignatius's words and insights. He gave a fresh reading to the life of Ignatius and to the *Spiritual Exercises*. He stimulated a renaissance in Ignatian spirituality. Arrupe's theological reflections and mysticism profited from the work of Jesuit theologians, such as Karl Rahner and Juan Alfaro, and spiritual writers such as Hugo Rahner, George Ganss, Jean Calvez, and a multitude of others. In other words, there was a wellspring of creativity, traceable back to at least the 1930s that had sprung up within the Society. Arrupe and his counselors, who presumably were often his ghostwriters, could draw on a vast array of scholarship for a profound renewal of Jesuit religious life.

Arrupe's assimilation of ecclesial events, such as the Medellin conference on justice in Colombia in 1968, the synod of Bishops' document "Justice in the World" in 1971, and then, of course, the Society's own confirmation of his leadership at GC 32 in 1974–1975, all shaped the tenor, tone, and texture of his writings and his contributions to the universal church. In fact, GC32 constituted a fresh new era in the Jesuit mission. For the first time the Society of Jesus, responding to oppression, poverty, and injustice, declared that our mission today is "the service of faith, of which the promotion of justice is an absolute requirement. For reconciliation with God demands the reconciliation of people with one another."[2] This decree became the shibboleth, the mandate, for Jesuits to reconstitute their lives, their mission, and their institutions around "the joys and hopes, the griefs and anxieties of the people of this age," as the Second Vatican Council had urged upon the whole Church. The other decree that had a lasting impact was the one on Jesuit identity, which declared: "What is it to be a Jesuit? It is to know that one is a sinner, yet called to be a companion of Jesus as Ignatius was." And it continues on to explain that we Jesuits are to be involved in the crucial struggle of our time: "the struggle for faith and the struggle for justice which it includes."[3]

In fact, GC 32 was a pivotal moment in the life of the Society and in the leadership of Arrupe. If it had not been for the warm, fraternal relationship that already existed between Pope Paul VI and Arrupe, some of the Society's finest efforts among the poor and the leadership of Arrupe

2. "Our Mission Today," Decree 4, no. 2.
3. "Jesuits Today," Decree 2, no. 1.

himself might have been undermined, even abrogated, by a few recalci-trant cardinals in the Curia who can only be described as enemies of the Society of Jesus. The more public fractures between the Society and the Vatican at GC 32 are well known. But I have been fortunate to gain an insider's view of the conflicts by being privy to the diary of the Oregon delegate Fr. Leo Kaufmann. Leo kept a day-by-day account of the en-tire Congregation. He sprinkled his diary with trenchant remarks about some of the delegates, especially those with whom he disagreed. Leo was bright, even brilliant, and a fine philosopher, specializing in linguistic analysis. He didn't have much patience for ineptitude. His diary gives a firsthand flavor of the proceedings of GC 32.

Like many Americans, he was impatient with those from the Latin culture and their loquaciousness. Commenting on the speeches in the general session, he said, "Give a Latin the floor and it's like giving the ball to Joe Namath. He dashes through a hole and runs for the whole length of the field." He continued his critique of "the Latins" when the document on Jesuit Identity came up for discussion. "Some of them," he observed, "made fun of the poor Latin" of the Americans. And then he added, "They are just beginning to realize that the tyranny of the Latin language has been broken." By contrast, he says, that the English-speaking group was very favorable to the document.

Leo had a bulky frame and complains, "The Italian food is not going too well at the moment. I feel like I have a lump of dough in my stomach much of the time."

At the outset of the Congregation, all the delegates traditionally made the trek across St. Peter's Piazza and up a multitude of stairs to the Aula Clementina to hear the Pope's discourse to the Society. If there were to be a severe criticism of the Society or a message to have it shape up, the pope would give the signal at this command performance. Leo picks up the narrative: "We climbed many steps and then crossed an interior courtyard. The room held 300 with very high straight back chairs. I was about sixty feet from the Pope. He looks frail and old. He read to us for seventy minutes. I got about half of what he said. His Latin is very Itali-anate, and I think his dentist might fit his teeth better. His talk showed great affection for the Society. We got the text in English later that after-noon. It's hard to know the nuances of the Pope's message, but certainly there's no call for more radical changes."

Later though, major fractures occurred in the relationship between the Holy See and the Society. During this crunch time, Leo explained the situation at length:

Leo identified that before the Congregation started, the Secretary of State [Villot] had sent three letters to the General about complaints and problems with the Jesuits. "Much in the letters was true," Leo affirms, "and we should take it to heart, but unhappily, the bill of particulars was a mishmash, some of it ridiculous. Had it been planned politically, it could not have been done better to get sympathy for the General in the Congregation. It was a 'collection of raw data,' as the FBI would call it."

Leo was no fan of Arrupe going into the Congregation, but by the time it finished, he was definitely supportive and realized that the complaints about Arrupe were broadside critiques of everyone at the Congregation as well. Harold Small, the American assistant to the General and an Oregonian, explained, "All the problems listed had already been looked into and explanations sent to the Congregation of Religious." But the Congregation on Religious had not shared these reports with the Secretary of State. The lack of communication within the Vatican itself was the point of disconnect.

Another bill of particulars had been given to the General the year before on February 15, 1973. The General asked for an appointment to respond, but two years later had still not received a response to his request. Leo commented that this additional bill of particulars sounded like "a culling of reports about Jesuits from the *Wanderer*, *Twin Circles*, and *Triumph*, well-known, right-wing critics of the Society." Leo concluded this contretemps, "You can see now why there has been a closing of ranks around Arrupe. Our General, with all his faults, has been ill-used, and the Society has been calumniated." Later he adds, "One has to be a Catherine of Siena not to get anti-Roman amidst all this Byzantine intrigue."

But clearly the Pope and the Holy See did not like what they were seeing. "Justice and Peace," Leo observes, "are not the thing in the Vatican these days—at least not what the Pope wants from us." *Humanae Vitae* [the encyclical on birth control] is at the center of it all. "Uncle Hal Small" thinks that what the "Holy Father wants is a rousing affirmation from us of *Humanae Vitae*." [Many of us called the avuncular Father Small "Uncle Hal" or "Uncle Ozzie." His middle name was Oswald.] "If so," Leo continued, "I certainly hope the Pope doesn't intend to keep us here until he gets it. I have always gone along with *Humanae Vitae*, though I don't like it. But there are a lot of holy and learned men here who cannot in conscience accept it." Leo summed up, "Everybody seems so tired and beat and frustrated, that they don't know whether they like the documents we have written or not. What a mess."

After three months of grueling discussions, the Congregation came to a close on March 7, 1975. Surprisingly the dark cloud that Leo had been battling lifted. He affirmed, "The Congregation, a great grace, a great experience. But something I am glad I will never have to endure again. We accomplished a great deal, to give balance and direction to the impetus of Congregation 31. Now might Jesuits once again be one. So, dear diary, until we meet again on the Day of Judgment, when the Lord will convince me fully of his unconditional love for me and my Society by natural birth and adoption. Farewell."

Clearly, GC 32 was a profound affirmation of Arrupe's leadership, a rallying around his prophetic stance, and a solidification of the progress already made to advance the preferential option for the poor as a hallmark of the Society, just as the Synod of Bishops had already affirmed for the universal church in 1971.

Though some might dispute the claim that Arrupe was a second founder of the Society, I believe that the convergence of evidence is so strong that you have to do cartwheels to dismiss the claim. A further comparison with Ignatius is helpful. Nadal says that if you wish to understand the Constitutions, then look to the life of Ignatius. Likewise, I would say, if you wish to understand the modern revision and updating of the Constitutions themselves, then look to the life of Pedro Arrupe. Arrupe is the key to the revival of the Jesuits, which sprang from the heart of the Church in the Second Vatican Council. He perceived that if the Society were to undergo the call for renewal issued by Vatican II, it would need above all "to revitalize its own practice of making and giving the Spiritual Exercises." His dynamic leadership upset Jesuit traditionalists and some of those in the Vatican. Curial types were especially defensive whenever principles of social justice were applied to the church itself.

At the same time, they rightly feared the excesses and the naïve enthusiasm for liturgical innovations that had no grounding in theology or tradition. I had a first-class example of such innovative liturgy when I traveled with a group of Jesuit seminarians and priests to the Holy Land in 1972. On our second night in Athens in one of the bedrooms, the young priest—no vestments, of course—spontaneously created a prayer that seamlessly flowed through what might have been the Homily, Offertory, Preface, and Canon of the Mass. Suddenly we were receiving

Communion. Jim Dugan, another scholastic, and I stared blankly at each other afterwards. Jim said, "What was that?"

"I think that counted for Mass," I dryly responded.

Liturgical innovations, marked by both creativity and abuse, were widespread in those early years after the Council, but they were also leading to a profound revival of active engagement by the laity in liturgical prayer that had been lost for centuries.

Bureaucracies seek stabilization, so the upheaval coming both from within and without the church in the period 1965–1985 was bound to raise consternation. Add to this, the election of a pope in 1978 who had spent his lifetime confronting Communism, and you have a formula for an inevitable showdown—with all the juridical power stacked up on the side of the indomitable Vatican bureaucracy.

"Great risks have to be taken in many places," Arrupe affirmed. The Society of Jesus made a communal discernment, he said, and set out in a certain direction. No discernment gives us 100 percent certitude. We make mistakes, we move on. Arrupe amplified, "The elasticity of this experimentation and risk-taking should be all in one direction—the direction pointed out by the Holy Spirit."[4]

The last time I encountered Arrupe was in 1980. He was in Spokane, Washington, for a meeting of all the American provincials. Shortly after he arrived on Sunday May 18, Mt. St. Helen's volcano exploded and sent ash spewing out in a northeasterly direction for hundreds of miles. Spokane was directly in its path. As I came out of the Baccalaureate Mass for our seniors graduating from Gonzaga Prep, I saw a gargantuan, ominous black cloud to the southwest. I said to a Jesuit scholastic mowing the lawn, "You'd better hurry before that rainstorm hits." I still had not heard about the volcanic eruption.

Very soon, five hours after the volcano blew, tons of ash were descending, and Spokane was wrapped in total darkness. Neither the sun nor any glimmer of light could be seen. At 2 p.m. all the streetlights came on, and an eerie, ghostly presence filled the air. Cars could not drive in the ashy mix because the carburetors quickly gave out. A most unhelpful expert from Washington State University, interviewed on the radio, blithely said, "Well, the last time this happened, it lasted for twenty years." What he meant was that there had been a series of eruptions over two decades, but his unqualified claim prompted me to calculate how quickly

4. Pedro Arrupe, SJ, Letter to Jesuits in Jesuit Relief Services.

I could get to the Oregon Coast and escape the mayhem predicted to last for twenty years. For three days we huddled inside, playing bridge for hours on end. Finally, by Wednesday we were able to muster all our forces, bring out the fire hoses, and start cleaning up the school.

Arrupe and all the ten American provincials arrived that night for dinner. They had been on the edge of town "eating ash" for almost four days, so they welcomed our little oasis with great relief. We presented Arrupe with a crafted T-shirt: "I Survived Mount St. Helens." Included in the group of visitors were the three officials of the Jesuit School of Theology in Chicago—looking haggard and anxious. I immediately intuited that a decision was about to be made to close the Chicago theologate since the number of Jesuits in formation was still rapidly declining, and the cost of subsidizing these centers was soaring. Sure enough, within a month the American provincials announced its closure. The decision left the Jesuit School of Theology at Berkeley and Weston College in Cambridge as the two remaining centers out of the original five. Thirty-two years later even these two sought financial refuge by joining with Santa Clara University and Boston College. These choices were painful, but necessary steps in consolidating Jesuit formation needs.

Arrupe looked pale, thinner, and worn, when I saw him. But the next morning when we hosted an extensive breakfast for Gonzaga Prep friends, parents, and students, he exuded his customary warmth and care. In my last moments with him as I had my photograph taken with him, I thanked him for all he had done for me and for the Society. I had no premonition that within a little more than a year, he would have a massive stroke and the Vatican power brokers would rein in the Society and curb its apostolic dynamism.

For my generation of Jesuits, Arrupe was our inspiration. He was our true north. He embodied our Way of Proceeding, which he acclaimed as our Ignatian method of discernment, moving forward step by step under the guidance of the Spirit—together and in community. Indeed, great risks had to be taken.

Don Pedro suffered a stroke in August 1981. This great communicator and linguist was struck silent, though he could haltingly struggle his way through some Spanish. As he continued to live in the Jesuit Curia attended by a Spanish brother, he was a sacred tabernacle in our midst. He died ten years later on February 5, 1991.

6

Great Risks Had to be Taken: The Revolution in Jesuit Spirituality

ARRUPE WAS THE VISIBLE face of the transformation of the Society of Jesus, but the greater revolution in Jesuit life was hidden, intimate, and charged with promise. It was the transformation of Jesuit spirituality itself, which changed almost everything.

The Council gave an apparently simple mandate to religious orders:[1] 1) Return to the sources (*ressourcement)* and, 2) in the light of the signs of the times and the needs of the contemporary world update everything (an *aggiornamento). Ressourcement* and *aggiornamento*—these two words—one French, the other Italian—symbolized the retrieval of the very best of the tradition to address modern ills and the wretched state of much of humanity. These two methods were the pillars of reform for the Council. They became paramount to our Jesuit way of proceeding, that is, our discernment in the midst of the storms that followed.

In addition, the Council underscored that "the Gospels are the supreme rule of life," but, unlike the Protestant insistence on *sola scriptura*, the Catholic Church held for the ongoing revelation of God through the Spirit, through the life of the church, and indeed through God's providential care for all of creation up to and through this very day. So the return to the sources meant not just a return to ancient biblical times, but to the whole history of the church—the tradition—in order to discern and retrieve the Spirit-movements down through the centuries.

1. Pope Paul VI, "The Up-to-Date Renewal of Religious Life."

Many religious orders and congregations, both men and women, were simply unprepared in philosophy, theology, canon law—as well as, spiritually and socially—to alter so many aspects of their life so quickly. The Roman Curia was equally unprepared to assess all the revisions. Because of the intellectual tradition of the Jesuits, however, scholarly research, already underway, provided a framework, amidst rapidly advancing changes. And fortunately, Arrupe's spirituality led him to see reality with the eyes of Christ and to discern the best possible way for the Society to move forward.

THE ARRUPE REVOLUTION

The depths of the revolution, led by Arrupe, were realized in the recovery of the original purpose and dynamic of the Spiritual Exercises of St. Ignatius. By having the *Constitutions* translated into English (finally!), they became accessible for the first time to the young Jesuits in training. Instead of reliance on the Summary of the Institute, which was simply a terse distillation of the *Constitutions,* providing a long list of rules without much élan or spirit, Jesuits could now mine the authentic Ignatian insights in their original context.

During all this time I was in close contact with Joe Conwell, my early mentor at Gonzaga University. In 1957 Joe had published *Contemplation in Action: a Study in Ignatian Prayer,*[2] which was the earliest monograph by an American to explore the model of prayer advocated by Ignatius for the Jesuits. Nadal's claim that the graces of mystical prayer, which Ignatius experienced, were also accessible to every Jesuit was astounding and deeply consoling. Years later I assisted Conwell with endless revisions of his classic *Contemplation in Action*, which became a whole new book *Walking in the Spirit* (2003). Joe realized that his original translation of *contemplativus simul ac actione* as "contemplative in action" was misleading. The better translation was "contemplative simultaneously in action." Jesuits were meant to be contemplative in every moment of our day. The prior translation led some Jesuits—with adverse results—to believe that their action was their prayer and that time devoted specifically to contemplation was superfluous. Joe acknowledged with a wry smile, "I have learned quite a bit since I wrote that first book forty years ago."

2. Joseph F. Conwell, SJ, *Contemplation in Action,* and *Walking in the Spirit.*

In the aftermath of Vatican II and especially after GC 32, our spirituality became radically regrounded in the mystical prayer experience of Ignatius himself and in his apostolic actions. Both movements—contemplation and action—took off together. Some Jesuits delved into the Exercises and rediscovered the personal retreat. Others engaged in more radical actions addressing the systemic social evils of our time. Several activists linked arms with other reform activities or borrowed heavily from confrontational strategies, such as those engineered by the social activist in Chicago, Saul Alinsky. At times the two major energies of contemplation and action seemed to be on a collision course.[3] Joe Conwell kept asserting that for Ignatius they were meant to be one and the same. Contemplation also in action was the core of the Jesuit vocation. Eventually, with time, experience, and wisdom hallowed by mistakes, these seemingly different energies became integrated into the vital mission that we experience today. In this chapter, I explore the spirituality revolution; in the next chapter I will take up the complex picture of the multiple movements for social action on behalf of justice.

A MORE AUTHENTIC IGNATIAN SPIRITUALITY AND SPIRITUAL GOVERNANCE REDISCOVERED

A few years ago some of the principal leaders in the transformation of how the *Spiritual Exercises* were given met at Georgetown University for a lively exchange on how the rediscovery of the *Exercises* in their authentic, Ignatian form had occurred.[4] Guided by Tony Moore, they recounted their early personal experience of making the thirty-day Spiritual Exercises as a preached retreat with four talks for prayer and a daily conference. They had minimal interaction with the director, if for no other reason than that the numbers of novices, ranging from twenty-eight to fifty and mostly eighteen-year-olds, prohibited it. Although these men entered the Society about fifteen years before I did, they perfectly

3. L. Patrick Carroll, SJ, and Katherine Dyckman, SNJM, creatively linked these two dimensions in their *Inviting the Mystic, Supporting the Prophet.*

4. Interviewed in 2008 by Tony Moore, special assistant to the president at Georgetown, the notable spiritual directors included: Walt Farrell (Detroit), John O'Malley (Detroit), Howard Gray (Detroit), Joe Tetlow (New Orleans), Dom Maruca (Maryland), and Bill Barry (New England). I'm grateful to Tony Moore for sharing the unpublished text with me.

described my own experience of the age-old, preached retreat during the first decade of my Jesuit life.

From the extensive dialogue among these six trailblazers, I will draw comments from just two of them, both good friends: Howard Gray, who was provincial of Detroit Province and later rector of Weston theologate, and John O'Malley, internationally recognized historian of the Catholic Church and the Society of Jesus. Gray began by cautioning against simply dismissing the previous era of the Society. "A lot of good was done. It gave the novices a common vocabulary, a symbolic world, and a sense of loyalty to the Society's traditions." But, he added, it was far distant from the intense personal, spiritual experience that Ignatius had in mind.

The group concurred that the one-on-one dialogue between director and retreatant became the norm by 1975, about ten years after the Council. The six Jesuits summarized the long history which preceded this change. Much of the charism of St. Ignatius was buried when Pope Clement XIV, under extreme pressure from the Bourbon monarchy and other factions in the church, ordered the worldwide Suppression of the Society of Jesuits in 1773. Historian John O'Malley explained that when the Society was restored forty-one years later, the documentation of the early Society was exceedingly meager. Jesuits in the English-speaking world had available the text of the *Spiritual Exercises*, the so-called Common Rules, which were a distillation of traffic regulations common in the early Society, and a set of rules called a Summary of the Constitutions, which were excerpts from the *Constitutions*. There was also St. Ignatius's letter on obedience and another letter to the Jesuit school at Coimbra in Portugal—only two of the 7,000 letters of Ignatius. The poverty of sources directly impacted the restoration of the Society and led to a narrower, more rigorist spirituality.

We now have twelve huge volumes of Ignatius's correspondence, O'Malley said, the largest extent correspondence of anyone in the sixteenth century. None of this was available in 1814. The other major breakthrough was the publication of most all of the early documents of the Society in the *Monumenta Historica Societatis Iesu* (MHSI), a collection of scholarly volumes (157 volumes—so far). The Jesuit scholars pulled together the primary sources so that, thereafter, other scholars could mine what was published. Another great resource, O'Malley said, were the three volumes of the Practice of the Spiritual Exercises in the early Society from the time of Ignatius up into the seventeenth century, published by Ignacio Iparraguirre, SJ. Throughout that earlier time the

Exercises were given in a one-on-one format, whereas from 1814 onward, they were given as a preached retreat.

Howard Gray recalled his own personal experience of the transformed Spiritual Exercises when he went to North Wales in 1962–1963 to make tertianship, the last stage of Jesuit formation. "Paul Kennedy, the tertian director, was starting the directed retreat and had a great influence. His whole insistence was on one-on-one dialogue." "Kennedy would encourage you to follow your own way," Howard explained, "to stay where you found fruit, light, insight, peace, and harmony. When you found unrest, when you found discouragement—you looked at yourself and you felt a certain 'dis-ease', then stay with it and see what was there." Howard underscored the importance of tracking consolation (moving towards God) or desolation (a feeling of movement away from God). They were the "eye of the needle of affective movement," where you were going to find God. All this accommodation to a person's unique individuality, Howard concluded, led to the *Exercises* becoming liberating and revelatory.

The changes in my own experience of the annual eight-day retreat began in 1966. That summer we had a preached retreat at the College of the Holy Cross for sixty of us scholastics. But six of us decided to gather each evening to pray, reflect, and to share our lives and spiritual movements together. The retreat became remarkably different. The insights of the others illuminated our own inner darkness or confusion. The intimacy of the group led to greater intimacy with Christ. We were each a tremendous grace to each other, channels of Christ's love and mercy.

During this same time my contemporaries at Mount St. Michael's in Spokane had a communal retreat given by Fr. David Asselin, SJ, a noted spiritual director at Regis College, Toronto. Asselin, along with a team of young priests for one-on-one spiritual direction, used short clips and documentaries from the Canadian film board as meditation points in order to engage the scholastics more intimately in their own unique relationship with God. Asselin explained later that short films, slides, and symbols may help reveal the divine involvement in human experience.[5] During these years of creativity and adaptability, multiple innovations with the Spiritual Exercises brought the Gospels alive and fostered one's personal encounter with Christ.

In my own province of Oregon, one Jesuit, who was highly critical of the changes in the church and Society, rather astutely fingered those

5. David T. Asselin, SJ, "Notes on Adapting the Exercises of St. Ignatius."

who were most influential in our province. In a definitive tone, he said, "Three men destroyed the Oregon Province." I would have expected him to name a certain provincial or perhaps a couple of rectors, or a few radical activists, but no, he went right to the heart of the matter. "They were Pat O'Leary, Jim Weiss, and Joe Conwell," he announced. Initially I was stunned, but then I reflected that all three of these men were intimately involved with Jesuit spirituality and in the training of the younger men. They revolutionized Jesuit formation in the Oregon Province. So ironically, I had to agree with the insightful critic about the "destructive" influence of these three exemplars.

Every province had similar trailblazers. The Detroit province, in particular, provided great leadership in this spiritual renewal: we have to think of Jules Toner, Howard Gray, John O'Malley, and Frank Houdek. And in the Missouri province George Ganss, David Fleming, and John Padberg made major contributions. George Ganss, in fact, dramatically captures the monumental shift in the Church and in the Jesuits: "The Church . . . is now passing through a transition as momentous as that of the Reformation and the Council of Trent. She is moving from an era of authoritarianism, when most of the impulses came from the top downward, no less than in the civil commonwealths under absolute monarchs, to an epoch far more democratic, when most of the ideas and initiatives are coming from members upward. . . . One manifestation of this trend toward increasingly democratic procedures in the Church is the growing use of 'communal discernment.'"[6] Ganss prophetically encapsulates the core of my thesis about the centrality of discernment in the historical development of the Jesuit mission over the last fifty-some years.

Michael Buckley of the California Province provided a foundational spirituality for young Jesuits when he was rector of Alma College after it became the Jesuit School of Theology at Berkeley. In a much-quoted article he challenged young scholastics preparing for ordination: "Are you weak enough to be a priest?" The question to ask, Buckley explained, is not, "Am I strong enough to be a priest?" But rather, "Am I weak enough?" That is, am I weak enough to recognize my own humanity and failings so that I rely on God? Am I weak enough to depend on others and know that I don't have all the answers?[7]

6. George Ganss, SJ, ed., "Foreword" to the article by Ladislas Orsy, SJ, "Towards a Theological Evaluation of Communal Discernment."

7. Michael Buckley, SJ, talk replicated in atlantadiaconateformation.com/weak-enough.pdf.

An Irish Jesuit on the occasion of his fiftieth year as a Jesuit succinctly captured the dynamics of transformation. "Seemingly overnight,"
he recounted, "we went from domestic exhortations to encounter groups;
from clerical dress to more relaxed secular clothes; from preached to
directed retreats; from the ascetical to the affective; from the academic
to the experiential; from polemical arguments to personal faith sharing;
from perfection to human development; from body and soul to embodied spirit; from devotions and dogmatics to dialogue and dialectic; from
silence is golden to talk or die!"[8]

CENTRALITY OF THE SPIRITUAL EXERCISES

As the years went by, Jesuits and their lay colleagues became more and
more aware of the great gift that the Spiritual Exercises provided, not only
for their own spirituality, but for the whole church. Lay people began to
be trained as spiritual directors and eventually they took ownership for
promoting, advancing, and transmitting the Exercises. As early as 1982,
Sister Katherine Dyckman, a Holy Names sister, and Father Pat Carroll,
still a Jesuit at the time, founded the Spiritual Exercises in Everyday Life,
(the SEEL program) in Seattle, Washington, which offered the thirty-day
retreat in a nine-month format to about fifty lay people each year.[9] In
addition, they simultaneously trained lay people to be directors for the
Exercises. The program flourishes to this day and has become a major
vehicle for transforming spirituality and for ecumenical dialogue, since
Lutherans, Episcopalians, Methodists, and people of other faith traditions
have made the Exercises and adapted them to their own communities.

In fact, the second revolution was the "giving away" of the Spiritual
Exercises to lay people and advancing the role of women in appropriating
and giving the Spiritual Exercises. It was a great boon to the spiritual life
of all types and manners of people. Three Holy Names Sisters, in particular, uncovered "liberating possibility for women" at the heart of the
Spiritual Exercises.[10]

In the summer of 1985 as I was finishing my doctoral studies at
Catholic University, I attended a four-day workshop on the Spiritual

---

8. Brendan Staunton, "Fifty Years a Jesuit," 24. I have abridged his quote.

9. L. Patrick Carroll, "The Spiritual Exercises in Everyday Life."

10. Katherine Dyckman, Mary Garvin, and Elizabeth Liebert, *The Spiritual Exercises Reclaimed.*

Exercises offered by Howard Gray at the Colombiere Center in the rolling hills outside Detroit. Howard was warm, compassionate, and so deeply immersed in the Exercises that he had the knack for letting them sing. Thirty years later when I talked with him at Georgetown about this book project, he generously spoke at length with me about his own personal life since he entered the Society at age eighteen in 1948. By now at eighty-six, never that tall, he had shrunk a few inches, but his wit and insight had expanded.

Here's a summary of the Exercises, relying heavily on Howard's insights and my own experience: Ignatius organized the Exercises into four "weeks." These are not seven-day weeks, but rather four stages on a journey to spiritual freedom and wholehearted commitment to the service of God. Our Jesuit spirituality, which is personal and social, individual and communitarian, has a clear set of developmental patterns which help us discern whether our quest for God's will is sound or sick. These patterns of development are freedom, discipleship, labor, and transcendence.[11]

First Week. The First Week of the Exercises is a time of reflection on our lives in light of God's boundless love for us. We see that our response to God's love has been hindered by patterns of sin. We face these sins knowing that God wants to free us of everything that gets in the way of our loving response to him. The first pattern of development is spiritual freedom, "the ability to donate oneself because I know my history, temperament, and talent. I am capable of giving myself, even as sinner, because Christ has freed me, graced me, to journey with him."[12] The Jesuit Pope Francis would say Christ had "mercy-d" him a sinner.[13]

Second Week. The meditations and prayers of the Second Week teach us how to follow Christ as his disciples. We reflect on Scripture passages: Christ's birth and baptism, his sermon on the mount, his ministry of healing and teaching, his raising Lazarus from the dead. We are brought to decisions to change our lives to do Christ's work in the world and to love him more intimately. The Second Week takes the free man or woman and asks whether the Redeemer can become the Exemplar, the one who dramatizes the only human strategy for the true pilgrimage of grace. Discipleship is the spiritual developmental issue. Do I buy into the

11. Howard Gray, SJ, "An Experience in Ignatian Government," 23.

12. Ibid.

13. *Miserando atque eligendo*, the pope's Latin motto is practically untranslatable in English. "Mercy'd and chosen by God," would be a rough approximation.

liberating strategies of Jesus to follow him as disciple, or am I enveloped
in the wily stratagems of the enemy of our human nature?

Third Week. We meditate on Christ's Last Supper, passion, and
death. We see his suffering and the gift of the Eucharist as the ultimate
expression of God's love. The Third Week, according to Howard, takes
the "free person who lives and desires to serve Christ by accepting his
strategy, that is, poverty, humiliations, and humility, and says, 'Will you
now labor with him, carry the Cross of the consequences of living as
one who even faces hatred and rejection?'"[14] One can see Pope Francis as
an exemplar of this call to humility, to reach out to the hurting and the
marginalized, to labor in the "field hospital" for those in dire need.

Fourth Week. We meditate on Jesus' resurrection and his appari-
tions to his disciples. We walk with the Risen Christ and set out to love
and serve him in concrete ways in our lives in the world.[15] In the myster-
ies of the Gospels about the Risen Christ and in the Contemplation to
Attain Divine Love, this Fourth Week invites the "free disciple who has
totally identified with Christ to let go, to move beyond even the present
mission to the wider designs of God. This transcendence, this spiritual
dissolution, is the death we all will face, but also the many deaths which
anticipate that final death. . . . Can I so live that even after strenuously
doing the work which is God's present will, I can leave it to others in
order to accept the new stage of God's will for me?"[16] Howard notes that
we have magnificent examples of this in Jesuits, such as Pedro Arrupe,
the El Salvador martyrs, those who surrender to age and infirmity with
quiet dignity, and those sent from a comfortable life to some new beginning. So we Jesuits are called to journey together as friends in the Lord
in freedom, discipleship, labor (compassion), and self-transcendence.
These stages are those which I would hope would be reflected in my own
life, but my interior certainly looked ragged; a lot more hits and misses,
falls and rising ups, than would be anticipated from this grand outline of
the journey.

14. Gray, "An Experience in Ignatian Government," 23–24. Quote is slightly
amended.

15. See "What are the Spiritual Exercises?" from Ignatian Spirituality, a service
of Loyola Press at http://www.ignatianspirituality.com/ignatian-prayer/the-spiritual-
exercises/what-are-the-spiritual-exercises#sthash.GCwtjeoL.dpuf.

16. Gray, "An Experience in Ignatian Government," 24.

OTHER DIMENSIONS OF THE TRANSFORMATION IN RELIGIOUS LIFE

To live in that period immediately after Vatican II was to live in the eye of the storm, but many of us did not see how radically different it was going to be once the storm subsided. A day-by-day progression—which at times seemed boringly predictable—marked the enterprise. Pedro Arrupe captured it well in an enduring phrase when he spoke to us Jesuits in Spokane in 1980. He recalled how once a journalist had asked him what was the vision that guided his choices throughout those tumultuous fifteen years.[17] He shook his head and said simply, "We had no vision. God guided us, and we made our paths by walking on them."

SENSITIVITY GROUPS

Several misdirections occurred during these rambunctious years. Some abandoned their own stiff, staid, rigid spirituality for more secular self-help, personal enrichment, and psychodynamic methods. A proliferation of sensitivity groups occurred. Carl Rogers was the psychologist of choice with his client-centered therapy. His approach resonated well with the Ignatian guidelines for spiritual directors to listen attentively to the person's inner being. Rogerian psychology offered a supportive, nonjudgmental atmosphere in which a person could begin to flourish. Acceptance was at the heart of his approach.

Other types of psychological approaches were more dynamic, often more aggressive. T-groups, which originated in Tavistock, England, became the rage. At times they were destructive because they broke down a person's natural defenses with highly charged interchanges. On the other hand, they could also allow a person—perhaps for the first time—to claim his or her own anger and to gain access to the deeper realms of one's own emotional makeup, including one's sexuality. The person could then move on towards a fuller appropriation of who he or she was as a person. In the scatological words of my crusty friend Fr. Jim McDonough critiquing the multiple ways humans have of hiding, "They could no longer put whipped cream on crap."

17. May 23, 1980—five days after Mt. St. Helens blew. I was there for his talk at Gonzaga University.

Some of the same techniques were taken over in Clinical Pastoral Education (CPE) programs, which became mandatory for many young Jesuits during their formation years. Superiors sometimes saw this route as an avenue for breaking through the rigid defenses of emotionally stunted Jesuits. When it produced negative effects, superiors backed off from making it mandatory. Some bolder Jesuits ventured into total body therapy, for which Esalen in California was notable, perhaps even notorious. People were ready to try anything. Some of it was destructive, but out of this experimentation, much good occurred. All in all, Jesuits were playing with fire, but also warmed and expanded by it.

TENTATIVE REFORMS AND MISSTEPS

Immediately after the Council, Jesuits were grasping for straws about how to reform our governance structures. In the past when authority was highly hierarchical and most everyone fell within the parameters of the long black line, the provincial staffs were small and sleek. The provincial curia might comprise five Jesuits at the most: the provincial, his socius or assistant, a secretary, a prefect of studies to oversee the studies and assignments of scholastics, and a fundraiser. Governance was straightforward and direct. Often a Jesuit did not know his marching orders until the "status" or assignments were posted on a bulletin board on July 31, the Feast of St. Ignatius. For instance, Fr. Frank Logan, who had entered the Society in 1919 and was stationed at Seattle College in 1938, told me that one year he received a call from the provincial on a Thursday to report to the Jesuit parish in Havre, Montana, for the weekend and to plan on being there for a year. Frank packed up a cassock, a clerical suit, a couple of shirts and pants, a weeks' worth of underwear and socks, a black overcoat, a breviary, a few books, and off he went by train to Montana. Today it takes anywhere from a week to a month for any one of us to pack up and move.

Some provincials opted for the secular governance model offered by the Arthur D. Little Company of Boston, which, in my view, dumped a mess of "management by objectives" on us. What was often obscured by this import of external expertise was the strength of our own spiritual governance. Our solid traditions were set aside, rather than reinvigorated. It took another decade for us to see the folly of unwittingly adopting secular models. By then, the annual manifestation of conscience, when each Jesuit discloses his interior spiritual life and apostolic life to the provincial, provided the basis for a genuine discernment about mission. Provincials used assemblies of Jesuits to sort through, absorb, and discern what was happening locally and how the province should respond to the mandates of the Society following the Council. Many Jesuits, especially those raised in the old ways of just having intelligent superiors make the decisions, found these gatherings god-awful. Inevitably, clichés would abound. Leo Kaufmann, a gifted philosopher, strung these together at the end of one of these assemblies and left everyone laughing uproariously with examples such as this: "We have to take the bull by the tail and look reality straight in the face." Steve Lantry, working off the same genre, offered: "This is a real red herring—we better nip it in the bud before it snowballs and blows up in our face!" Jesuits typically used wit and humor to survive arduous times.

Provincials shifted focus to national priorities beyond their own parochial regions. Consequently, they met together at the national level at least three times a year to form the National Jesuit Conference. Each provincial also served on the governing board of one of the two theologates. In addition, as lay people took over leadership of our institutions, the provincials had to meet with each of them as well as their governing boards and the local bishops. The proliferation of meetings devoured them.[18]

Early on, a shortage of Jesuits began to occur, further complicating governance. The numbers of Jesuits peaked at 701 in the Oregon Province in 1962 and reached their acme worldwide in 1965, though by then, a significant decline had already begun in Europe.[19] By the fall of 2016 the Oregon Province had 181 members. The critical factor, however, was not so much the shortage of Jesuits, as it was a vision stunted by relying almost exclusively on Jesuits to lead and staff our major institutions. The lack of a revitalized vision exacerbated the reliance on old ways.

When I entered the Jesuits in 1961, the Oregon province had 271 scholastics, 361 priests, and 59 brothers. Those on the missions included 42 in Alaska, 24 on Indian reservations in Montana, Idaho, and

18. Gerald McKevitt, SJ, unpublished notes shared with this author. Jerry interviewed about thirty provincials, who served in the era from 1966 onward about their roles in leadership. Santa Clara University Archives.

19. Joseph M. Becker, SJ, "Changes in U.S. Jesuit Membership, 1958–1975," offered an early statistical assessment of the dramatic exodus of scholastics and priests from the Society. Becker agreed with the analogy offered by Pedro Arrupe that "the Society had been ill—both before and during the collapse in membership—but that the patient is showing strong powers of recuperation." (3)

Washington, 5 in Japan, and 2 in the new commitment to Northern Rhodesia (Zambia). In subsequent years, the Native American ministries took a heavy hit in manpower. Numbers in Alaska, where we had 3 high schools—St. Mary's, Copper Valley, and Monroe, Fairbanks—took a heavy hit when they closed. For some years, the Jesuit Volunteer Corps had been a vital ingredient in the success of these schools. A Sister of St. Ann provided the inspiration to attract young college grads to volunteer for a year or two of teaching. Subsequently in 1957, Jack Morris, SJ, then a scholastic, founded the Jesuit Volunteer Corps. My second cousin Mick Byrnes and his future wife Sylvia were in that first class of JVC at Copper Valley. Initially, the JVs were confined to Alaska, but then they spread to the whole Oregon Province. Now, sixty years later, the JVC Northwest has 148 volunteers and another 300 volunteers in the separate, national organization with another 50 volunteers internationally.

Of course, changes needed in the formation of young Jesuits were vital. And the murky confusion at the top created a muddled pattern within formation. The genial Fr. Pat O'Leary, novice master in our province, 1976 to 1982, famously said, "If I only knew where the Society was headed and what young Jesuits could expect for their mission, then I would know what to do with formation. I barely know what I'm preparing them for."

By the 1970s most novitiates, located in an idyllic rural setting, were moving into urban settings. First Studies and Theology were relocated to a university campus. Tracking the where's and why for's of these decisions would be worth a chapter in itself, but here are a few examples: New England's Shadowbrook novitiate in Lenox, Massachusetts, moved into Boston. Oregon's Sheridan novitiate moved to an old convent school in Portland. The Shrub Oak philosophate moved to Fordham University. The Weston philosophate moved to Boston College and the Weston theologate joined an ecumenical consortium in Cambridge. Alma College in the Santa Cruz hills moved to the ecumenical center of Graduate Theological Union in Berkeley. St. Mary's theologate in Kansas had already moved to St. Louis University. A further irony was that often enough some fundamentalist group or schismatic Catholic sect bought the former Jesuit properties. The breakaway Tridentine Catholics moved into Mt. St. Michael's philosophate in Spokane, and the schismatic Lefebvre St. Pius X Catholics bought out the theologate in Kansas. We retained ownership of some places, such as Los Gatos; Weston; Colombiere, Michigan; and

Wernersville, Pennsylvania, which became a combination of assisted care homes for aging Jesuits and spirituality centers.

The renowned Woodstock College in Maryland, the oldest and most prestigious Jesuit theology school in America, where Avery Dulles, Gustave Weigel, John Courtney Murray, and other Jesuit luminaries had taught, moved to Union Theological Seminary in Manhattan. With the number of scholastics drastically falling, however, provincials soon decided they could no longer justify the expense of supporting five theologates. So they closed two of them: St. Louis University and Woodstock College. The latter decision had more twists and turns than one would have expected. After a lengthy discernment the provincials and their staffs had opted to close Weston College in Cambridge, rather than Woodstock. But when they referred it to Rome, Arrupe declared that Woodstock would close. What undid Woodstock was not the academic caliber of the program, which was stellar, but the chaos in the formation program. The former Woodstock theologate in the Maryland countryside had gone from rigid, formal, predictable structures to near total freedom in Manhattan—with casual dress, sunbathing on rooftops, and easy tolerance of female guests for coffee, dinner, and conversations. Garry Wills, a former Jesuit, recounted these adventures in a revealing, near scandalous, article in the *New York Times* magazine section. His article probably undid Woodstock. In addition, two Woodstock Jesuits about to be ordained by Cardinal Terence Cooke, the archbishop of New York and the military ordinary for the American Armed Forces, mounted a public confrontation of the Cardinal's role with the military right in the middle of the ordination ceremony. The other ordinandi were burnt to a crisp at how the two had hijacked the whole solemn ordination and what should have been a wonderful celebration of their priestly ministry.

The heady freedom of Woodstock led to mounting questions about "Why be a Jesuit at all?" And more intimate encounters led to deeper questions about celibacy. Personal crises and uncertainty mixed with ill-defined formation goals led to a stew of doubt, anger, and loss of direction. When I visited the Woodstock complex in 1971 a couple of years before it closed, the place seemed incoherent; it was difficult to identify any center.

The upheaval at Woodstock did have its humorous moments. One of them related to Avery Dulles, the son of the distinguished Secretary of State John Foster Dulles. Avery had undoubtedly grown up in a family with servants, and when Woodstock was out in the woods, a team of brothers, along with the scholastics, had done all the household chores. So when he got to New York, he had to wash his own clothes for the first time in his life. One morning a scholastic came down into the kitchen area, and there was poor old Avery in front of the dishwasher wringing out his sopping wet laundry. He turned to the scholastic for help: "Could you show me how to operate this blasted washing machine?"

After the decision was made by Arrupe to close Woodstock, one of the New York Jesuits quipped that "discern" was an irregular verb and that its conjugation was:

I discern	We discern
You discern	You discern
He decides	They decide

A highly irregular verb. But I should add—totally in keeping with our Jesuit vow of obedience and the Jesuit way of proceeding. The superior is the ultimate decision-maker.

Even in Rome, we had our own protests and demonstrations. My good friend Fabrizio Valetti led a "pray in" in the Basilica of St. Peter's. About twenty Jesuits and supporters knelt in the main nave of the church to protest the promulgation of *Humanae Vitae,* the encyclical on birth control. The Swiss guards were so startled that it took them awhile to realize what was going on. In a former day, Fabrizio might have been thrown out of the Society, but "the times they were a-changin.'"

One indication of the incredibly rich, new time in the church was the golden age of Catholic publications after the Council. The Jesuits clambered on board this train of commentary, Scripture study, and historical studies. For many years the *National Jesuit News* and the Oregon Province's creative *The General Exchange,* begun by Pat Twohy and thoroughly advanced by Brad Reynolds, kept everyone abreast with lively articles, dialogue, and controversy. Twohy led off the inaugural issue in Thanksgiving of 1971 with a full-page cartoon of the provincial staff as turkeys. That set a tone! Good humor, serious stuff, and a family gathering á la Thanksgiving for sharing our lives together.[20]

---

20. The Vatican Revolution could be richly tracked through the history of publications, such as *America, The National Catholic Reporter,* and *The Wanderer.* And the plethora of theological insight could be mined through the publishing outlets of The Liturgical Press, Orbis Books, Paulist Press, Sheed & Ward, Ave Maria Press, and others.

My own transformation in Jesuit spirituality took another step forward in the summer of 1971 when I made an individually directed retreat for the first time. I had as my director the wild and crazy biblical scholar Fr. Bill Fulco, a truly exuberant character. He seemed as nervous as I was in our daily encounters in which I shared the fruit of my prayer. He had brought along a parrot with him, named Hot Beak. And whenever he was at a loss for words, which wasn't often, he would turn to the parrot: "Hot Beak, what do you think? What do you recommend to Pat?" After a little conversation with his avian companion, Fulco would interpret Hot Beak's squawk or chatter and relay it to me. It was quite entertaining, but also freeing. More importantly it allowed me to delve deeper into my own spiritual interior with greater freedom.

The next significant step was my ordination retreat the following year. Our spiritual guide for the retreat was Federico Arvesú, former Jesuit provincial of Cuba. He was both kind and shrewd. He based the retreat on *dinamico di gruppo*, group dynamics. We prayed individually through the day and then the twelve of us briefly shared the movements of our prayer in the early evening. Arvesú helped us discern how God was working in and through the group and in each of us individually. About the fourth day of the retreat I had a profound, intimate experience of God's presence symbolized by a shower of camellia petals. Since the full range of my Italian vocabulary was lacking, I translated my experience to the group as *una pioggia di rose*, a rainfall of roses—close enough. By the sixth day the group itself was experiencing a bout of desolation—which Arvesú identified as a deepening anxiety over the prospect of a lifetime commitment as a priest. *How could we take on such a long, uncertain commitment?* Then he described how when he first went to philosophy studies in Pullach, outside Munich, Germany, he was told that before he finished his studies in Germany, he would have eaten 100 kilometers of *wurst* (wieners or sausage)! It was a daunting, even revolting vision of his future. But, he continued, "We took it day by day and I managed the impossible!" The wild analogy broke the tension, and we had a great laugh. A few weeks later we were ordained as deacons at the Gesú Church by Archbishop Paul Marcinkus, president of the Vatican Bank. Later Marcinkus was notoriously at the center of one of the most clamorous Vatican scandals because of shady deals perpetrated by the bank. Many thought smarmy Italian financiers had hoodwinked this generous American.

An ominous turning point in my spiritual journey came three years later after my first difficult, tension-filled year as principal of a boys

Jesuit high school. Once school let out, Jim McDonough and I gave two eight-day personally directed retreats to Maryknoll Sisters in Hawaii. We dropped the customary, long-established preached retreat and adopted a much more personally tailored, one-on-one retreat.[21] Giving these retreats was consoling and intimate because of the personal relationships. They confirmed God's gracious goodness.

After my return to the mainland, I was relaxed, receptive, and eager to make my own retreat, which was directed by a good friend with whom I was easily able to open up and be myself. I was also able to do some vigorous exercise each day, something I had been missing during the stress-filled days of my first year as principal. As the retreat progressed, I felt more and more consoled and drawn to a deeper intimacy with God. The Gospels came alive, and I felt placed immediately in the scenes with Jesus. At night though, I had nightmarish dreams. In one I heard this haunting buzzing sound and woke to a huge beetle on the screen window. The next night I felt I was in mortal combat with a jungle of beasts and a gigantic ape. During the day consolation and peace returned in my prayer, but I felt surges of emotion and the beginnings of some unnamed eruption. At some point my dream world, my imagination, and the dynamics of the retreat all merged and from then on I was overwhelmed by the onset of a major psychosis. It was as if I had moved into the imaginative world of the Exercises and was acting them out. My normal psychic defenses collapsed, and I could no longer differentiate the real from the imaginary. Surprisingly, on the outside I functioned well enough for a few more days so that many didn't know the difference.

But interiorly, my incipient psychosis was becoming more and more acute and frightening. Fortunately, three Jesuits intervened and committed me to a psychiatric unit at Providence Hospital, Portland, Oregon. I was in the hospital psyche ward for a month—back in the days when insurance was generous! Then I was in intense, outpatient psychotherapy for another two years. My whole interior had unraveled because of a false start in my psychospiritual development somewhere along the way, and then I was knit back together again. In the aftermath my emotional life, my sexuality, and my spirituality were more grounded, less driven. Ironically, looking back on the disruption, I felt that the psyche ward was more real, more human than many other avenues of my life. I developed what I called my "psyche ward spirituality," almost as if I had done a second

21. The commentary by John English was also immensely helpful: *Spiritual Freedom*.

novitiate, but this time my interior was more congruent with God and the world around me. I could live in my own skin at peace, without feeling driven. My rector, the curmudgeonly, kind Jim McDonough, visited me every couple of days; he would describe some of the outlandish behaviors exhibited at the high school and drolly claim, "You're the sanest person I've met all day!" I have recounted this whole experience at much greater length in my autobiographical account *Reducing the Storm to a Whisper,* so there's no need to dwell on it all here. I bring it up here to demonstrate the power as well as the danger of these privately directed retreats—most often with far less dramatic results.[22]

Three years after the breakdown, I became principal of Gonzaga Prep in Spokane, Washington. The ensuing five years as principal were a terrific experience, some of the best years of my life, which undoubtedly brought much further healing. The culmination of this period came during yet another retreat—my thirty-day tertianship retreat made under the guidance of Joe Conwell (once again!).[23] During this time I experienced a quiet, inner peace—as if the glow of a candle in a dark room were illuminating and soothing my own interior darkness. The divine presence enveloped me. A verdant love gave way to a ripening, mature love in my life.

In subsequent years I became an advocate for people with mental illness and especially their families—frequently sharing my own story of breakdown and recovery. What had been a nightmare became a surprising gift. Was my psychosis a mental breakdown or a mystical, religious experience? Perhaps both. The acute psychosis I experienced was debilitating and impairing. But through medication, psychotherapy with a gifted psychiatrist, and strong, caring support from Jesuits and family, I came out the other end stronger, healthier, and more self-confident. Years later I could say, "It was one of the best things that ever happened to me, but I would not recommend it to anyone." Healing of the breakdown was certainly a religious experience. So it's not an either/or; it's not either mental illness or a religious experience, but, in my view, a *tertium quid,* a third alternative, namely God acting in and through multiple players and resources. The human person is too complex for a solitary explanation of

22. Howell, *Reducing the Storm to a Whisper.*

23. Tertianship is the final stage of formation for a Jesuit, sometime after ordination. It is the third ("tertius" in Latin) probation period, which a Jesuit undergoes after a long period of study, formation, and apostolic work. It culminates with full profession in the Society of Jesus.

all that might be occurring. The danger of claiming a mystical, religious experience is that a person might not seek the normal, available human resources, such as competent psychiatric help. But certainly the ultimate healing that I experienced was at the nameless core of my being an encounter with mystery, with God, for sure.

ARRUPE: REFLECTING ON THE MYSTICAL HEART OF OUR SPIRITUALITY

To close out this reflection on the dynamic evolution of Jesuit spirituality, I turn once again to Pedro Arrupe, who late in his time as general provided a theological reflection on the mystical and Trinitarian heart of our spirituality. "I am firmly convinced," Arrupe energetically said, "that the Society, in virtue of the Trinitarian inspiration of its Ignatian charism, rooted and grounded in love, is providentially prepared to enter the struggle and is engaged effectively in curing the spread of *anomia* (destructive lawlessness) and working for the victory of love. The plight of the world so deeply wounds our sensibilities as Jesuits that it sets the inmost fibers of our apostolic zeal a-tingling."[24]

That was vintage Arrupe—setting our "apostolic zeal a-tingling!"

Arrupe helped the Society of Jesus rediscover its fundamental call to discernment. Through a series of high-risk discernments, Jesuits found that they were not so much called to abandon their schools or missions or retreat work, as to do all these things in new ways. At General Congregation 32, the Society of Jesus had asked itself this question: What is it to be a Jesuit? The answer it gave was memorable. "It is to know that one is a sinner, yet called to be a companion of Jesus as Ignatius was."[25] It's not surprising then that Pope Francis, who attended this Congregation as provincial of Argentina, later on famously described himself as a sinner, like St. Matthew, shown mercy, called and loved by God.[26]

Over and over, Arrupe referred to the crucial mystical experiences in the life of St. Ignatius Loyola, especially his vision at La Storta in 1537 while on the way to Rome. So too, he observed, we in our day were being placed with Christ carrying his cross, being invited into service of humanity with Christ, with the firm promise that God would be with us

24. Burke, ed., *Pedro Arrupe*, 147.
25. GC 32, Decree Four.
26. "A Big Heart Open to God," interview by Antonio Spadero, SJ.

wherever he sent us. The vision at La Storta links the mysticism of Ignatius to a spirituality of service with a particular sensitivity for suffering. These are the characteristics that Arrupe himself helped recover—this practical mysticism so central to the Society.[27]

DISCERNMENT OF SPIRITS

The other highly significant feature of a recovered Jesuit spirituality was the renewed emphasis on discernment. An Ignatian guideline for a genuine discernment was "indifference" or spiritual freedom realized in contemplative prayer. Without this freedom, all the biases rutted in the past were bound to recur.[28] Some of the misdirections in the Society came from narcissism, clericalism, authoritarianism, and sexism—lots of isms, absence of spiritual freedom.

My friend and spiritual confidante Joe Conwell was fond of dissecting the origins of a word down to its marrow in order to unfold more fully the intent of the language. "Discern," Joe noted, comes from the Latin: *dis* (apart) + *cernere* (to perceive), to perceive apart from or "to tell the difference." But if we go deeper it means to cut away, divide, separate, and sift. In Joe's memorial words it means "to cut the crap."[29] Late in life, when he was writing his last book,[30] his major insight was a resounding declaration that desolation has a positive element. God has something to teach us through these dark, painful experiences, Joe declared. Desolation should not be ignored; it should be sifted and tried. By now in his nineties, he said to me ruefully, "I wish I would have known this a long time ago. It would have saved a lot of anguish and pain."

The Church itself went through considerable desolation from about 1980 to 2005. We should not dismiss or ignore the events of this dark,

---

27. Joseph Tylenda, SJ, "Commentary," in *A Pilgrim's Journey*, 113. For Arrupe's commentary, see Burke, ed., "Introduction" to *Pedro Arrupe*, 123.

28. Jules Toner, SJ, *A Commentary on Saint Ignatius' Rules for the Discernment of Spirit*. In this magisterial book, Toner provides a guide to the principles and practices of the discernment of Spirits enunciated by Ignatius.

29. See also: Burke, ed., *Pedro Arrupe*, 158–59.

30. Joseph F. Conwell, SJ, *Darkness in Light*. Unpublished manuscript on the Rules for Discernment of Spirits in Jesuit Oregon Province Archives (JOPA). The Oregon provincial assigned me to review all of Joe's papers and final book. I decided that his 530-page manuscript was not publishable, but it rests intact in the Oregon Province Archives (JOPA) for someone to mine its riches.

even tortuous, time; rather they have something to teach us. So now it is
time to explore some of the messiness and graces arising within the Society during these years of transition. As I said at the outset, the Society has
with careful attention been wending its way through these last fifty years
of confusion and renewal, of diminishment and flourishing, of sinfulness
and graced choices, through the lens of spiritual discernment and the
bold adherence to the inspirations of the Holy Spirit. Indeed, "great risks
had to be taken."

7

Commitment to the Faith
That Does Justice

THE RESPONSE OF THE Society of Jesus to the mandates of the Council moved forward in two simultaneous trajectories, parallel at first and then converging. The first was the renewal of Jesuit spirituality by a rediscovery of the genuine Ignatian method for the Spiritual Exercises and, the second, a more radical commitment to social justice based on the teaching and practice of Jesus (Matt 25:40) and the preferential option for the poor articulated by the Synod of Bishops in 1971. Both trajectories were integrally connected. Faith without justice was not credible. Justice without faith was not sustainable. So when the Society accepted Pope Paul VI's charge to the Society in GC 31 (1965–66) to combat atheism, it wholeheartedly addressed the injustices that lead so many to ask, "Where is God in all this?" Or even, whether there is a God at all. The pope's vision was for a church that was much more in touch with the poverty, oppression, and hardships of the poor and how they were vulnerable to atheistic communism. Pope Paul succinctly captured the essence of what was needed: *If you want peace, work for justice.*

The Jesuit commitment to social justice came painfully hard, most especially where the Jesuits had a strong institutional commitment to education. The high schools made the adjustment swiftly; but the universities, with a few notable exceptions, mainly among individual Jesuits, greeted the changes with reluctance or even resistance. Eventually, however, a notable transformation in all Jesuit apostolates took off with increasing acceleration. By now—in 2018—it's assumed by all our students that Jesuits have *always* been committed to a faith that does justice. That's what a Jesuit education is all about! And certainly all of our schools now have a strong reputation for social justice. If they only knew what a struggle it was to get here!

Unlike my intense experience of transformation in Jesuit spirituality, my engagement with social justice emerged over a longer period of years. Some pivotal events stand out: in 1956 when I was fifteen and just two years after the landmark Supreme Court decision of *Brown vs. Board of Education*, which mandated that all public schools be integrated with all "deliberate speed," my parents took my brother Mike and me on an extended trip from our home in North Dakota to Mardi Gras in New Orleans. The trip made a lifetime impression on me. We left the snow-swept tundra in the north, and mile after mile we enjoyed the increasingly warm weather and eventually the bright, joyful spring of Louisiana.

"White only" and "colored only" signs began as early as Kansas. For the first time, I witnessed the prejudice, bias, and oppression of Negroes—the name used in those days. I was shocked. I had seen the violence and persecutions of Negroes in movies, but this was real. While we were in New Orleans, Archbishop Joseph Rummel ordered the integration of all the Catholic schools.[1] "Racial segregation as such," Rummel announced in his pastoral letter which I read years later, "is morally wrong and sinful because it is a denial of the unity and solidarity of the human race as conceived by God." We watched some of the ugly scenes on television as die-hard segregationists in New Orleans—Catholic parents—angrily protested the Archbishop's order. My dad asserted, "It's a hundred years since the Civil War; it'll take another hundred years for real integration to occur." As a teenager, I thought he had to be wrong. But Dad's sense of the violent nature of racism was certainly right. And, in fact, despite Rummel's mandate, the Catholic schools in New Orleans did not integrate until 1962.

Some years later in 1964, my summer in Roxbury in the inner city of Boston provided another indelible mark. Five other Jesuits and I fanned out in pairs, dressed in our clerics, taking a parish census. We encountered the stark rawness of poverty. It smelled poor. The projects housing hundreds of people in the same sterile environment lent themselves to

---

1. See the Rummel papers (February 11, 1956). Notre Dame Seminary Library.

crime, filth, and danger. They encouraged passive endurance. Survival was the key.

Another powerful event was the movie *The Pawnbroker*. My friend George Murphy and I managed to escape the confines of Weston in the woods and under the guise of going to the Boston Art Museum, we headed for the movie. Set in Harlem, the movie portrays Sol Nazerman, a Jewish pawnbroker, played by Rod Sterling. He is an emotionless man, which makes him effective in negotiating with his desperate customers because he has no feeling about their plight. Nazerman is bitter, viewing the people around him as rejects, scum. Through a series of flashbacks we learn that his detached attitude results from his dreadful experiences in Auschwitz during World War II, which included the rape of his wife and the murder of his family by the Nazis. A parallel process occurs now between what happens on the streets of Harlem and what happened to him in the concentration camp. And in a painful, awakening moment Sol becomes acutely aware that he is exploiting his desperate customers in a manner similar to how the Nazi guards treated him and his family. In this moment of awareness and self-torture, he plunges his hand through a metal letter file holder.

Another pair of tragic events hit me when I took a biblical tour of the Middle East in 1972. On the bus through Central Turkey, we came across a village where thirty people had frozen to death the winter before. And in one of the Turkish cities I witnessed a little girl of three struck dead as a huge truck ran over her. Turkey had a harsh, primitive feel to it at the time. When we flew from Istanbul into Tel Aviv, we saw the Israelis' pervasive oppression of the Palestinian people—already. But the occupation was mild in 1972 compared to what I saw later in 2000, by which time the settlements had mushroomed across the occupied territory. By then, the Israelis had become exceedingly aggressive in condemning Palestinian land and seizing their homes, olive groves, and gardens. Soldiers insulted revered elders. Israel was treating people who had lived in the region for centuries as illegals. For the slightest infraction, the occupiers would bulldoze a Palestinian home and seize the property. They were relentless in "creating facts on the ground." And meanwhile the United States was still pouring billions of dollars into Israel each year despite the increasingly harsh occupation.

Most of all, my worldview and my sense of structural injustice came from day-to-day rubbing shoulders with other Jesuits—many of whom were on the front lines of addressing poverty, exploitation, worker harassment, and the relentless machinations of war.

The Jesuit awakening broke wide open in 1989 with the assassination of the six Jesuits and two women by paramilitaries of the El Salvadoran government, whose military leaders had been trained at the School of the Americas in Ft. Benning, Georgia. With this violent assault on the heart of the university, American Jesuit universities finally awoke to the need for an institutional commitment to social justice—not as just another academic exploration or a piece of research but as a challenge central to our identity. We embraced our mission. And our alumni did too. Speaker of the US House of Representatives Tom Foley, who had graduated from Gonzaga Prep and attended Gonzaga University, was instrumental in appointing the Moakley Commission to investigate the assassinations and the role of the paramilitaries and US government in the violence. I had meet Speaker Foley seven years earlier when I was principal at Gonzaga Prep and also a member of our local Faith and Justice Commission. We met Foley in our attic quarters to argue the case for the United States to cease and desist its military aid to the El Salvadoran right-wing government, which was feeding the raging fires of civil war. Foley was a big man, a large presence who filled the cramped room. He was supportive, but was skeptical and realistic. "We don't have the votes yet." After the assassinations of the Jesuits, he had the votes.

During that same time, I wrote a letter to the editor of the *Spokesman Review* critiquing the linking of the Lilac Parade in May with the jingoistic celebration of Armed Forces Day. Military weaponry and armed forces overwhelmed what could have been a grand folk festival. Oooh! What an uproar. After my letter was published, many of our alumni wrote or called the Prep: "How could you?" Another alum, who was an air force colonel, asked to see me. He was cordial but firm. I had touched a nerve in the military complex.

My own education as an undergraduate at Gonzaga University had not emphasized social justice. The exception, as I mentioned before, was the course on St. Paul with Archbishop Thomas Roberts of Bombay, who lectured almost exclusively on the nonviolent movement of Gandhi and of Martin Luther King, Jr. in the incipient civil rights movement. For the most part, I was saturated with Thomistic philosophy and Christian humanism. Our theology tended to be apologetic, a schooling in how to defend the faith against Protestant incursions. Justice was a Thomistic virtue, but not action oriented. Prudence dominated.

COMMITMENT TO THE FAITH THAT DOES JUSTICE

Proud alumni from those years still express their appreciation for their Jesuit education and its emphasis on philosophy. They boast, "The Jesuits taught me how to think, but not what to think." I wince when I hear this, since the claim may be made by a well-heeled alum touting his or her success, comfortable lifestyle, and political aversion to supporting the poor in their aspirations. Some seem to have cast aside the Thomistic focus on the common good in favor of a muscular American individualism. But they are "thinking for themselves."

Admittedly, many other alums live a life committed to justice, and they strive to create opportunities for the poor and marginalized. For instance, the founding of Nativity schools, middle schools for inner city, at-risk kids, beginning in lower Manhattan in 1971, would not have been possible without the vigorous support of alums from Jesuit high schools and colleges. Today over sixty-five Nativity schools in twenty-six states are thriving. Often our alums are leaders in their Catholic parish or major players in making a Catholic education accessible to as many as possible. The lay leadership envisioned by the Council took root, so that the gifts of all could flourish. Today—ironically—many of our Jesuit high school and college alums seem to think that the Jesuits are an advance guard of the Church, and that the rest of the Catholic Church just needs to step on the gas and catch up. The historical truth is a far different reality. The Church itself was in the vanguard for the reform of its own teaching. And consequently, the Church inspired the Society of Jesus to go deeper, to reflect more carefully on the gospel of Jesus, and to learn firsthand what it means to be in solidarity with the poor.

CATHOLIC SOCIAL TEACHING

I need to take a detour at this point and bracket my own personal experience so that I can give a wider perspective on the impact of Catholic social teaching on me and my fellow Jesuits. The strongest church statement which explicitly condemned "unjust systems and structures" was the 1971 statement by the Synod of Bishops, "Justice in the World."[2] It contains one of the clearest statements on justice ever proclaimed in official Catholic social teaching: "Action on behalf of justice and participation in the transformation of the world fully appear to us as a constitutive

2. *Justice in the World*, 270 and 276. Synod of Bishops, 1971. https://www1.villanova.edu/content/dam/villanova/mission/JusticeIntheWorld1971.pdf.

dimension of the preaching of the gospel, or, in other words, of the Church's mission for the redemption of the human race and its liberation from every oppressive situation."[3] Here the bishops insisted that Christian faith and justice cannot be separated. If one claims to be Christian, she or he must work for justice. Faith without justice is not credible. This first major example of worldwide, episcopal collegiality reflects a forceful refinement of previous papal pronouncements.

The Catholic Church began its marathon race towards social justice 128 years ago with the encyclical of Pope Leo XIII in 1891's *Rerum Novarum*. Pope Leo XIII was concerned that Communism and socialism were gaining strength and a newly industrialized Italy caused long, dangerous work hours for little pay for workers. Fear of Marxism and a potential revolution led Leo to seek social and economic reforms.

The Society had had a long, distinguished history, for instance, of defending indigenous peoples; most notable was the establishment of the Reductions or compounds in Paraguay and Brazil for the Guarani Indians. Many Jesuits, such as John LaFarge, Michael Twomey, and others were early advocates in the 1940s and 1950s for social justice in the United States, especially regarding race relations, but it was not a Jesuit institutional commitment, nor was it at the forefront of the formation for young Jesuits. As early as 1949 the Superior General Jean Baptiste Janssens issued his famous *Instruction on the Social Apostolate*, considered a milestone in the Society's road toward commitment to the so-called "social question." In bold language for those days, Janssens spoke of completely uprooting the spirit of caste among Jesuits and their students. They should not appear "to be allied with the rich and the capitalists." Those especially who labor in the educational ministry should manifest "an interest and concern for the proletarians that is equal to, or even greater than, that shown to the rich." One can imagine the impact of these words on the American Jesuit schools in that era. Shades of Communism!

My personal impression was that Janssens did his best to bring the Society into the modern era, but most of his efforts were thwarted. In 1957, for instance, after eleven years in office, Janssens summoned the 30th General Congregation to provide him with a vicar general because of his affliction with asthma and increasing ill health. The delegates elected Canadian John Swain to the position. Janssens had also hoped to do some updating of the Society, but Pope Pius XII derailed him. After the

3. Ibid., #6.

pope asked the Jesuits to give up smoking, all the energy centered on this triviality. As a consequence, our novice master spent formidable energy on how the ban on smoking came under the vow of obedience, and that infractions could be mortal sin.

As the twentieth century unfolded, it was clear that Christian humanism and a clear grounding in philosophy were not enough for a Jesuit education that engaged the justice issues of our time. Worldwide poverty was accelerating and even in wealthy, developed countries the poor went to bed hungry, children were undernourished, the violence of poverty was increasing. The remarkable history of the breakthrough in Catholic understanding is readily available elsewhere so I will just allude to a few key moments.[4]

Following Pope Leo XIII's *Rerum Novarum* (1891), Pius XI's *Quadragesimo Anno* (1931), Pope John XXIII's *Mater et Magistra* (1961), and Pope John Paul II's *Centesimus Annus* (1991) promulgated further reflections on the linkage between faith and justice on the occasion of the fortieth, seventieth, and one-hundredth anniversaries of the original document on Catholic Social Justice. The impetus for the Jesuits' eventual commitment to social justice as central to our mission was Vatican II and the papal encyclicals *Mater et Magistra (1961)* by John XXIII and *Progressio Populorum* (1967) by Paul VI. These two documents formed the pillars for much of the rapid advances in the church's increasingly strong commitment to the poor and marginalized. But at this stage of my life as a young Jesuit, I had only a passing twinge of conscience, "These are documents I should be reading." But the ponderous tomes slipped on by me. By 1971 Catholic social teaching was articulate, well developed, but it needed to be activated. Too often, as Jesuit Pete Henriot and Joe Holland announced, it was our best kept secret.[5] Even today, when I teach this history in my graduate course on the Theology of Vatican II, many exclaim, "Why haven't we ever heard about all this?"

These movements inspired the Jesuits in GC 32 to make "the service of faith, of which the promotion of justice is an absolute requirement" the central calling of our mission today. Even prior to this time Pedro Arrupe had used the phrase "option for the poor" in a letter to the Jesuits of Latin American in 1968. And the Catholic Bishops of Latin American (CELAM) advanced this cause and its theological underpinnings at the

4. Peter J. Henriot, Edward P. DeBerri, and Michael J. Schultheis, *Catholic Social Teaching*, 31.

5. Ibid.

influential conferences in Medellin, Colombia (1968) and later at Puebla, Mexico (1979). So Arrupe was clearly leading the Society towards generously embracing the call of Christ to serve the poor, the imprisoned, the orphan, and the widow. In the early seventies, I cannot say I was aware of these struggles except through conversations with Fr. Phil Land over breakfast at the American cafe in Rome. Between mouthfuls of scrambled eggs and a pinch of bacon, Phil, who worked in the Pontifical Peace and Justice Council, explained his role as one of the two drafters of the 1971 Synod document on "Justice in the World."

THE SOCIAL APOSTOLATE

Tension mounted between the universities and the social apostolate. A few of the older fathers looked with disdain upon valiant efforts to enact social justice and, missing the point entirely, would piously assert, "I wasn't trained to work in a soup kitchen." Several younger Jesuits, however, did become involved in direct ministry to the indigent and homeless. Some trained in the aggressive, confrontational tactics of Saul Alinsky in Chicago. One of these was my Jesuit classmate Greg Galluzzo. Alinsky, a cultural Jew, explained that his reasons for organizing in black communities were that Negroes were being lynched with regularity in the South. And many of the white civil rights organizers who had started to work with them were tarred and feathered, castrated or killed. Most Southern politicians were members of the Ku Klux Klan and had no compunction boasting of it.[6]

Ordained a priest in 1974, Greg was a fireball and passionately committed to organizing for structural change to empower the poor and the homeless. He left the Society a few years later and returned to Chicago, where eventually he was instrumental in helping to found the Developing Communities Project. For three years in the mid-1980s, Barack Obama worked with Galluzzo and was influenced by Alinsky's work. Obama later wrote, "It was the best education I ever had, better than anything I got at Harvard Law School," an education that was "seared into my brain." Galluzzo said to me shortly after Obama's election as president, "Obama's time with us and his identification with the tribulations of the black people began his political journey."

6. Serge Kovaleski, "Obama's Organizing Years."

These were also the years of the Great Exodus out of the Society. I had entered the Society with twenty-seven other men. Of the original twenty-eight of us, seventeen took first vows after two years of novitiate and only eight of us were ordained. And three priests left after that, leaving the remaining five of us—two of us at Seattle University, two in Zambia, and our only African American Jesuit serving as chaplain in Tacoma. From 1966 to 1986 the number of Jesuits in the United States slipped from 8,237 to 5,168, and the biggest decline came among the scholastics, that is, those in formation from the time of first vows to ordination, 2,229 in all. The Vatican developed an arduous process of "return to the lay state" for the ordained priests. But to receive approval, the person had to acknowledge that he had never had a vocation whatsoever. By confessing to negligence and other faults, the man could grease the skids for a positive approval. Despite our novice master's fine explanation of the difference between Jesuit life in the novitiate and a Chinese concentration camp, a few similarities endured, in this case a public confession of malfeasance.

In November 1974 when Father Arrupe held a press conference to explain why men were leaving the Society, the numbers worldwide had declined already from 36,038 in 1965 to 29,462, and greater attrition was on its way. Don Pedro said that 0.8 percent of Jesuit priests were leaving each year. Though obviously he did not relish this trend, he was completely unfazed by it. He did not blame it on the modern world, and he refused to wring his hands in impotent grief. He learned from the departures, he said. Some people leave to sort out personal psychological problems. They go with blessings on their head, and their departure, though sad, is not tragic. After all, there are other ways of serving God. "Our mission has many ministries," as the Council says. Even so Pope Paul VI expressed profound anguish at the departure of so many priests. In an unusually harsh statement for him in a famous Maundy Thursday homily, he likened defecting priests to Judas. He quickly followed with: "I know! I know!" the Pope exclaimed, "One must distinguish case by case, one must understand, be compassionate, forgive, maybe wait for the return. And one must always love." [7] Don Pedro, on the other hand, said he was more worried by another kind of departure. Just as pain can be a sign of malfunctioning of the organism, so the losses of bright young men could be a warning that change must come or decline would set in

7. Paul Hoffman, "Pope Paul Compares Defecting Priests to Judas." By then about 25,000 priests had left the priesthood in the previous seven years.

irrevocably. Don Pedro always held firmly to this principle: "The voice of the young Jesuits is the voice of the modern world within the order." And he wanted to give that voice a hearing.

REVERSALS AND RETRENCHMENT

With the election of Pope John Paul II in October 1978, reactionaries and conservatives took firm, solid control of the Roman Curia and set about appointing bishops of like mind. Cardinal Joseph Ratzinger, later Benedict XVI, imposed the Vatican's doctrinal authority throughout the Catholic world. In 1984 and 1986, the Holy See twice condemned elements of liberation theology, especially the Marxist elements.

Even so, some reform initiatives continued for a while. In 1986 the bishops of the United States, still reflecting the caliber of episcopal appointments made under the earlier popes, wrote *Economic Justice for All*, in which they analyzed and criticized the United States economy for allowing increasing poverty in the midst of plenty. They acknowledged that, rather than being accidental or inevitable, social and economic structures are human constructions and, therefore, can be made more just.

APOSTOLIC INITIATIVES

Cataloguing the immense amount of creativity and outburst of new apostolic initiatives that occurred after the Council would alone constitute several volumes. All I can do here is feature some of them—obviously those of which I was most aware or even engaged with.

In the United States the culmination of the civil rights movement coincided with the conclusion of the Council. The assassination of President Kennedy in November 1963 paved the way for the master of Congress Lyndon Johnson to cajole the faint of heart to ram through passage of the Civil Rights Acts of 1964 and 1965, but these landmarks would not have been possible without a nationwide movement of civil disobedience led by the valiant Martin Luther King, Jr. and the black community. As the movement persisted, they often marched arm in arm with clergy and with white college students from the North. A few Jesuits were on the streets with them. But more often, Jesuits were incorporating the cause of justice into their classrooms and research. Michael Twomey in New Orleans and Horace McKenna and Richard McSorley in Washington, DC were outstanding and inspirational. Jesuit scholastics, because of their youth, energy, and idealism, were also more apt to be directly involved. Some of my classmates, for instance, flew to California in the early seventies to join up with Cesar Chavez in his fight for immigrant farm workers, and returned brimming with excitement about their arrest and overnight in jail. Though admiring the cause, I was always ambivalent about "fly in" justice advocates. Closer to home my friend Father John Topel, a young theologian at Seattle University, in order to support the cause of Cesar Chavez among farm workers protested the selling of grapes at the local Safeway and made headlines in the *Seattle Times*. His actions and identification as a Jesuit at Seattle University angered some of our trustees, one of whom withdrew a $25,000 donation.

The second major American movement was the whole series of protests against the Vietnam war, which gathered momentum and burst out onto almost every college campus after Nixon authorized intrusion into Cambodia in May 1970, and the National Guard shot and killed several students at Kent State. Once again I was remote from the scene. Living in Rome studying theology, 1969–1972, I ducked these protests. When I returned to the United States in August of 1972 for my ordination and my first assignment as a priest, the political protests and militaristic counter measures bloodied the streets. Nixon was on his way to a second term, and the Watergate scandal had not yet broken the barriers.

Fr. Bernie Tyrrell, a newly minted philosophy professor at Gonzaga University, created a *cause célèbre* when he mounted a campaign supporting presidential candidate George McGovern in order to halt the determined march of Nixon towards arbitrary power. Bernie solicited 100 Jesuit signatures and ran an advertisement in the *Spokesman Review* entitled "100 Jesuits for McGovern." It was a futile effort, but it stirred up the wrath of donors and alumni. I voted for McGovern, who was inept, but a decent man. I was convinced that Nixon was corrupt. My wise old grandmother lamented, "Who am I to vote for? One is an idiot, and the other is a crook." I don't recall precisely, but I suspect I was simultaneously sympathetic to the urgency of stopping the war and dismayed at the chaos in the streets. Unwittingly, I was a modern Hamlet—betwixt and between—decision and indecision. Or as T. S. Eliot might have said, "Between the lip and the cup falls the shadow."

So my own growth in awareness and increasing activism advanced slowly but steadily. By 1985 when I finished doctoral studies in pastoral theology at Catholic University of America in Washington, DC, I had seen enough and absorbed the thrust of the new Society. Consequently, I was strongly drawn to Seattle where Archbishop Raymond Hunthausen was known for his prophetic stance against the militarization of the United States and our national obsession with more and more nuclear weapons.

Another inspirational, charismatic presence in our midst was Jesuit Father Bill Bichsel, who participated in a four-decade crusade against what he called the "unabated works of war" and "forces of militarism." Just months before he died in 2015 at age eighty-six, he still mustered enough strength to participate once again in a nonviolent peace action at Naval Base Kitsap near Bangor, Washington, home of the nuclear submarines. On his death Fr. Scott Santarosa, our provincial, wrote, "Bix fearlessly proclaimed a message of peace and worked tirelessly for the poor and the least in our society." Several times Bix was sentenced to prison. Ironically he spent almost two years in the federal minimum-security prison in Sheridan, Oregon, the little town where he had spent his Jesuit novitiate years. Bix explained of his work, "I know it sounds idealistic, but I believe strongly in my heart in the power of God and the power of creation and the Resurrection. They are much stronger than the powers of death." Though he and I never worked together, we were soulmates because of our accompaniment and advocacy for people with mental illness.

Meanwhile the Jesuits within their higher education institutions kept evolving and becoming more sophisticated and strategic in the mission of the faith that does justice. Greater hope was emerging. But above all, the Spirit's inspiration was taking hold; a more intelligent, vigorous faith was responding. We pick up the threads of this story again in chapter 10 where I detail the resistance and eventual reform among the Jesuit universities.

Howell family in 1964.

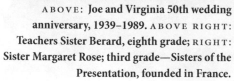

ABOVE: **Joe and Virginia 50th wedding anniversary, 1939–1989.** ABOVE RIGHT: **Teachers Sister Berard, eighth grade;** RIGHT: **Sister Margaret Rose; third grade—Sisters of the Presentation, founded in France.**

TOP: Presidential candidate Jack Kennedy speaks at Gonzaga University in April, 1960. I'm looking on from the left side—the guy in glasses. MIDDLE: 50th anniversary of the first Gonzaga Honors Program students; I'm on the far right. BOTTOM: Pat Howell, SJ, and Joe Conwell, SJ, mentor, teacher, life-time friend.

TOP: **Greeting parishioners of St. Aloysius Church, Lisbon, ND on ordination day, August 19, 1972. Bishop Justin Driscoll of Fargo gestures from my right;** TWO MIDDLE PHOTOS: **Ordination to the diaconate at the Chiesa del Gesú, Rome.** BOTTOM: **Baptism of Linda and Victor Mora's son.**

TOP: **Protesting the Trident Missile Base at Bangor, WA.** MIDDLE: **Vietnam Protestors engaging Fr. Ken Baker, SJ, president of Seattle University;** BOTTOM: **Fr. Frank Wood with ROTC cadets during World War II.**

TOP: Delegates for General Congregation 34 (1995) in Rome; I'm in the second tier down from the top with hand propping up my chin. MIDDLE LEFT: we gave a special award to the provincial from Chile for greatest improvement in spoken English; RIGHT MIDDLE: I'm making some point or other. BOTTOM: Tertianship class, Spokane, 1980–1981, final stage of Jesuit formation.

TOP LEFT: a relaxing day at Ocean Shores
WA. TOP RIGHT: Greeting Jesuit General
Pedro Arrupe, SJ, in May 1980 at Gonzaga
Prep where I was principal . LOWER LEFT:
Fr. Ed McDermott, SJ, first president of
Jesuit Secondary Education Association.
LOWER RIGHT: Jesuit classmates—Steve
Sundborg, Pat, Joseph McGowan, and Ron
Hidaka. Roy was in Zambia. Of the 28 who
entered in 1961, only we 5 remained.

TOP: El Salvadoran boys saluting "Presente!" three months after the 1993 peace accords. MIDDLE LEFT: Woman in procession with name of her murdered daughter Lucia, commemorating the martyred Archbishop Oscar Romero

MIDDLE RIGHT; I'm with husband of Elba, father of Julia, who were martyred by government paramilitaries, along with six university Jesuits. BOTTOM: A guerrilla describes his military actions with rebel forces

TOP: I met Pope John Pope II, introduced by Fr. Frank Case, SJ. MIDDLE LEFT: At *America* magazine, I helped translate the Pope Francis interview from Italian to English (Sept. 20, 2013)

MIDDLE RIGHT: As dean of our School of Theology and Ministry, I helped dedicate our new home in honor of retired Raymond Hunthausen, archbishop of Seattle, 1975–1991. BOTTOM: Two Jesuit Superior Generals: Adolfo Nicolás, 2008–2016, and Peter-Hans Kolvenbach, 1983–2008.

8

Jesuit High Schools Stumble, Scramble, and Thrive

I SPENT A TOTAL of thirteen years in Jesuit high schools from 1966 to 1983, with an interlude of three years to study theology at the Gregorian University in Rome. So from ages twenty-six to forty-three, I was intimately involved with Jesuit secondary education—at the same time that all the cultural, theological, and political upheavals were racking the country.

The high school world can seem rather small. Jesuit conversations inevitably centered on the sports teams. At Jesuit High School in Portland, Oregon, Crusader football was king. Though the school was only ten years old, we won the state championships two years in a row. Football put us on the map as an "excellent school." Students were the other prime topic of conversation—whether they were excelling or causing grief. A little relaxation after dinner might involve watching CBS *Evening News* with Walter Cronkite, followed by *Hogan's Heroes*. The high school pace was rapid, intense. It was hard to gain perspective on the wider issues facing society. Yet storm clouds were rapidly closing in on all of us.

One of my awakenings came through a student. During my first year, I taught senior English honors. The students were all racehorses. I was rather amazed when Greg submitted a paper about his spring break trip (1967) hanging out in the Haight Ashbury district in San Francisco. From him I discovered that it was the birthplace of the hippie movement

with peaceful protests and psychedelic experimentation. The era's luminaries, such as Jerry Garcia, Allen Ginsberg, and Jimi Hendrix, all lived
nearby. The infamous Summer of Love was still a few months away when
young dreamers converged by the thousands on the area. Soon after, the
district was nearly trashed and laden with drugs and homeless people.
The movement rose and died quickly—no longer a hub for music, poetry,
and art. I was rather repulsed by what I saw.

The next year the Vietnam war protests intensified. In the New
Hampshire primary, Senator "Clean Gene" McCarthy upset the pundits
and, fueled by an army of young people, came close to winning. He had
announced, "I am concerned that the administration seems to have set
no limits to the price that it is willing to pay for a military victory." Some
conservative die-hards, of course, accused him of kowtowing to Hanoi
and caving in to Communists. President Johnson had raised US troop
strength in Vietnam to 486,000 by the end of 1967. In October 1967, tens
of thousands of demonstrators gathered at the Pentagon calling for an
end to the war. In addition, a growing civil rights movement pointed out
injustice and continued racism throughout America. In the larger, youth-
driven society, countercultural music, fashion, and values were challenging convention. And television brought all this fresh turmoil to people's
living rooms as never before. Society seemed to be unraveling. More
darkness and tragedies soon followed, firing the nation to the boiling
point.

Gene McCarthy's strong showing in New Hampshire opened the
door for Senator Robert Kennedy to announce his candidacy a few weeks
later. Then LBJ dropped a bombshell on March 31 when he declared he
would not run for reelection. Just before the Oregon primary in May,
Kennedy operatives called Jesuit High and asked whether we could host
Teddy Kennedy. The entire student body and faculty gathered in the gym.
Ted spoke, took some questions, and then roared off to the next event. It
was a thrilling moment. But Bobby lost the Oregon primary. I was still
a Rockefeller Republican and cast my vote for Rocky—a wasted vote.
Nixon was already on a roll to wrap up the Republican nomination. It was
my last year as a Republican. Barry Goldwater had made the clarion call
for true conservatives in 1964, and the party became increasingly radi-
calized. Once Nixon dipped into racist politics to capture the Southern
states, I crossed the aisle to the party of Roosevelt and Truman, which my
parents had opposed ever since they voted for Wendell Willkie in 1940.
The assassinations of Martin Luther King, Jr. and Robert Kennedy were

the public events that profoundly affected most everyone that year. They triggered riots all over major cities. Later in August I was in Washington, DC and drove up to Columbia City, Maryland, with Jesuit friends to attend a Gene McCarthy rally. The highway was jammed. Cars overheated and stalled. Traffic was barely inching forward, so we arrived just as McCarthy finished up his crowd-rousing speech.

The in-fighting among Democrats reached a bloody culmination at the Chicago convention at the end of August. I watched on TV the brutality on the streets of Chicago when Mayor Daley shut down the protesters and imposed his version of law and order.

Even so, all these events seemed rather distant from the cocoon of high school teaching.

By the next year, I was studying theology in Rome for three years, 1969–1972, so I was even more remote from the social upheavals throughout the United States. I had no inkling about their effect on Jesuit educational institutions.

Rome had its own protests, which often enough were rallies of labor unions or teachers or political parties. I rarely understood the issues. We had frequent strikes of a day or more. A "white strike," what the Italians called *uno sciopero bianco*, or a hiccup strike, was my favorite. One such strike for buses was scheduled to last a minimum of five minutes and a maximum of fifteen minutes, merely to make the point about some arcane issue. The length of time was up to the driver. I was on one of those buses. We shouted encouragement to the driver, and all cheered after a mere five-minute stall. Postal strikes were the painful ones, because they stopped all communication with home. One year the mail stacked up so high over a three-week period that the postal clerks stored it in rail cars, which then got shuttled around to vacant tracks and lost!

After my ordination to the priesthood in 1972, I returned to Jesuit High School in Portland. I was shocked to find how much had changed in such a short time. Everything seemed more ragged. Pictures in the yearbook told the story. Instead of photos of seniors in the formality of shirt and tie, they were now "expressive"—whatever pose or style they chose. Significant numbers of lay people had been hired. My good friend Fr. Mike Merriman was now the principal—a warm, accepting priest who leaned on me a great deal in my new role as academic vice principal. I was starting all over with my teaching. I felt tested and tried, but, of course, I wasn't. I still had remnants of the fear I had internalized from my first year of teaching six years earlier, but now discipline was not a problem. I

am not certain what my aura was, but it was sufficient. I must have conveyed authority, and the students liked me. Discipline across the school,
however, was looser, more chaotic, and challenging. Teachers were more
uptight and cranky.

Across the United States similar upheavals had happened—all in
a short time. Jesuit education was unmoored from its traditional ties.
More electives were introduced. Biology was finally included in the Jesuit
high school curriculum. Its absence had always struck me as a strange
anomaly. The Jesuits had placed a premium on the classics as the primary
humanizing element in the Jesuit arsenal. Now Latin was no longer required. Modern languages, such as French, Spanish, and German, came
into prominence. Considering the four centuries of adamant adherence
to the classics, this shift was monumental, but it passed practically un-
noticed by students and parents. The fact that Latin was no longer used in
the Catholic Mass provided another reason for letting it fade away.

All the elements of a crisis were upon us and rapidly accelerating. In
those short, critical years, five major factors seemed to propel the doubts
and pressures on Jesuit secondary education.

1. Loss of Jesuit manpower. The rapid decline of Jesuit vocations
and the huge exodus of young men from the Society meant that the Jesuit
high schools were severely hit because they relied so heavily on the young
Jesuit scholastics for replenishment of their faculty. The total number of
scholastics, including novices, in 1966 was 2,599. Twenty years later in
1986 it was 590. By 1996, it was 364.[1] A rapid acceleration in the hiring of lay people began as early as 1970. Often enough, the new teachers were idealistic young men who were graduates of Jesuit high schools
themselves, but soon this changed. And faculty, often without any understanding of Jesuit education or the Catholic tradition, were hired. In
the Oregon Province, the apostolates hit the hardest by the decline in
numbers during those first two decades were the high schools and Native American ministries. If enough Jesuits were not available in a high
school, that is, about twenty or more, some Jesuit superiors judged that
it was no longer viable and obviously had to close. An implicit arrogance
in some of these decisions seemed to be, "If we can't do it, nobody else
can either."

1. Numbers from *The Society in Numbers, 1996,* in *Rome: Curia Generalizia della Compagnia del Gesú,* published anually. For the years 1966 and 1986, I have culled them from each of the individual USA province catalogues. The USA Assistancy did not have a combined province catalogue in those early years.

2. Rapid Rise in Tuition. Hiring more lay people increased all the costs. Schools could not depend on Jesuit-contributed services. By way of one example, Seattle Prep's tuition for 1964–1965 was $180. By 1973–1974 it was $700. And by the year 2016–2017, it was $17,900 with a $250 activity fee. With increased costs came higher tuition and consequently, fewer applicants. In addition, Jesuit leaders had deliberately kept tuition lower than actual costs, in order to make a Catholic education more accessible to those least able to afford it.

3. Religious Education Hit a Wall. The full integration of Catholics within the American culture meant the loss of a Catholic subculture. And correspondingly, the loss of nuns teaching in the Catholic grade schools diminished these feeder schools for a Catholic high school. More importantly, the dramatic shifts in the Church meant that religious education had to be reimagined and severely updated to appeal to the student in these new times. Tremendous creativity occurred. Innovative Jesuit teachers, such as Bill O'Malley of New York, Mark Link of Detroit, and Don Driscoll of Wisconsin penned excellent resources for high school religion.

4. The Raison d'etre for a Jesuit High School Seemed up for Grabs. Other Jesuits—internal critics—started to question the nature and purpose of our high schools. Weren't we simply educating the wealthy elite and perpetuating a cycle of failing to enfranchise the poor? A more telling critique was that our schools tilted toward white, traditional Catholics. The inclusion of minorities seemed minimal. Some Jesuits, most often those not directly involved in secondary education, were inspired by the Mexican Jesuits' decision to close its prestigious high school in Mexico City because it had served an almost exclusively rich clientele.

5. The Upheaval in the United States and among the Jesuits Themselves. As I suggested above, massive political differences tormented the country. The protests against the war now hit the high schools. Disruptions increased. Differences about the Church and the Vietnam war split the Jesuits among themselves. Generally, the younger Jesuits and the Jesuits leading the Society in governance and formation welcomed the changes. Older Jesuits, whether in the classrooms or on the missions, struggled with, and often resisted, the changes. The liturgy itself became a battleground. And when pastors started to remove statues from the sanctuary, change church décor to accommodate the shift of having the priest facing the people, and dismantle the communion rails, many of the laity were up in arms. "My grandparents donated all the money for that marble altar rail and now they're ripping it out like so much junk."

So Jesuit education, which had been slowly heating up, now reached a boiling point.

DARK NIGHT OF THE SOUL

In 1969 a long, overdue split of the Jesuit Education Association (JEA) into a university network, American Jesuit Colleges and Universities (AJCU), and a high school network, Jesuit Secondary Education Association (JSEA), occurred. In January the next year Jesuit high school leaders met in Scottsdale, Arizona, to regroup and to chart a new time, a new direction, and to create the JSEA, inaugurated in 1971. All but one of the attendees were Jesuits. Three years later in 1974 when I was elected to the national JSEA board, several of those pioneers described the "dark night of the soul" in Scottsdale and their near despair. They had gone round and round in their discussions, making no headway whatsoever. They were faced with the demise of the Jesuit school system as they had known it. They had not developed any viable program for incorporating lay faculty into the Jesuit ethos, and the outlays for lay salaries were formidable. In addition, the leadership knew only too well that American culture and political system were up for grabs.

A key person in the turnaround was Fr. Jerry Starratt, SJ, who had a recently minted PhD in education from the University of Illinois. He became the architect for the new vision of the JSEA. Years later Jerry recalled that as he was preparing to fly out to Scottsdale, a Jesuit principal in New York told him, "Morale in my school is at an all-time low. If you don't come back from Scottsdale with any sense of direction, I'm going to close the school." Starratt also recounted that during the discussions in Scottsdale, he summarized an essay by Fr. Jim Connor, SJ, the Maryland provincial: "No matter what ministry Jesuits were engaged in, they are basically giving the Spiritual Exercises." So Starratt imagined for the Scottsdale group what this integration of the Spiritual Exercises into the curriculum might mean in a high school setting. He cited themes from the Exercises, such as the Call to the Kingdom, Finding God in all things, Ignatian Discernment, Contemplatives in Action, and Carrying the Cross with Christ. Starratt recalled, "I spoke off the top of my head about how to translate the Exercises into the curriculum and pedagogy of a Jesuit school and thereby to recapture the Jesuit identity of our work." Jerry's peers were enthusiastic. They told him to go aside and put those ideas into writing. Meantime, they all relaxed and watched Super Bowl

VI. Jerry said later, "I went to my room and said, 'My God, what have I gotten myself into.' The trouble was that I couldn't remember what I had just said." But when he returned, Starratt had in hand the six-page Preamble to the Jesuit Secondary Education Association's Constitution (JSEA), which gave a rationale and dynamic direction to Jesuit high schools.

The response to the Preamble was electric. It became the rallying cry and transformational point for Jesuit high schools. The JSEA itself became a catalyst for change throughout the next decade and beyond. Fortunately, three bright Jesuit stars had just finished their doctorates in education: Jerry Starratt, of course; but also Bob Newton at Columbia, and Vinny Duminuco at Stanford. They became the brain trust for advancing the redefined Jesuit mission and identity. I was fortunate to work with them through those formative years.

Fr. Ed McDermott, SJ, a genuine energizer bunny and veteran principal of two California Jesuit schools, was elected the first president of the JSEA and became the heroic leader who kept us on track, vigorously helped to promulgate the Preamble far and wide, and to make it practical. By 1975 or thereabouts, the high school apostolate was on the move again. It was a dramatic reversal.

The Preamble challenged the schools to "go beyond the criteria of academic excellence, important as this is, to the far more challenging task of bringing about a true *metanoia* [the Greek word for a change of heart] in their students." It also asked the schools to "honestly evaluate their efforts according to the criteria of both the Christian reform of social structures and the renewal of the church." When I was on the national JSEA board, we continued the pattern of brainstorming and then commissioning a couple of us to draft the next document.

That same year the JSEA Board asked me to research the advantages and disadvantages of coeducation at the high school level. The coed environment had clear pluses for the boys—better social integration, less wild, and more respectful of women. But all-girls school often proved better for teenage girls. They were more likely to flourish if they didn't have to compete for the attention of their heart's desire, and they easily assumed leadership roles. Already Scranton Prep had gone coed in 1971 after a disastrous fire destroyed Marywood Academy. Driven by economic and demographic imperatives, Bellarmine Prep in Tacoma went coed with a courageous combining of resources with St. Leo's High School and Aquinas Academy in 1973. Other Jesuit schools soon followed suit in going coed, including Gonzaga Prep in Spokane in 1975. When I arrived at Gonzaga Prep as principal three years later, the senior class boys chauvinistically declared they were the last genuine Gonzaga Prep students.

On the continuing search for an authentic mission, many Jesuits felt that if Jesuit schools were simply providing good college prep, they should leave the enterprise to far wealthier independent and public schools. We were all searching for distinctive, identifiable qualities in our schools which would legitimize naming them *Jesuit*. A key moment became the shift of the Jesuits to having the laity as full partners in the secondary education ministry. We could clearly affirm, "If the faculty at a Jesuit school are men and women whose lives are inspired by the Ignatian vision, then the question about the percentage of Jesuits on the faculty is not an overriding issue." Could the teachers exemplify and communicate the vision of Ignatius to the students? Hence formation of faculty in the Ignatian tradition became a pivotal point.

Some of the reforms came too late to save some institutions. A pattern of diminishment came about abruptly. So, for instance, Xavier High School in Concord, Massachusetts, where I had done my student teaching, was a good example. The highly successful school had been founded in 1962. But two Jesuits—the local superior and the principal—impulsively announced the withdrawal of the Jesuits in 1971, without even consulting other Jesuits. So it closed. The school was only ten years old. It was situated in a wealthy suburb, so with thoughtful planning, it could have been turned over to lay leaders.

Another early closure was the popular, highly selective Brooklyn Prep in the New York Province. Founded in 1908, it was strong in religious values, in the classical roots of Latin and Greek, and had a demanding dress code (ties and jackets). It touted a well-rounded educated student with most of its graduates continuing on to four-year colleges. Although I am not cognizant of all the factors leading to its closure in 1972, the alumni mourned its loss for years after. But they were sufficiently imbued with Jesuit values to be instrumental in sponsoring a Nativity school— Brooklyn Jesuit Prep, rising like a phoenix from the ashes—for at-risk, minority middle school students in Brooklyn.

The high-classed boarding school Cranwell Prep in Lenox, Massachusetts, also closed in 1975. On the former grounds of the Berkshire Hunt and Country Club since 1939, Cranwell prospered by catering to sons of diplomats, international businessmen, and the wealthy. But then it declined. My good friend Charlie Allen taught there both as a scholastic and a young priest. His description of the closing of Cranwell Prep in the accompanying sidebar captures the mood of surprise and upheaval:

Charles H. Allen, SJ—Cranwell Prep closes

It was my good fortune to have taught at the Cranwell School in Lenox, Massachusetts, as a scholastic from 1966 to 1969 and later as a priest from 1974 to the school's closing in 1975. Because I loved the boarding school atmosphere and the opportunity to live in the beautiful Berkshires, I presumed that I would spend most of my teaching career at Cranwell. So much for the plans of man!

When I left Cranwell in 1969 to study math at Brown University and then complete my theology studies at the Gregorian University in Rome, the Cranwell School seemed to be surviving the upheavals of the late sixties without great difficulty. A new, dynamic chapel had been built—very much in the spirit of Vatican II—a new dormitory had been completed and another dormitory was being planned for an expected increase in the size of the student body.

When I returned in the fall of 1974, the situation had changed drastically. Rather than increasing, the number of students was decreasing and a much larger percentage of financial aid was being offered to this smaller number of students. The school was in serious financial difficulty.

The decrease in the number of students was attributable in part to the chaos of the times—Vietnam, Watergate, Richard Nixon's resignation, the growing drug culture and a general sense of rebelliousness, especially among the young. The decrease in the number of Jesuits in the New England Province was not an immediate problem. But the departure from the Jesuits of Cranwell's charismatic director of admissions and the general loss of enthusiasm by other Jesuits for educating the sons of very wealthy families certainly added to the difficulties. And, always in the background, was the heavy debt taken on for earlier building projects.

In a sign of support for Cranwell, the New England Province appointed one of its most skilled administrators, Fr. Raymond Swords, SJ, a former president of The College of the Holy Cross, as the school's president. Fr. Swords, no novice at fund raising, announced that the school would have to raise some impossible sum of money by May or close. Fr. Swords' attempt at fundraising fell far short of its goal and so in May, 1975, the final graduation was held, the underclassmen enrolled in a variety of other schools, and Cranwell quietly closed its doors. Today, the school is a posh Berkshire resort and still a wonderful place to visit and contemplate what might have been.

Charlie Allen, SJ, assistant to the president, Fairfield University, July 5, 2016

Another boarding school, Campion High School in Prairie du Chien, Wisconsin, also closed in 1972.[2] In still other schools, often owned by the local diocese, we withdrew Jesuit manpower, relinquishing schools such as Bishop Connolly High school in Fall River, Massachusetts, and Chaplain Kapaun Catholic School in Wichita, Kansas. Others were restructured and continued on after the Jesuits left, such as St. John Berchmans (later Jesuit High School) in Shreveport, Louisiana (1982); Loyola High School in Missoula, Montana; and Monroe High School in Fairbanks, Alaska. When the New York Province announced the closure of McQuaid Jesuit in Rochester, the alumni and parents vigorously rallied and reestablished the school on solid financial footing.

When I began my regency period of teaching at Jesuit High School in Portland, Oregon in 1966, we had eight scholastics. In the three years I taught there, fourteen scholastics rotated through the school. Of these, nine left the Society. At least twice during those three years, my teaching schedule changed after one of the scholastics left the Society. No replacement was hired. The Jesuit principal simply shuffled the pieces around (that was us) to cover the vacancy. During my very first semester

---

2. Though a great many Jesuit high schools had housed boarders in their early days, they were becoming a thing of the past. Examples include Gonzaga High School (Spokane), Georgetown Prep, and Bellarmine Prep (San Jose).

of teaching, I picked up a senior English class from an experienced priest-teacher so that he could fill in for the Jesuit scholastic who had been teaching French. I was fed to the wolves. They ate me alive. It was the worst class I ever had. By the second time two years later when a scholastic left the Society, I was an experienced third-year teacher. I picked up a C-level, sophomore English class. We had a ball. These rambunctious boys were so relieved to get a good teacher after enduring a boring class that they responded to practically everything I offered. For the required drama unit, for instance, I had them put on skits and dramatize some of the material we were reading. They thoroughly got into it, creating their own costumes and dramatic scenes. I'm afraid we caused a bit of a ruckus because it was all so much fun.

By the time I became principal at Gonzaga Prep in Spokane in 1978, coeducation was an accomplished fact, and a bright new time had dawned on Jesuit secondary education. We were now in a phase of continuing to advance, consolidate, and build on a solid foundation. Prep already had a great tradition weighted towards the past. The old timers told stories of the separation of the high school from the university in 1954. Gordon Toner, the principal, wanted to locate the school in a poor section of town so he and Father Wilfred Schoenberg hired a charter plane to fly over Spokane, and they spotted the blue collar section, not far from Gonzaga University. "Build here." And it happened. Frank Corkery, the president of both the university and high school, had earlier designated Father John Hurley as fundraiser for the new high school. John fondly related to me that Frank beckoned him to his room and was shaving when he arrived. "He gave me a beat up old car and $5,000 to start the high school." In the last days of Prep on the university campus, the school inhabited army barracks, surplused from World War II. The roof regularly leaked during a heavy rain. A scholastic would send a student down to the principal's office to report a sizeable leak, and the Father Toner would show up with a drill in hand, locate the leak, and drill a hole through the wooden floor for drainage. "There, Mister, that'll take care of it."

A REFLECTION

We need to ask, why did the Jesuits in the high schools, in contrast to their brothers in higher education, get on so quickly with the renovation of their apostolate and with a freshly articulated Jesuit mission? As early as 1971, the Jesuit high schools had a direction, they had a mission—even though there were bumps and hiccups ahead of them. But it took the Jesuit universities and colleges another twenty years before they began, as institutions, the serious, arduous shift to a new era, a new time, and into the transformative possibilities in Jesuit education. That's not to say that there were not significant university leaders—both Jesuits and lay— urging the renovation. But the obstacles, inertia, and resistances were formidable. One answer is that from the very beginning the split of the former JEA (Jesuit Educational Association) into the AJCU and the JSEA had different purposes. All twenty-eight Jesuit presidents comprised the AJCU university board, and the primary purpose of the AJCU was to be a lobby with Congress to secure funding for Jesuit higher education. By contrast, the JSEA featured a highly representative, grassroots endeavor. It was an elected body of presidents, principals, faculty, and at large members. Initially, all were Jesuits; but it rapidly evolved into including lay men and women.

Another significant reason for the alacrity of response by those in secondary education is that the Jesuits and lay people in the high schools are typically the marines of the Society. They are the doers—men and women of action, rather than pondering all the possibilities and consigning it to research and committees. They are experimenters and risk takers. In addition, high school students quickly pick up on the enthusiasm of their teachers. Teenagers are immediate in their response.

Furthermore, during those years the high schools were uniquely blessed with strong Jesuit leadership. Men such as Bill Woods and Vinny Duminuco (New York), Tom Healy, Dan Weber, and Bill Hayes (Oregon province), and Ed McDermott and Bob Mathewson (California) stand out. These were the ones I knew personally, but there were many more. And on the knotty religious education front, talented teachers, such as Bill O'Malley, Mark Link, and Paul Fitterer, inaugurated a new era in high school religion teaching. They revamped the curricula so that religion courses were no longer didactic and apologetic. They were exploratory and invitational. They tapped into the experience and affective life of the students, rather than just their intellects. The courses were more congruent with contemporary adolescent development—psychological, spiritual, and moral. They adapted the pioneering research of Jean Piaget in adolescent development and Lawrence Kohlberg's stages of moral development. A dam of pent-up creative energy burst out. It was long overdue.

BY WAY OF CONTRAST

Meanwhile, the Jesuits in higher education were slow to embrace the reforms, though certain individuals warmly embraced the mission. A few Jesuits and their lay colleagues formed study groups to read and reflect on the implications of the Second Vatican Council and of General Congregation 32. Campus ministries welcomed the liturgical reforms and inaugurated a wide degree of experimentation, too often done on a whim and a prayer, without much liturgical sensitivity or knowledge. Some genuinely nutty stuff happened in campus Masses, which further triggered a reactionary impulse among the *patres graviores*.

So it's time now to turn to the arduous, seemingly insurmountable challenge that faced Jesuit higher education.

9

Jesuit Universities Flounder, Hit the Wall, Break Through, and Thrive

THE CRISES FACING THE Jesuit universities and colleges by 1970 were multiple, and they arose from several, often competing, factors. Notable treatises have been written on this,[1] so I need not dwell on every detail. Instead I'll offer a sketch, necessarily with several gaps.

As early as 1899, Charles Eliot, president of Harvard, had critiqued Jesuit education (*Atlantic Monthly*, July, 1899) as being embedded in the past, wedded to and overly reliant on the classics, and lacking adequate academic challenge. No doubt, some anti-Catholic bias crept into his critique, but Eliot kept that out of sight. An anti-intellectual atmosphere had crept into the Church. The condemnation of freedom of religion, freedom of the press, and freedom of conscience by Pope Pius IX in 1864 had sent a chill through any Catholic attempt to integrate the faith with modern science and intellectual inquiry. Some relief came when the scholarly Cardinal Pecci was elected as Leo XIII (served 1878–1903), which led to some breakthrough documents such as *Rerum Novarum* in 1891. The first of many social encyclicals, in it the Pope critically addressed the plight of the laboring class in the age of exploitative industrialization. This short-term relief from anti-intellectualism was followed by

1. See the bibliography in Paul A. Fitzgerald, *The Governance of Jesuit Colleges in the United States, 1920–1970*. Also Michael J. Buckley, *The Catholic University as Promise and Project*.

the ascendancy of Pius X, a pious, devoted man, suspicious of innovative, creative thought. His condemnation of Modernism in 1907 probably set back the intellectual life of the church for at least forty years.

By the 1930s the Jesuits themselves were feeling the urgency for equipping their faculty with substantive professional degrees. American provincials were starting to send qualified men to first-rank academic institutions for doctorates. The American intellectual historian Perry Miller at Harvard would claim in the 1950s that the two most outstanding doctoral students he ever had were William Costello, SJ (Oregon Province) and Walter Ong, SJ (Missouri Province).

Up until the 1940s, the highest degree that most of the Jesuits and their lay colleagues achieved was a master's level qualification. When I attended Gonzaga, 1958–1961, the era of theological ineptitude was over. I did have four or five teachers who had attained no more than a master's degree, but were nonetheless outstanding pedagogues. Teaching was primary. Research was something you did in your spare time—which was rather minimal if you were teaching eight or nine semester courses each year.

Another crucial factor in the post-World War II era that stimulated a vast enlargement of Catholic higher education was the GI Bill, which made it possible for service men and women to attend a Jesuit university at minimal cost. Enrollments doubled, even tripled, within a very short time. Many Jesuit universities also went coed during this same time. Yet, when my sister Margaret attended Gonzaga in 1964, she said it was still skewed towards favoring men. Later I discovered that when Gonzaga went coed in 1948, an informal agreement existed that men and women be admitted at a ratio of two to one.

The rapid expansion meant that faculty and resources were stretched thin. Library holdings were paltry. Enthusiasm, dedication, and youthfulness made up for the dearth of resources. One famous example at Gonzaga University illustrates the can-do spirit. As was the custom, Father Frank Corkery, president from 1945 to 1957, gathered the faculty together at the beginning of the school year. There was a scattering of laymen along with sixty or so Jesuits. Father Corkery said, "Well, we have most everything covered. The only class for which we still need a teacher is Torts in the Law School." One of the Jesuits piped up, "I can take it." Corkery exclaimed, "Terrific." The newly inscribed law professor then queried, "So Torts, what is it?"

Monsignor John Tracy Ellis in his famous critique on American Catholicism and the intellectual life would assert in 1955 that Catholic higher education was second-rate and lacked academic integrity. Ellis offered a number of explanations for the backwardness of Catholic colleges and universities. As Thomas Shelley explained, "Some of the reasons [Ellis] mentioned were beyond the control of American Catholics, such as the anti-intellectualism of Americans in general, the persistence of anti-Catholic bigotry in the United States and the long-standing need of the American bishops to devote their limited financial resources to the elementary education of poor immigrants."[2] But Ellis touched a more delicate nerve when he focused his attention on the intellectual shortcomings of the American Catholic community itself and criticized American Catholic scholars for their failure to cultivate a love of learning for its own sake.

A decade later, Fr. Ted Hesburgh, CSC, already well-known president of Notre Dame, convoked a gathering of all the presidents of Catholic universities and colleges at the Land o' Lakes conference in Wisconsin in 1967.[3] They issued a mutual challenge to begin hiring and staffing their universities with the best qualified faculty, aiming to compete with the top universities in the country. This Catholic universities summit was certainly one of the key turning points in Jesuit higher education, and the quest for academic excellence became yet another factor in the unraveling of the traditional identity of Jesuit institutions.

The history of Jesuit higher education during these years has been extensively reported over the last two decades.[4] The ever insightful Howard Gray, SJ, and energetic Joe Appleyard, SJ, offer a first-rate analysis for what has occurred. They postulated three periods in Jesuit higher education.[5]

The growth of Jesuit colleges and universities after World War II took place within a Control Model, 1946–1968. All the principal administrators, including deans, were Jesuits, often explicitly appointed by the Jesuit

2. Thomas J. Shelley, "John Tracy Ellis and Catholic Intellectual Life," 23.

3. See *Land O'Lakes Statement: The Nature of the Contemporary Catholic University* as cited by J. M. O'Keefe, ed., *Catholic Education at the Turn of the New Century*.

4. For two of the best overviews of the movements and history of Jesuit Catholic higher education, see Charles Currie, SJ, "Pursuing Jesuit, Catholic Identity and Mission at U.S. Jesuit Colleges and Universities," and J. A. Appleyard, SJ, and Howard Gray, SJ, "Tracking the Mission and Identity Question."

5. Appleyard and Gray, "Tracking the Mission and Identity Question."

provincial. They made all the decisions about governance, policy, curriculum, and student formation. This top-down model was congenial to the pre-Vatican II Church. It produced alumni who were sure of what the church taught. It focused on philosophy and apologetics for the Catholic faith, and had a modest suspicion of the rest of the world. It celebrated having the right theological and philosophical answers, exercising sexual restraint, and ambitioning a prosperous career in the postwar US.

Professional Model, 1969 to present. Jesuit institutions responded to the pressures for reputation, ratings, and research; they were sensitive to the critique that they were merely mediocre colleges and universities. Departments started to recruit for the best and brightest faculty members. Their religious affiliation or their commitment to the mission as Catholic and Jesuit was generally not a factor. Jesuits themselves were finishing PhDs at Yale, Harvard, Princeton, Stanford, and the like. Other Jesuits were earning degrees in theology from Duke, Emory, Louvain, and Vanderbilt, rather than the Roman universities. Professors concentrated more on research and publication than on teaching and student religious/ethical formation. The Professional Model was coupled with the Permissive Model. Principles of free choice reigned. Core requirements were reduced, especially those in philosophy and theology. Regulation of student behavior was minimalized to the point where it amounted to little more than observing civil law. *In loco parentis* was a thing of the past.

Mission Model, 1990 to present. Elements of a new model began to appear in the nineties. Voices were raised asking what was distinctive in a Catholic Jesuit education. Professional expertise, academic excellence, and personal freedom were undoubtedly good things, but the most Ignatian of questions began to be asked: "Good for what?" The mission model wants to abandon the supremacy of the professional model that relegates all discussions of faith and meaning, of justice and service, of vocation and discernment to the marginal activity of campus retreats or to service programs. It asks the fundamental questions: how do faith and learning mutually challenge and enrich each other?

But it is a model in process, something being developed. And the outcome hangs in the balance. It honors the craft of research and publication, but cares more about the heart of education as wisdom. It is a model that sees the Jesuit/Ignatian character of the college and university as central to being Catholic—and to being Jewish and Muslim and Buddhist and agnostic. It trusts honest dialogue as critical to holistic education.

It refuses to bracket out religion as a privatized, individualistic prefer-
ence. In the new mission model, a shift has occurred in what it means
to be a "whole person." Fr. Peter-Hans Kolvenbach's definition of it as an
"educated solidarity" with the poor and oppressed has taken hold in the
Jesuit enterprise.

FOUR ERAS IN JESUIT HIGHER EDUCATION

Over the last eighteen years I have given many presentations on the
history of Jesuit education at Seattle University. And I think that the
framework that I have developed represents a typical pattern for American Jesuit higher education, which does not deny the Gray-Appleyard
scheme, but provides more concrete, more nuanced factors. And I take
into account the social, political, and cultural conditions as well. In my
scheme of things, the Jesuit mission/identity of the universities falls into
three main periods with the fourth one yet to be determined. I will use
the developments at Seattle University as indicative. The dates are arbitrary. They will vary according to the dynamics of each institution.

1891–1965, Jesuit founders and builders

Seattle University was a *Jesuit college within a Catholic subculture within a
Protestant country*. In this first era Seattle College began as a high school
with a grade school. Only forty years later in 1931 did it become a *bona
fide,* college-level institution. It then quickly evolved into a university
by 1948. Across the Protestant United States, Catholics were tolerated
but held with suspicion. The presidential campaign of Al Smith in 1928
surfaced some of the most virulent anti-Catholicism in the history of the
country. The two world wars started a dramatic shift in Protestant con-
sensus, and Supreme Court decisions in the 1940s led to a greater and
greater secularization of American society in order to avoid any constitu-
tional obligation to support the Catholic school system.

   In the aftermath of World War II, Seattle University flourished, often
with make-shift buildings repurposed from post-World War II surplus
and with an overworked faculty. By 1965 65 Jesuits and 188 lay faculty
worked in the university, which numbered 4,163 students. Eighty-five
percent of the students lived within 100 miles of the campus. Seattle University was a small, regional Catholic enterprise with a focus on excellent

teaching. It shared in the exuberance of the 1950s and 1960s. The enduring highlight of that era and often recounted by nostalgic alumni was the
1957–1958 Seattle basketball season when Elgin Baylor led the team to
the national championship and came within a whisker of beating Kentucky in the finals.[6] Alumni also recall with fondness memorable Jesuit
teachers.

1965–1975, Upheaval, Rapid Change, and Stabilization

The second era brought incredibly rapid change and realignment. The
Second Vatican Council, 1962–1965, released the Catholic Church from
its deadly grip on all its old wounds, suffered from the Enlightenment
and from the French Revolution, and brought it into a generous dialogue
with the contemporary world of science, technology, world cultures, and
world religions. It broke the impasse between Catholic and Protestant
churches. Simultaneously in the 1960s in the United States, all hell broke
loose culturally and politically! Martin Luther King, Jr. led a nonviolent
revolution to press home civil rights reforms, which President Johnson
signed into law in two dramatic breakthroughs 1964 and 1965. But the
Vietnam war and subsequent protests radically divided the country. The
assassinations of Martin Luther King, Jr. and Robert Kennedy in the
spring of 1968 unleashed further riots and antipathies.

When the highly respected Fr. Arby Lemieux retired from the presi-
dency in 1965 at the age of fifty-five, Fr. Jack Fitterer, SJ, the well-liked
academic vice president, picked up the presidential reins to continue the
legacy. Already several new buildings were in the works: two residence
halls and an athletic center. The university was riding a wave. Enrollments surged from 3,451 in 1955 to 4,163 by 1965. But just as Seattle
University was finally building out facilities to accommodate the influx of
students, the State of Washington launched the community college system. Overnight freshmen and sophomore enrollment plummeted, and
total enrollment took a free fall. The first year (1966) Seattle University
lost over 500 students and came in at 3,610. The decline continued for
six years and bottomed out at 2,884 in the fall of 1972. It was a huge hit.
Not until 1974 was the enrollment back to 3,728, approximately the same

6. The Seattle Chieftains were leading by 60 to 58 with seven minutes remaining,
but then Kentucky surged to win by 84 to 72.

number as twenty years before.[7] In addition, the university started to hire many more lay people, mostly men, so that the line item for faculty salaries notably increased.

The otherwise capable Fr. Fitterer was in over his head and unable to cope with these new circumstances. So the Board of Trustees, composed entirely of Jesuits, decided that Fitterer had to go. In 1970 they brought in a talented young theologian with absolutely no administrative experience—Fr. Ken Baker, SJ, a faculty member at Gonzaga who had done his doctorate in theology in Innsbruck, Austria. The situation immediately went from bad to worse.

On May 1, 1970, protests erupted in Seattle following the announcement of President Nixon that US Forces in Vietnam would pursue enemy troops into Cambodia, a neutral country. Anti-war protests and disruptions swept the country, especially on college campuses. Four days later, the Kent State massacre of five students by the Ohio National Guard set off riots on almost every college campus. Seattle University was no different; it was a hotbed of rebellion.[8] Students at Seattle University and the University of Washington joined forces and marched in solidarity onto the arterial freeway running through the city and totally shut down traffic.

A bomb was detonated between Garrand and the Liberal Arts building, shattering windows throughout the campus. No one claimed responsibility. William Cooley, who chaired the faculty's urban affairs committee, claimed that the campus was permeated by racism. Because of decline in enrollment President Baker announced "reductions in force" of the faculty. Baker set more teeth on edge when he welcomed Senator Barry Goldwater to campus for a speaking engagement. One hundred students marched through Seattle University shouting, "Shut it down." Students tried to occupy the president's office, but were forcefully removed. Black students, led by charismatic student activist Emil Wilson, staged a campus-wide call to action. But here the dark days were not without their light side. The redoubtable Fr. James McGoldrick managed to convince Emil to hand him the microphone, and Emil deferred to the priest. McGoldrick then launched into a long exposition about the history, the beauties, and benefits of a Jesuit education. As he droned on, the

7. These numbers are taken from the Oregon Province catalogues, 1956 to 1975.

8. Events during 1970 were exceedingly disruptive and hot. Walt Crowley in his chapter "To the Brink and Back" does a highly credible job of tracking all the riotous forces and winds of change.

crowd drifted away and the storm was over. Later McGoldrick, recogniz-
ing Emil's talents, befriended him. He personally coached him such that
Emil became the first Rhodes Scholar in the history of the university.

Meanwhile Fr. Ken Baker was not faring so well. Threats were made
on his life. He had an armed guard wherever he went out on campus. He
made an infamous trip to Rome, the purpose of which never was clear,
but in the course of it, Fr. John Navone introduced him to Gore Vidal,
Muriel Spark, Morris West, and others. When a photo of Fr. Baker and
Gore Vidal hit the pages of the local newspapers, the fat was in the fire.
Socializing with a public homosexual was a bridge too far for the sedate
Seattle readers.

Both Fitterer and Baker had used the Control Model, as explained
by Gray and Appleyard. They censored the student newspaper, attempted
to quell faculty dissent, and operated from a hierarchical stance. As Fr.
Frank Wood, who had sought Baker's appointment a year earlier, ruefully explained, "He would have been a great president—forty years ago.
The Lord just did not give him the art of diplomacy."[9] The university was
teetering. By the fall of 1970 the university could not make payroll for
faculty and staff.

At this point Jesuit leaders from both Gonzaga University and Seattle University met with the provincial Fr. Ken Galbraith and the province
consultors at a hotel in Yakima (Central Washington) on October 10,
1970.[10] Both universities were in a financial crunch. Ken Baker explained
that Seattle University was under water financially. The fall tuition had
already been spent to meet debts. He offered four alternatives: 1) Volun-
tary bankruptcy; 2) Lease the SU property to the State for a community
college; 3) Sell the property to the State; 4) or major retrenchment of degrees, programs, and the selling off of buildings. In the meantime, however, Bill Boeing had offered a gift of $750,000 contingent on: a change in
leadership, disposing of Marycrest Hall and Campion Hall, retrenchment
of programs, and reduction in student body and faculty. Several Jesuits
at the Yakima meeting voiced concern about being coerced by having a
gun held to their heads. Meanwhile, Gonzaga had its own challenges and
Fr. Frank Conklin proposed the sale of Waikiki Retreat House, closing
the music school, a moratorium on Jesuit retirement and health pay-
ments to the province, and by borrowing $250,000. A major difference

9. Crowley, "To the Brink and Back," 91.
10. JOPA [Jesuit Oregon Province Archives], "Emergency Meeting," 1–2.

seemed to be that under Father Dick Twohy's leadership as president, the morale issues that had plagued Gonzaga the previous year were much diminished.

The provincial and the two presidents emerged from the Yakima Summit with no clear decisions. Their public statement reasserted the Jesuit commitment to higher education, simply highlighting the obvious: "as fewer Jesuits enter the field of university education so also does the risk increase of our universities losing their traditional Jesuit character."[11]

In desperation the Seattle Jesuits turned again to their lay friends. Three men stepped forward; all had been regents and supporters of Father Arby Lemieux: the president of Paccar Bob O'Brien, Bill Boeing, and Bill Woods. They agreed to arrange for a line of credit with the banks, provided the Jesuits agreed to three conditions:

1. fire the president;

2. establish a lay board of trustees;

3. and divide the responsibilities so that the Jesuits operate the University, but the lay trustees would run the finances.

They also wanted to tone down the Catholic identity and emphasize Christian humanism.

The Jesuit readily agreed to the first three conditions and implemented them. The heroic Father Lou Gaffney, the academic vice president for just a few months, stepped into the breach as president with an up-front commitment to serve for a maximum of five years. A cash flow from the banks stabilized the rocky situation. Bob O'Brien served as chair of the new board. In fact, with an iron hand he held sway for the next eighteen years. He brought financial credibility and savvy to the university. It was a new dawn.

During some of those same years while being an administrator at Jesuit High School in Portland, I became a trustee of the university, 1973 to 1976. In that short span we had three Jesuit presidents: Lou Gaffney, Ed Ryan, and Bill Sullivan. By 1975 it was clear that Lou Gaffney had served well, but that we needed someone more dynamic and more at home in the job. Lou's anxiety would soar and his sciatica flare up whenever a trustees' meeting was about to occur.

The board recruited the highly talented Fr. Ed Ryan from Georgetown. Soon Ryan's expansive plans and near megalomaniac hopes came

11. Ibid., 7.

to naught, and he started to unravel psychologically. So after seven months, the board had to ask Fr. Ryan to resign and once again seek out a president. Fortunately, one of the very positive things Ryan had done was to recruit Fr. Bill Sullivan from St. Louis University as the provost. Bill had been fired by an inexperienced Jesuit president when Bill was dean of the divinity school at St. Louis and was momentarily rudderless. As the first Catholic priest to receive his doctorate in theology from the School of Divinity at Yale University, he was highly intelligent and pioneering. In addition, he was strong, articulate, and strategic. He righted the ship and served as president for the next twenty years. Those early 1970s were turbulent. Other Jesuit universities had similar turmoil although the precise circumstances were colorfully different.

1976 to 2008, Great Expansion, Academic Excellence, National Prominence, and Search for Identity

These years were the defining moment for all Jesuit universities for whatever they would become in the twenty-first century. In striving for academic excellence, they hired top quality professors, mostly from state universities. Initially, Seattle University made little effort to hire for mission, that is, to attract faculty who could articulate and sustain the Jesuit Catholic tradition. The first two decades of this period of professionalization marked the gradual erosion of the nature of a Jesuit Catholic university. Seeking to play down Catholicism and to emphasize the Jesuit emphasis on humanism in its educational tradition, the university catalogue, circa 1976, described Seattle University as "a private university in service of the public." It had no up-front mention of the university being either Jesuit or Catholic. That identity was buried in subsequent pages.

Only gradually did the Jesuit leadership, in its pell-mell striving for sheer survival and for academic excellence, realize that the very identity of the university as Jesuit and Catholic was at risk. Beginning in 1989 and over time, it inaugurated multiple programs for new faculty to get on board with the mission once they arrived. Weary Jesuits observed that most often they were continually offering "Jesuit 101" to faculty and staff for whom this was their first acquaintance with the Jesuit tradition. Similarly, the trustees were largely secularized, although some notable Catholic leaders were in the mix. These lay people were sharp business people, chosen for their philanthropic potential. But many had no inkling of what the Jesuit Catholic tradition was about, though they admired it.

From 1989 to 2009, Jesuits and key lay people were bent on articulating and inculcating the Jesuit vision and mission of "the faith that does justice" within faculty and staff. But it had a long ways to go towards recovery.

I have marked the close of this period as 2009 with the inauguration of Barack Obama as president because it marked a time of exponentially greater racial and multicultural awareness. His election came exactly forty years after the assassination of Martin Luther King, Jr. and sadly reminded us of a dream yet unfulfilled—though glimmers of hope had been breaking through. But ten years later, Donald Trump threatens to destroy that promise; he has unleashed torrents of hate and monstrous lies. Republican Senator Lindsay Graham of South Carolina in the summer of 2016 said Trump was totally unqualified to be president because "he was a xenophobic racist and religious bigot."

In 2008 Fr. Kolvenbach turned eighty and resigned as Superior General of the Jesuits. Fr. Adolfo Nicolás, SJ, of the Japanese province was elected. He was the first superior general to have been ordained after the Second Vatican Council reforms were inaugurated.

I have given two sketches of how the Jesuit charism has played out in the Jesuit institutions of higher education. Naturally schema like these will trigger nods of agreement or negative shakes of the head indicating "that wasn't the way it was." That's fine. Let the dialogue begin, or rather continue. Now I want to conclude this section with some of my personal, thiryt-four-year history at the university so that some meat might adhere to the boney frame I have offered above.

Personal involvement

I arrived as a faculty member in the fall of a 1985 and joined the Institute for Theological Studies (ITS), a wonderful new enterprise to train Catholic lay leaders for leadership in the church, namely for parishes, chaplaincies, and sometimes social work. It was a creative joint effort by the Archdiocese of Seattle, led by Archbishop Raymond Hunthausen and by President Fr. Bill Sullivan, SJ. Sullivan had continued to dream of a first-rate divinity school after his thwarted efforts at St. Louis University.

The new institute bolstered the leadership role of the laity in the Catholic Church.

I could not have been in a better place. Our ITS faculty was dynamic, forward looking, and on the cusp of creating a whole new chapter in the Catholic Church. Hunthausen's vision of shared leadership in ministry and Sullivan's commitment of resources wedded two great traditions, and our new Institute welded academic excellent, pastoral leadership skills, and spirituality into a coherent, dynamic, holistic formation. Vatican officialdom quickly brought a chill to the whole enterprise as Pope John Paul's restoration efforts and quelling of the spirit took hold. I will treat this story extensively in the next chapter.

By the time I arrived in the Jesuit community in 1985, the community still had about sixty men, but half of them were either retired or in some other ministry, such as hospital chaplaincy. These retired men had gone through the battles and were spent. They resisted the efforts of the Society to incorporate a strong justice component. Schooled in the Renaissance tradition of the humanities, they eschewed social activism. And they certainly could not see why that obvious misstep in the 1970s of redefining the Jesuit mission as "the service of faith, of which the promotion of justice is an absolute requirement"[12] should be incorporated into the academic enterprise. Their inane mantra "we are not a soup kitchen" somehow heightened their academic superiority.

Nineteen-eighty-nine was clearly the pivotal year. In that year three events conspired to motivate Seattle University, as an institution, to embrace the freshly defined Jesuit mission of the service of faith and the promotion of justice. I was involved with all three: 1) The Georgetown Assembly of 1989, highlighted by Father Peter-Hans Kolvenbach's address on the nature of a Jesuit university, birthed the National Seminar on Jesuit Higher Education, publisher of *Conversations,* where twelve years later I took the helm of the Seminar as chair and general editor. 2) The assassinations of the six Jesuits and two women at UCA in El Salvador in November 1989 brought home what our mission was all about: harnessing the intellectual and research capacities of the university as a transforming engine for creating an inclusive, diverse society and giving voice to the poor and the oppressed. Around that same time every Jesuit university inaugurated a position for a mission and identity officer, and many years later I was Seattle University's Vice President for Mission and

12. "Our Mission Today," *Documents of the 31st and 32nd General Congregations,* Decree Four.

Ministry. And 3) the Jesuit Community founded Colleagues, a conversation group on our campus, which met five times a year to explore the Jesuit mission. It's worth dwelling on some aspects of these movements.

Embracing our Jesuit Mission

The seismic tragedy of the El Salvador assassinations on November 16, 1989, shook the foundations of all Jesuit universities. But, in fact the president at Seattle University at that time was still passive, even resistant on the issue of incorporating the "faith that does justice" into the mission, and the administration had done nothing at the public level to commemorate or engage the tragic events in El Salvador. So another Jesuit and I initiated a letter to be sent to the Board of Trustees in which we critiqued the university leadership's passivity about commemorating this tragedy and advancing the mission. All Jesuits, except the three who were trustees, signed it, including the incoming rector and the about-to-be-inaugurated provincial. Well, that created quite a stir. I was told it precipitated a full-blown, heated discussion among the trustees. Three weeks later I received a letter from the chair of the trustees chiding us for not addressing all these issues through regular channels. Of course, that was the problem! Regular channels were clogged with inactivity. The president felt he had been blindsided, which was true. In any case, from then on multiple initiatives on campus received significant support. At the macro level, our efforts still seemed rather tepid, but many professors and staff were now "getting it" and mounting initiatives. Still we had a long ways to go towards recovery of a mission-driven university.

The next big step for us came when Fr. Bill Sullivan resigned after a successful run of twenty years as president. "The see was vacant," I told some colleagues. "*Sede vacante*," as we say in Latin when the Pope has died. The moment was opportune. So I convened a group of ten of us, which met in the basement of the campus ministry building in order to create a platform for the new president, whoever that would be. Over a series of several meetings, we wrote a "white paper" to bring about the transformation of the academic programs and institution orientation so that Seattle University would, at its core, be driven by the Jesuit Catholic mission of "the faith that does justice." Our efforts were well received. After my Jesuit classmate Fr. Steve Sundborg, SJ, was appointed president in April, I contacted him, and he quickly lent his support to our project, even assigning his own secretary to staff our committee after he took office that summer.

Our Faith That Does Justice committee continued for another three years sponsoring lectures, workshops, surveys, and raising consciousness on the campus.[13] Our work was extraordinarily well timed since meanwhile three other Jesuit universities—Boston College, University of Detroit Mercy, and Santa Clara, with crucial leadership from Pat Byrnes, Art McGovern, SJ, and my friend Bill Spohn, SJ—had combined forces to host a national conference at Santa Clara in the fall of 2000. I was invited to join the group—seven of us in all—to plan and sponsor three regional meetings leading up to the national meeting at Santa Clara where Father Peter Hans Kolvenbach, SJ, gave his second major address on the mission of Jesuit higher education today. Bill told me afterwards that Father Kolvenbach used only about 10 percent of the talk he had drafted for him.

I have always been struck by how a small group—say ten or fifteen—of dedicated faculty and staff with a purpose, dedication, and a sense of direction, can effect such a large change. Perseverance is crucial because often it takes five years or more.

By 2000 Jesuit universities across the spectrum had developed multiple programs to inculcate the Jesuit spirit and tradition into staff and faculty—at least for those who were receptive. At Seattle University Joe Orlando began a highly effective faculty immersion program in Nicaragua, which acquainted our faculty with another Jesuit university in the context of extreme poverty and social/political upheaval. Out of these exchanges came some highly creative efforts. A chemistry professor, Dr. Susan Jackels, for instance, instituted a simple lab test, operational in the field, to test the ph-factor (level of acidity) of the coffee so that poor campesinos could certify their own coffee and avoid paying the exorbitant fees of a warehouse.

Then in 2008 Heartland/Delta universities—in the midwest and the south—inaugurated the Ignatian Colleagues Program (ICP) and invited other universities to join as well. By then I was Vice President for Mission and Ministry, and I jumped at the chance to send some of our key leaders. I convinced our business dean and our engineering dean to join the first cohort of fifty. The ICP incorporated many of the same components that we had already initiated at Seattle University: 1) immersion in a Central

13. Patrick J. Howell, SJ, ed. and Faith and Justice Committee, "Education for Justice at Seattle University: A Self-Study in Progress" (June 16, 1999)—available in Seattle University archives, Lemieux Library.

American country; 2) a six-day retreat with the Spiritual Exercises; 3) an online course in Jesuit history; and 4) the bonding and familiarity that come through a cohort. ICP is the single most effective program available. A vice president at Loyola University Maryland said it well: "I was first attracted to the Jesuit mission at Loyola; it resonated with my own values; secondly, I became involved and understood it increasingly better through reading, through seminars, and by participating in activities; and now, after doing the Ignatian Colleagues Program, I 'own' the mission. I realize I'm responsible to build and advance the great Jesuit legacy that has gone before us."

It has been a long journey, and the outcome is not at all certain. So let me now posit the fourth and last stage of my analysis of our history of the Jesuit higher education mission.

2009–2020, Significant Shift in Mission to Worldwide Perspective

At this current juncture, the future is murky. We are now *a Jesuit university in a secular society in a worldwide context.* The Jesuit hallmark of the "faith that does justice" seems in practice no longer to be directly linked to the Catholic faith. All people of faith, whether Jewish, Muslim, Hindu, or Buddhist; Catholic, Protestant, or Anglican, are invited to a vigorous interfaith dialogue to address urgent human needs related to poverty, racism, sexism, and discrimination and bias in whatever form. Concomitantly, the university's Jesuit identity is ambiguous. In practice it keeps shaking off its Catholic roots, despite the best efforts of the Jesuit leadership and certain key Catholic faculty members to sustain the tradition. David O'Brien's seminal article in *Conversations* over twenty years ago still has validity. "Jesuit, Si!, Catholic, Not So Sure." It is not at all clear whether future university leaders and faculty will embrace the originating Jesuit Catholic mission. They will certainly create something new, and it will be excellent in its own right, but they may cast off the original religious moorings as they set off into uncharted waters. The risk is that it will no longer be Jesuit because it will no longer be Catholic.

As I mentioned at the outset of this chapter, the changes in the American Jesuit universities and colleges since 1965 were multiple, complex, and found variant incarnations in each of the twenty-eight institutions. During that time the total enrollment of students went from 139,969 to 216,218, with the greatest percentage increases coming in graduate schools. At the same time the total number of American Jesuits plummeted from over 8,200 to 2,150. And correspondingly the number of Jesuits in the universities descended from 1,530 to a few hundred.[14] And, of course, their average age is significantly increased. As the number of lay faculty, administrators, and staff soared, costs multiplied, and tuition rates mounted from fairly modest, affordable rates of about $2,000 per year to $40,000 to $60,000 per year.[15] A couple of examples will highlight the differences in Jesuit presence. Canisius College in Buffalo had thirty-five Jesuits in 1965; it will have only one in 2018. Xavier University in Cincinnati dropped from forty-five Jesuits in 1965 to nine in 2018; of the nine, most were half-time or emeriti. Larger places like Boston College were more stable; it dropped from 134 to thirty-five during the same period.

In this chapter I have attempted to demonstrate the incredible, transformational changes that occurred during these dense fifty-plus years. The astute theologian Monika Hellwig, the president of the Association of Catholic Colleges and Universities (1996–2005) and former faculty member at Georgetown, probably described the challenge best: "We are not trying to recover something that has been lost, some neatly packaged, precisely described and circumscribed identity, or even a museum piece. Rather, we are trying to create something that has never existed: a Jesuit, Catholic identity combining Ignatian spirituality, the Catholic intellectual tradition, and Catholic Social Teaching, all forged with diverse colleagues, in a pluralistic, postmodern university setting, while facing all of the challenges of a globalizing world."[16]

And with her customary generosity, Monika closed with a paean to hope and with confident faith: "Nothing is clearer, from the history of Jesuit educational practice, than that it was endlessly adaptive to time and place and the needs of those who sought it."[17]

14. Precise statistics are almost impossible to arrive at since each institution has different ways of reporting these numbers.

15. Figures from the AJCU. I am grateful to Michael Burns for his generous labors in digging out these numbers from the AJCU Archives, housed at Boston College.

16. Cited by Currie, "Pursuing Jesuit, Catholic Identity and Mission," 355.

17. Appleyard and Gray, "Tracking the Mission and Identity Question," 15.

10

Jesuits Under Siege:
Trauma and Recovery

IT'S TIME NOW TO treat the biggest trauma that the Society faced over the last fifty-plus years. In October 1981 Pope John Paul II usurped the normal governance of the Society and installed two of his own appointees to lead and corral the Society. To delve into this traumatic time, I need to lay considerable groundwork about the Vatican and hierarchy and how they were relating to the Society and especially to Pedro Arrupe during the previous fifteen years.

By 1980 Pedro Arrupe's health was clearly failing. When he came to Spokane for the meeting with the American provincials, we could see he was more frail, his skin translucent. But even so, he was still buoyant and enthusiastic. After securing the support of his consultors, he had asked John Paul II's permission to resign as general, a possibility that had been foreseen in 1966 by General Congregation 31. All previous generals had served in office until they died. With modern medicine and better health care, all of us were living longer—on average as much as fifteen years. Up until 1966, a Vicar General could be appointed when the general was incapacitated. But ever since GC 31, the general can simply ask to resign and, with agreement of his consultors and a nod from the pope, have his resignation accepted by a General Congregation.

Despite the clear option for resignation, Pope John Paul refused permission to Arrupe. Later when I had a lengthy visit with Fr. Vinnie

O'Keefe, SJ, at America House in Manhattan, he related that Vatican cardinals were preparing for a more drastic intervention in the Society's leadership, but they weren't ready yet. Vinnie was an extremely close confidante of Arrupe and was appointed Vicar General after Arrupe had his stroke. In his private room at America House, Vinnie explained some of the machinations that led to the drastic intervention by John Paul II.

Here's the story about the papal intervention, as best as I can reconstruct it. Already in 1978, prior to the conclave to elect the short-lived Pope John Paul I, multiple cardinals had had a rare discussion on "the problem of the Society of Jesus." Many were not happy with the leadership of Pedro Arrupe. His charisma and well-known popularity among the people intruded on their own jealously guarded prerogatives. More importantly, the Society's commitment to social justice, its critique of existing social structures, including the arbitrary, oppressive structures within the Church itself, stirred the wrath of some leading cardinals. And, of course, a few zealous Jesuit critics of Arrupe regularly wrote to the Vatican dicasteries about failures or apparent aberrations of Jesuits.

Don Pedro had worked tirelessly to fulfill the mandate of the Council for renewal and the adaptation of the Society to the changed conditions of the times. Instead of a wooden repetition of what had always been done, he promoted the Ignatian charism of spiritual discernment to read the signs of the times, to find God in all things, and to risk living the gospel to the full. "Great risks had to be taken,"[1] as he said repeatedly. "What to do, what to do?" He was especially attuned to the suffering and dire situations of the least of our brothers and sisters. The Congregation that elected Arrupe in 1965 had mandated that "those things may be removed from our body which could constrict its life and hinder it from fully attaining its end . . . and to be ready for every form of the service of God."[2] Arrupe had the instincts, the leadership, and the grace to do just this. He embodied a creative fidelity to the Ignatian charism, and his joy permeated every conversation.

But still criticisms of particular Jesuits kept rolling in.[3] At synod after synod, bishops would come up to Father Arrupe and ask him what he was doing about Father So-and-So who had joined the guerrillas in Latin America or who said Mass in coveralls or who questioned *Humanae Vitae*

1. Pedro Arrupe, SJ, Letter to Jesuits in Jesuit Relief Services (August 6, 1981).

2. *Documents of the 31st and 32nd General Congregations*, no. 17, 72.

3. Peter Hebblethwaite, "Pedro Arrupe in History."

and urged the faithful to follow their own conscience. The English writer Peter Hebblethwaite, who had been a Jesuit until 1974, said that whenever he was writing about the Vatican, he was liable to get a letter from the Vatican Secretariat of State charging him with "'offending against Truth and the Apostolic See,' as though the two terms were synonymous."[4] In 1966 Pope Paul VI had issued grave, but murky, warnings to the Jesuit leadership about "clouds passing over that were not entirely dissipated." Especially later on in his pontificate, Pope Paul seemed wreathed in dark clouds himself and angst about all the upheaval in the church.

During GC 32 (1974–1975) there was a serious misunderstanding between Pope Paul and the Jesuit leadership about abolishing traditional distinctions between solemn and simple vows in the society and allowing the brothers to be professed with solemn vows. Pope Paul had told Arrupe privately that there should be no change in the vows, but then he put Arrupe in an impossible bind by commanding him to secrecy— that is, he forbad him to say anything about his injunction. So when the Congregation duly took up the matter because so many provinces had urged it, a painful confrontation ensued and cast a permanent pall over all the proceedings. Some delegates, such as our own Oregon provincial Ken Galbraith, came home exhausted, even depressed, by the clandestine maneuvers.

Don Pedro and Pope Paul normally got along well. Though different in temperament, they mutually respected each other and were on the same spiritual wavelength. Later, relations with Pope John Paul II were not so cordial. From the beginning the Polish pope was cold, aloof, and even hostile to the Society. Some knowledgeable Jesuits attributed it to the fact that he did not know the Jesuits in Poland, had little contact with religious orders, and often viewed the religious orders of men as an untapped pool of priests who could fill the mounting vacancies in parishes. As early as 1972, John Paul—still Cardinal Karol Wojtyla—had proposed an examination of religious life because of the defections in vocations and infidelity in keeping the vows. He urged a reform to insert them more fully into the life of the Church, a euphemism for bringing them under control of the bishops.

On September 21, 1979, Pope John Paul II addressed Father Arrupe and his top advisers in menacing fashion: "I'm not unaware—drawing on a few other sources of information—that the crisis which in recent

4. Ibid.

times has troubled religious life and is still troubling it has not spared your Society, causing confusion among Christian people and concern to the church, to the hierarchy and personally to the Pope who is speaking to you."[5]

The charges were typically imprecise and vague. The pope was worried by secularizing tendencies and a lack of austerity in community life. He exhorted the Jesuits to greater "fidelity to the magisterium of the church and to the priestly character of your apostolic work." In papal code language, this meant unwavering support for *Humanae Vitae* and absolute silence on the desirability of the ordination of women. In fact, these two touchstones of orthodoxy were prominent in the confidential document for calculating a priest's aptitude to serve as a bishop that I was asked to fill out a couple of times for priests that I knew. Adherence to the Vatican's position on these two neuralgic points became a mark of one's fidelity to the church.

Much of the ecclesial conflict came because the Jesuits' analysis of the present state of the Church was so at odds with the Vatican analysis. In 1972 in an address to the German Katholikentag, Don Pedro declared: "For hundreds of millions of Catholics the real crisis of faith comes not from materialism or from unrestricted theological discussion, but from the brutal misery of their existence." But, in stark contrast, the Vatican's take was that the crisis of faith was caused by "materialism and unrestricted theological discussion." On yet another front, the Vatican ignored the first anniversary in March 1981 of Archbishop Oscar Romero's death. But the Union of Major Religious Superiors, led by Father Arrupe, celebrated a Eucharist of commemoration in the Church of Saints Cosmas and Damian in Rome. "It was regarded as provocative," according to Peter Hebblethwaite, "by Cardinal Sebastiano Baggio . . . prefect of the Congregation of Bishops and president of the decisive Pontifical Commission for Latin America."[6] The event was a black mark against Don Pedro. He obviously was not a team player.

Perhaps the deepest chasm between the Society and the pope lay in a different interpretation of Marxism. Pope John Paul, of course, had lived under the oppressive regime of Communism, so Marxism was clearly the ideological enemy. When he heard Marxism, he envisioned Communism. He expected the Church, as an impenetrable phalanx of opposition,

5. Ibid.
6. Ibid.

to march forward in lock step against Marxism, namely Communism. But most Jesuits, especially in Latin America, distinguished between the Marxist analysis of the causes of oppression and Marxist philosophy itself, which had become the basis for totalitarian Communist regimes.

In 1979 Don Pedro went to Lima, Peru, to discuss with the Latin American provincials what to do about Marxism. Earlier the conference of Latin American bishops at Puebla had denied that it was possible to separate out various aspects of Marxism, notably its philosophy from its analysis. Based on widespread consultation organized by Jean-Yves Calvez, SJ, one of Father Arrupe's brilliant general assistants, Don Pedro produced his letter "On Marxist Analysis," dated December 8, 1980. It was a letter of considerable subtlety, which inserted all the necessary caveats: "It seems to me that in our analysis of society, we can accept a certain number of methodological viewpoints which . . . arise from Marxist analysis, so long as we do not attribute an exclusive character to them. For instance, an attention to economic factors, to property structures, to economic interests . . . or a sensitivity to the exploitation that victimizes entire classes . . . and attention to ideologies that can camouflage for vested interests and even for injustice."[7] Arrupe's comments did not mean that Don Pedro or the Society of Jesus had suddenly "gone Marxist." On the contrary, the rejection of Marxism as a whole package was clear and unhesitating. But perhaps the passage that most annoyed the critics in the Vatican was that which exposed the fraudulence of much anti-Communism: "Finally, we should also firmly oppose the efforts of anyone who wishes to take advantage of our reservations about Marxist analysis in order to condemn as Marxist or Communist, or at least to minimize esteem for, a commitment to justice and the cause of the poor."[8] The passage ended with the rhetorical question: "Have we not often seen forms of anti-Communism that are nothing but means for concealing injustice?"

In the spring of 1981, as Father Arrupe's letter on Marxist analysis began to be known, Roman dicasteries began their counter campaign. It was hinted that the General of the Jesuits had no business to pronounce on such matters of universal importance. With his earlier letter on priest-workers and now this on Marxist analysis, Arrupe was arrogating

7. Pedro Arrupe, SJ, "On Marxist Analysis."

8. As quoted by Hebblethwaite, "Pedro Arrupe in History," 162.

to himself the functions of the magisterium. He was setting up a rival magisterium.[9]

Since I was deeply immersed as principal in running a high school in Spokane, I was only vaguely aware of these tensions at the highest level of the Society. And though I was a province consultor, these larger issues were not part of our agenda. We were busy helping our new provincial Tom Royce to get his feet on the ground and to heal some of the divisive elements of the Oregon Province.

Then, in August 1981 Arrupe suffered a major, debilitating stroke as he was returning to Rome after a long, tiring trip through Asia. Many of us were saddened, even shocked, when we heard he was gravely incapacitated. He lost his marvelous command of languages and could no longer express himself orally. Fr. Vinnie O'Keefe, the vicar general appointed earlier by Arrupe, assumed command. Several weeks later, early on a Saturday morning in October, I received an urgent call from my Jesuit friend Tom Bunnell. The pope, Tom announced, was taking over the Society and had installed two of his own men to lead the Society of Jesus. He appointed Father Paolo Dezza, former rector of the Gregorian University and confessor to two popes, as his own personal Papal Delegate. And since Dezza was elderly and mostly blind, Father Giuseppe Pittau, the rector of Sophia University in Tokyo, who had made a good impression on the pope when the pope visited Japan, would assist him. Within two hours Fr. Tom Royce also called me since I was one of the four province consultors. Tom reported on how the ten American provincials were in urgent consultation with each other about what to do.

We Jesuits felt humiliated. Our regular government was suspended. Did that mean that our *Constitutions* were also suspended? How long would this last? What mandate was Dezza given? Would the Pope ever relent? Were some malcontent Jesuits involved in undermining Arrupe and the Jesuit leadership? We grieved for the admirable Vinnie O'Keefe, who had already smoothly taken over the role of ordinary governance of the Society.

Later I learned through a reliable grapevine, a source now buried in the fog of my memory, about how all this came about. Initially, the pope had contacted a retired Italian missionary Carmelite bishop, to become his Delegate to reform the Society. The poor bishop was disturbed—shocked really. He confided in Cardinal Carlo Martini, the renowned

9. Ibid.

Jesuit archbishop of Milan, and enlisted his help. The two of them made haste to Rome to lodge a vigorous representation to the pope. So the pope backed off and appointed the two Jesuits, which in retrospective was much more compatible. Even so, much consternation arose throughout the whole Society. When Paolo Dezza took over as Papal Delegate on October 31, 1981, there was a concelebrated Mass in the chapel of the Jesuit Curia in Rome. After the homily, Don Pedro, seated in the corner in his wheelchair, made a sudden gesture that at first was not understood. He called Father Dezza over and embraced him in front of the whole community—a visible sign of his and the Society's obedient acceptance.

In the fall of 1981, Father Dezza had other things on his mind than the purge, which some Vatican zealots and even some cranky Jesuits from the Gregorian University expected. Father Dezza kept the Jesuit curial team together, left all superiors in place, and continued all of Father Arrupe's policies, while making reassuring noises to Vatican officials from time to time.

Soon the absurdity of the suspension of ordinary government became apparent. For if the Jesuits really were the politically minded, semi-Marxist, dissident secularists they were imagined to be, then they should have risen in revolt, led demonstrations, or resigned *en masse*. None of this happened. The silence was profound. In fact, as the pope was going through the preparations for the suspension of the Jesuits, his cardinal advisers had told him to expect one third of all the Jesuits to leave the Society. When not a single Jesuit left—not one—the pope acknowledged privately that he had been poorly advised. But, of course, no apologies were ever issued.

Meantime, Father Dezza summoned an unprecedented meeting of provincials at which Pope John Paul II assured them that the Jesuits had "passed the test" (*una prova*). So supposedly that was what it was all about! "La prova" provided cover for a major papal miscalculation and abuse of authority. Successfully "passing the test" prepared the way for normal government to be resumed. Father Dezza, with the approval of the pope, convoked the 33rd General Congregation to elect a new general. When the delegates met in September 1983, it did something no previous congregation had done: It accepted the formal resignation of a general—Father Pedro Arrupe. All Jesuits in Rome at the time were invited to this unique event.

Father Arrupe had managed with help to write a few words, which were read for him by Father Ignacio Iglesias, provincial of Spain: "How I wish I were in better condition for this meeting with you," Arrupe wrote. "More than ever, I find myself in the hands of God. This is what I have wanted all my life, from my youth. But now there is a difference: The initiative is entirely with God. It is indeed a profound spiritual experience to know oneself totally in His hands."

This moving testimony has become one of my favorite prayers. It is the ultimate fulfillment of the Suscipe, recited by every Jesuit who makes the *Spiritual Exercises:* "Take, Lord, receive all my liberty, my memory, my understanding, and my entire will, all I have and call my own."

Strong men could not fight back the tears. Don Pedro's farewell went on: "It is to the Society at large, and to each of my brother Jesuits, that I want to express my gratitude. Had they not been obedient in faith to this poor Superior General, nothing would have been accomplished. To each one of you in particular I would love to say *tantas cosas*—so much, really. I am full of hope, seeing the Society at the service of the one Lord and the church, under the Roman Pontiff, the Vicar of Christ on earth. May she keep going along this path, and may God bless us with many good vocations of priests and brothers; for this I offer to the Lord what is left of my life, my prayers and the sufferings imposed by my ailments."

One of the great moments in the life of the Society came immediately after the election of Fr. Peter-Hans Kolvenbach, as the new superior general. Peter-Hans and Don Pedro gave each other a warm embrace. In all the photos Pedro is radiant, as if the divine light were already shining right through him. Thereafter, Don Pedro lived in the Curia, assisted by a Spanish Jesuit brother, for another eight years. I always sensed that he was like a luminous tabernacle at the heart of the Society.

Though Pope John Paul II never apologized, he as much as admitted by gesture and change of attitude that he had overstepped his absolute authority. He came over to the Jesuit Curia to celebrate Mass at the outset of GC33, and afterwards greeted each delegate in the Recreation Room. Even so, when Don Pedro was dying in 1991, it took considerable urging for him to come to Pedro's bedside to give him the customary papal blessing.

The siege on the Society lifted with the election of Kolvenbach. But the siege on the universal church and bringing it into line with the neo-orthodoxy was just beginning. The clamp down continued. That same year that the governance of the Society was suspended, John Paul II appointed Cardinal Joseph Ratzinger as his official doctrinal watchdog to head up the Congregation for the Doctrine of the Faith (the CDF).

From then on, Pope John Paul II and the Vatican Curia singlemind-edly set about restraining, drawing in, and even quashing the multiple pastoral movements unleashed by the Second Vatican Council. Many faithful Catholics dedicated to the Church felt the scourge. The pope quickly checked or silenced several leading theologians such as Fran-ciscan Leonardo Boff, Dominican Edward Schillebeeckx, the leading American moral theologian Charles Curran, and later on Roger Haight and Jacques Dupuis, among many others. It was a long, distinguished list.

In 1983, for instance, when John Paul II visited Nicaragua, he encountered Fernando Cardenal, SJ, who knelt to receive the pope's blessing. Instead, the pope waved a sharp finger at him and sternly told him, "Usted tiene que arreglar sus asuntos con la iglesia." (You must fix your affairs with the Church.) Cardenal was Minister of Education for the Sandinista government. He had worked nonviolently to support the overthrow of the tyrannical Somoza regime. The idea of a priest serving in the government, especially one built on Marxist analysis, did not sit well with the pope, and Cardenal was forced to choose between his two greatest loves: the marginalized poor and the Society of Jesus. John Paul II defrocked Cardenal in February 1984. Many years later, through the ministrations of Father Kolvenbach, Cardenal, who had still been living in a Jesuit community all those years, was reinstated as a Jesuit by making a novitiate all over again and once more taking vows. During his years in government, Cardenal helped raise the nation's literacy rate from 49 percent to 87 percent.

Two years after Cardenal was expelled from the Jesuits, Father Charles Curran, a diocesan priest from Rochester, was fired from the theology faculty of the Catholic University of America (CUA). Despite strong support from faculty groups, past and current students, and from the Catholic Theological Society of America, the Vatican's Congregation for the Doctrine of the Faith, led by Cardinal Ratzinger, withdrew Cur-ran's license to teach Catholic theology. It had been a long battle ever since the young, articulate Father Curran, age thirty-four, had led the theological faculty at the CUA in a counterargument to *Humanae Vitae* in 1968. Charlie knew the rich Catholic tradition inside and out, respected it, but also urged it forward with new perspectives and fresh theological insights for the new times.[10]

10. Dennis Coday, "Charles Curran to Retire from Full-time Teaching."

I had had a graduate seminar in moral theology at CUA with him, and I was amazed at his total command of the Catholic tradition. I once asked him at the beginning of class, "Who are the major moral theologians in Europe and could you give us a quick sense of what issues they are focusing on?" What followed was a spontaneous tour de force. One hour later Charlie had rolled on through all the leading European moralists and their thinking on a multiplicity of issues, their strengths and weaknesses. His comprehensive recall was stunning for all. His silencing at CUA was a great loss for the future of the Church since so many seminarians might otherwise have had exposure to this brilliant, faithful diocesan priest.

The pope was clearly on a mission to cleanse the Church. Though he repeatedly acknowledged the importance of the Council, his interpretation was so much more restricted than what the universal church needed. The Council had called for the reform of the Roman Curia, but Pope Paul VI had made only the slightest adjustments. And John Paul II had no interest in reforming or even overseeing the bureaucracy. Besides it served his purposes. It shared his inclinations to block significant internal reforms and to keep the bark of Peter on its traditional, predictable, authoritarian course. The most damaging aspect of the reign of John Paul II was not what happened to the Society of Jesus, but rather what happened to the universal Church. In the United States and frequently elsewhere, he appointed rigid, traditionalist bishops, which in turn spawned a whole new breed of priestly candidates more concerned about rules, rites, and ultra-orthodoxy than about compassionate care of people. Seminaries became hotbeds of reactionary ecclesial politics.

Though he was retrograde with regard to internal reform of the Church, the pope was progressive in building bridges with other faith leaders. He was superb in the external realm of the Church. The Jewish community deeply appreciated his visit to the Western Wall of the Second Temple in Jerusalem and to Yad Vashem, the Holocaust memorial museum, in the spring of 2000. And he repeatedly made overtures to the Eastern Orthodox Churches to move towards unity. In one memorial phrase, which I have used frequently in my classes, the pope said that the church needed to learn to breathe again with both lungs, both East and West—a remarkable metaphor since it suggests parity between each lung. In addition, his encyclical *Ut Unum Sint* (1995) set the table for a whole new look at ecumenical relations, one of the most positive encyclicals ever written up until that time.

On the practical, internal front of the Catholic Church, however, the pope continued to rein in reforms. Bishops were not beyond his reach. Among those arrested in their pastoral ministry was Raymond Hunthausen, the saintly, prophetic archbishop of Seattle, Washington, whom I was privileged to know exceedingly well.

Raymond "Dutch" Hunthausen had been president of Carroll College when he was appointed bishop of Helena in 1962. At forty-one, he became the youngest, sitting ordinary among the American bishops at the Second Vatican Council. Hunthausen once said to me, "It was the best possible formation any bishop could have had. Every day we were treated to the wisdom of these great theologians, and then after a lively dinner, several of us bishops might sit on the steps of a church pondering how we could bring this experience home, back to our local churches." A decade later when he arrived in Seattle in 1975 as the new archbishop, Hunthausen quickly created an inclusive model of shared ministry, which tapped into the gifts of all, especially the laity, both women and men. He reached out to the poor, provided sensitive ministry to people of diverse sexual orientations, and became deeply involved in ecumenical and interfaith friendships throughout the region. When the archbishop was under siege from the Vatican, a Jewish friend of mine said, "You know he's my archbishop too!"

Archbishop Hunthausen's thoughtful pastoral leadership in Seattle was well known for creating one of the most progressive places for implementing the documents and the vision of the Second Vatican Council. Hunthausen's quiet, but effective, protest of the massive nuclear weapon build-up under the Reagan administration provides the key to why the Vatican initiated an investigation. The Trident submarine base, located at Bangor, Washington, across the Puget Sound from Seattle, was the scene for the world's newest, deadliest nuclear weapon. People of faith converged to protest the monstrous weapons system. Among them were "Mennonites, a Methodist minister, a Nestorian Orthodox priest, a Native American shaman, and the head of the United Church of Christ."[11] As they converged at Bangor at one of these events, all were intent on hearing Hunthausen. He had no love for public speaking, but he spoke from the heart. He knew he would disappoint the crowd that day. He was going to tell them to love their enemies and to offer a blessing for the

---

11. John McCoy, *A Still and Quiet Conscience*, 2.

sailors and officers. When asked why he did this, he said, "Because the Gospel tells us to."[12]

Still later the archbishop decided to withhold and put into escrow half his income tax as a protest against the military build-up. In a famous address at an ecumenical gathering at Pacific Lutheran University, he described the nuclear submarine base as "the Auschwitz of the Puget Sound."[13] Needless to say, a cascade of protests from conservative, jingoistic Americans flowed into the Vatican. Meanwhile the Reagan government was concerned not only about Archbishop Hunthausen, but that the American bishops, who were writing a peace pastoral, would condemn outright nuclear weapons as a deterrent. Simultaneously Pope John Paul and President Reagan wanted a unified front for supporting the solidarity movement in Poland, and they were looking for the first-ever formal exchange of ambassadors between the USA and the Vatican City State.

Hunthausen was caught in the vise of geopolitical maneuvers. Rome launched an official papal visitation, headed by Archbishop (later Cardinal) James Hickey of Washington. I had known Hickey when he was rector of the North American College in Rome. I liked him when we served together on a committee of the Gregorian University to help structure a fourth-year program for Americans who would not be continuing on for the licentiate. In fact, when he was advanced from Cleveland to Washington, DC, as archbishop, I sent him a congratulatory note, and he had graciously invited me to stop in to see him whenever I came to DC. I never did.

By now though the man I had known seemed different—more keen on ascending the clerical ladder. Hickey's report on the Church in Seattle became the basis for an intervention into the ministry of Archbishop Hunthausen. So a month after I arrived at Seattle University to begin teaching pastoral theology, I was stunned to hear that Fr. Donald Wuerl was appointed auxiliary bishop in Seattle. As I mentioned before, I had met the young Father Wuerl fourteen years earlier when he was Cardinal Wright's personal secretary in Rome. Of course, Wuerl, Hickey, and others were all from the same clerical brew bubbling up out of Rome. Much more problematic for the Archdiocese of Seattle was that the Vatican had given Wuerl secret, juridical powers over five areas. It was an errand doomed to failure—not least because the laity and priests rose up

12. Ibid., 4.
13. Ibid., 26.

in protest about this draconian intervention into our local church. The shared ministry inaugurated by Hunthausen had truly taken hold, so this attack was not just on "our archbishop," but upon "our church."

The crisis led my colleague Gary Chamberlain and me to host a three-year series on the role of authority in the church today. With awareness of the irony, we drew our title for the series "Episcopacy and Primacy" from the progressive description of the role of authority by Karl Rahner, SJ, and the young theologian Joseph Ratzinger—way back in 1962.[14] When we inaugurated the series, several members of the Catholic Theological Society of America, including two of its presidents, gave us great support and were speakers at our symposium.[15] It was a booster shot for the much-admired archbishop and for our local church.

Throughout the whole trial precipitated by the imposition of secondary authority, Archbishop Raymond Hunthausen remained a sea of tranquility in the midst of the ecclesial storm. He was truly a "still and quiet conscience." He never sought to challenge the pope, the president, or the Holy See. That's not what he was about. He was simply an honest, prayerful man of conscience who risked the truth and sought out and cared for the least of our brothers and sisters. His gospel witness was the challenge that could not be accepted. It's telling that many said that the only friend Donald Wuerl had in Seattle was Raymond Hunthausen. Bishop Wuerl, to his credit, learned, listened, and became a better leader in the church through his scathing embroilment in Seattle. It was an impossible situation for him as well.

During this time I said to a Jesuit friend, "The oppression and the corruption of power are more heinous in the church, than they are in the Reagan government, though they are often enough running neck and neck." The difference was that the Church should have known better. Its mission was to live the gospel, which meant "giving up the power" and relying on the beneficence of God's goodness. In any case, John Paul II was doing to the Church, no doubt unconsciously, what Reagan was doing to the American people. Greed and power ascended to the top of the pyramid. In that same period, Margaret Thatcher was doing much the same for Great Britain, reversing the gains of the laboring, blue-collar workers and enriching the rich.

14. Josef Ratzinger and Karl Rahner, SJ, *Episcopate and Primacy*.

15. Patrick J. Howell, SJ, and Gary Chamberlain, eds., *Empowering Authority*.

Some years later when I was dean of our School of Theology and Ministry, I hosted a symposium on the fortieth anniversary of the opening of the Second Vatican Council, October 1962. We were fortunate enough to have Archbishop Hunthausen, now retired and living with his family in Helena, Montana, give the keynote and offer his personal reminiscences of the Council, some of them rather hilarious. He concluded his talk with this moving exhortation:

> What we really need in our church and our world today is an in-pouring of the Spirit. . . . We have a hard time waiting. . . . The Spirit is a gift. We cannot make the Spirit happen. But we need to have a sense of anticipation. We need a miracle. Expect one. Expect one, be people of hope. Always, because God is in our midst. There isn't any question about that. And over and over again we continue to pray, as honestly and as profoundly as we can, that the Spirit will touch our lives and touch our world. . . . The Spirit is there to help us understand what Vatican II was about because I have no doubt in my mind that Vatican II has a lot yet to be lived.[16]

In the summer of 2013 when I visited Archbishop Hunthausen, then ninety-two, in Helena, Montana, where he lives in retirement, I said, "I think that you and the new pope would get along very well." "Yes," he said with a quiet smile, "I think so too." The miracle had begun.

Later I told some friends that we had had a quiet, engaging, soul-filled visit. And I added, "It's always good to visit a saint at least once a year."

16. Raymond G. Hunthausen, "We Need a Miracle—Expect One," 13.

11

The Society Coalesces
Around New Leadership

PETER-HANS KOLVENBACH WAS AN unlikely, but brilliant choice to succeed Pedro Arrupe. He was Dutch, had spent most of his Jesuit life in
Beirut, and had been vice provincial of the challenging Near East vice
province for nine years. In 1981 he was brought to Rome to be the rector
of the Pontifical Orientale Institute, whose mission was theological training and research for the traditional Eastern Churches. The Orientale was
a center for fostering ecumenical relations with the Orthodox.

When Paolo Dezza, the pope's superimposed delegate, convoked
General Congregation 33, considerable trepidation rippled through the
Society. Would the pope interfere in the election and in the proceedings
of the Congregation? Would he demand certain reforms? Would he insist
on a certain profile or even a certain Jesuit to be elected as the new Superior General? It had happened before. Pope Gregory XIII (1572–1585)
told the Society in 1573 that he didn't want another Spaniard as General.[1]
"Someone like Father Everard Mercurian, SJ from Belgium would be
good." After some thorny negotiations, the obedient delegates duly elected Father Mercurian. None of this occurred at GC 33, but the delegates
were keenly aware that the Society needed an astute mediator, a man with
a lower profile than Arrupe, a Jesuit who had dealt with conflicting currents. The new general would need to deal with the Byzantine ways of the

1. Padberg et al., eds., *For Matters of Great Moment*, 6–8.

bureaucracy of the Holy See. Kolvenbach, with his Semitic wisdom from long experience during the civil wars in Lebanon and other conflicts in the Middle East, seemed ideally suited.

Prior to the election, the delegates gathered in prayer to make the best possible election. During this time a "murmuratio," or buzz about likely candidates occurs. The procedures are strict and formal. No one can campaign for himself. No one can campaign for someone else. If I were a delegate, I could ask someone about a likely candidate, what he was like as a leader, how apt he would be to govern the Society, whether he was a man of prayer, but I could not advocate for any given candidate. Generally six or seven candidates emerge rather quickly. Inevitably, they are currently a provincial or have been a provincial. For instance, I heard later that Simon DeCloux, the esteemed former provincial of Belgium, was considered electable at GC 33. Likely prospects are fluent in three or four languages, ideally English and Spanish. Their health is good, and they are vigorous enough to endure for ten or more years.

Peter-Hans, fifty-five, had an austere look. He wore rim glasses and a somewhat disheveled cassock, and sported a short goatee. His manner of speech and writing were gracious and to the point; he had a superb wit. My friend from New York Fr. Leo Donovan was an elected delegate, and he related to me years later his encounter with Kolvenbach during the "murmuratio." After a few preliminaries, Leo said, "I notice that you were at GC 32 eight years ago, as I was, but I don't recall that you made any interventions or comments in the Aula during the general proceedings." Kolvenbach replied, "Yes, that's correct. I did not. I didn't sense the need. But I recall that you made six interventions yourself." And then he proceeded to tell Leo precisely what each of them had been! Other delegates had the same experience, and soon the murmurs percolated through the congregation about what a prodigious memory Kolvenbach had, along with thoughtful, prudent, and measured responses. So when the voting came, he was elected on the first ballot! Remarkable since there are no nominations. Each delegate just wrote out a name. Ballots were then collected and tallied.

Avery Dulles, the well-known American Jesuit theologian who by now was on the faculty at Catholic University, was the one who announced who the new general was to me. I was walking along the mall near Caldwell Hall, where I had just started my doctoral studies, when Avery loomed up out of the morning mist. Though I didn't have him for a teacher, we had met briefly, and he knew I was a Jesuit. He told me that

a Dutchman—Kolvenbach—had been elected, commenting, "I have not
heard much about him, but I understand that he is a scholar and received
his doctorate in Paris." Of course, scholarship ranked high for Avery on
any list of qualifications!

Kolvenbach kept a prodigious schedule. He visited as many Jesuit
provinces as he could. He had a calming presence in the midst of continuing turmoil in the Church, in society, and within the Jesuits themselves. Whenever I heard him, he was witty, frank, and responsive to any
question asked.

Peter-Hans Kolvenbach had lived most of his teen years during the
German occupation of the Netherlands in World War II. In an interview
just before he completed twenty-five years as general, Kolvenbach noted
that experiencing war was not an uncommon experience in the formation of a superior general. He said, "Before his conversion, Ignatius of
Loyola defended heroically the fortress of Pamplona in Spain against the
French army in 1521. Father Arrupe, my predecessor, had the cruel experience of the first atomic attack on Hiroshima in Japan. To my formation belonged not only World War II, especially the violent defense of the
nearby German border from September 1944 until April 1945, but also
the long years in war-torn Beirut when Lebanon's independence was at
stake. War teaches you to live in complete insecurity and precariousness,
aware that coping with conflicts and tensions is more common than is
a nice, peaceful existence."[2] And then Kolvenbach poetically described
how peace and creative love breaks through the war. "After a night of
deadly violence, the birds sing again, announcing that in spite of destructive human hate, death will never have the last word in the Creator's will."
So these experiences of the paschal mystery are a good preparation for
becoming general, he added.

His reference to the paschal mystery of suffering and redemption
was about as close as he came to describing the formidable challenges he
faced as General of the Society. I was not on the inside track about how
he interacted with the Vatican, but I heard that immediately after his election, he set out each week to make his way through the Vatican dicasteries (cabinets) on personal visits to get acquainted with the key cardinals
and archbishops. These were much appreciated. A cardinal could later
boast to his peers, "The Jesuit General stopped by to see me today."

---

2. James McDermott, SJ. "Let Us Look Together in Christ," 10.

I asked one of Kolvenbach's close advisers Jack O'Callaghan how he would describe Pedro Arrupe and Peter-Hans Kolvenbach in a phrase or two. Jack said, "Arrupe was a creative innovator; Kolvenbach was a pragmatic diplomat. All those years in the Levant (the Middle East) prepared him well." Jack then went on to relate a story that Kolvenbach told about his Near East diplomacy. "Shortly after he was named vice provincial, Kolvenbach was invited to dinner by a powerful, local tribesman. Fortunately he was advised ahead of time how it would play out. All the men sat down to an elaborate, multi-course dinner. And not a word was spoken during the entire meal! Cued in, Kolvenbach adhered to the custom and remained silent and observant. At the end of the meal, the sheik-leader said, 'This has gone so well, you must come back soon.' At the next dinner, they had vigorous discussions and exchanges and worked out whatever political understandings and arrangements were necessary."

Later as general, when Kolvenbach caught wind that the writings of Jesuit liberation theologian Jon Sobrino of El Salvador were about to come under the piercing scrutiny of the Congregation for Doctrine of the Faith (CDF), Kolvenbach initiated his own review. He asked the respected Father Juan Alfaro, SJ, at the Gregorian University to give him a report on Father Jon Sobrino's writings. Alfaro probably had a few quibbles, but he gave Sobrino an excellent report—well within the bounds of orthodoxy. Kolvenbach then reportedly shared the report with the Congregation for Doctrine and the Faith and that was the end of their thumping and harrumphing about Sobrino.

By the time Kolvenbach was elected in 1983, an atmosphere of oppression, secrecy, and spying had seized the church. Neo-orthodoxy was in the ascendancy. It was not as nefarious as the underground network of spies following Pius X's condemnation of Modernism in 1907, but it had some of the same repressive features. Candidates for Church leadership were blackballed if they had written on certain topics, such as relaxing the Church's stance on birth control and ordination of women, or if they had ever protested Church policy, especially in writings that could be tracked down. The rigorous authoritarianism of John Paul II was seeping down into every layer of leadership in the Church. At the same time his charismatic power enticed young people and especially young clergy to imbibe the papal cocktail of rigid authority, restorationism, and liturgical fastidiousness. The Holy See also had a strong streak of homophobia and prohibited acceptance of men with "deep-seated homosexual tendencies" for ordination or seminary training. In keeping with his single-minded approach, John Paul said that women's ordination was clearly not in the church's tradition. And in a hermeneutic worthy of ardent fundamentalists he announced that since Jesus never ordained women, the church could never do so either. Not only that, but he forbad pastors and theologians to even speak or write about the question. Men aspiring to a priestly vocation were also picking up the new wave. Since they had been shaped in their early years by the rampant upheavals in the Church and in society, they were drawn to stability, orthodoxy, and surety of the faith. What had happened to the Society of Jesus, to Charles Curran, and to Archbishop Hunthausen was now affecting the whole Church.

I want to recall one incident as characteristic of what Father Kolvenbach did repeatedly, as a mediator, diplomat, and man of prayer. In those years Georgetown University was under scrutiny by both the local cardinal of Washington and the Vatican. I had heard reports from my good friend Fr. Phil Boroughs, the Georgetown vice president for Mission and Ministry, that he and Jack De Gioia, the first lay president of Georgetown, had been making annual visits to Rome, touching base with all the key dicasteries, especially the one on education. The Georgetown cocktail reception for cardinals and archbishops on the rooftop of the swank Hotel Minerva, near the Pantheon, was a major draw and helped to smooth troubled waters. Years later when I had the chance to ask Jack about it, he said that immediately after being named president, he had contacted Monk Malloy, the president of Notre Dame. "Monk said that he and Fr. Ted Hesburgh made an annual trip to Rome to burnish these relationships. So that's what I did," Jack said. "But each time the secretary archbishop in education would ream me out. A scorched-earth policy. I mentioned this to Father Kolvenbach when I met with him, and he said, 'The next time you're in town why don't you invite Father Frank Case, the American Assistant to the General, to join you and the archbishop for dinner.' It worked like a charm. The archbishop was all laughter and conviviality over an Italian dinner, and the critiques from his office softened!" "Now, however, a few years later," Jack continued, "the leadership has changed and the Austrian in charge no longer sees us as a problem, but as a resource. We have two or three contracts with the Vatican to provide resources around key issues, like dialogue with Islam. Kolvenbach initiated the difference."

Some Jesuits had difficulty shifting from Arrupe to Kolvenbach. They were habituated to Arrupe's charismatic leadership and regular conferences, news communiqués, letters to the whole Society. Kolvenbach, by contrast, had a studied reserve. His letters were a few short paragraphs. By contrast with Arrupe, he seemed to leave a vacuum at the top. But Kolvenbach was doing exactly what needed to be done: lowering the profile of the Society, mending fences where needed, and addressing issues with the Holy See discreetly. More than once he conveyed to provincials privately that he was opening up a space for Jesuits to freely practice their ministry and to take on vital issues for the Church and society today. He never once pulled back on the Society's freshly articulated mission of the service of faith, of which the promotion of justice is an integral dimension.[3]

He convoked the 34th General Congregation, which addressed key issues about the Jesuit mission in the face of a rapidly changing world and the revision of the Society's law following the new Code of Canon Law promulgated by the Vatican in 1983. I was a delegate to this congregation, and I will enlarge on my experience in the next chapter. For now, I wish to focus on a few issues related to the pope.

As delegates to the Congregation, we had a special audience with Pope John Paul II in the Aula Clementina, in the heart of the Vatican complex. Kolvenbach gave the customary address to the pope, respectful, deferential, coupled with a readiness for mission. We all applauded his talk, and then John Paul spoke. We could see that Parkinson's disease had already hobbled him, though the Vatican continued to publish official denials. There's an old Roman saying "the pope is not sick until he's dead." We had a taste of that. That evening, hours after the audience, the Vatican majordomo sent us an official reprimand. We should not have applauded Father General after he spoke. Applause should be given only to the pope. We were still in the presence of the medieval monarchy.

About ten years later I met the pope again in quite different and stark circumstances. Seattle Archbishop Alex Brunett had invited me to join his party of fourteen for his *ad limina* visit to Rome, the obligatory checking in with the pope and the Vatican offices, which occurs every five years. To my further surprise, I was the only one to accompany the archbishop going in to see the pope. Encountering the pope, now crippled up and even more wracked with Parkinson's, was a shocking event. He was all bent over and could barely speak above a whisper. Neither the archbishop nor I could make out whatever he was saying. He resembled a cardboard figure, propped up by all his aides, to continue to appear as

3. Over the years the original articulation of the Jesuit mission became more nuanced and better articulated.

pope, while others seized the power. Brunett did hear the pope mumble, "Give my blessing to Archbishop Hunthausen."

Archbishop Brunett was highly satisfied with his meeting with Cardinal Ratzinger in the Congregation for Doctrine of the Faith. He thought that Ratzinger was the only one in the Vatican who understood the scandal and devastation to the church of the sexual abuse crisis, and he was intent on assisting bishops to address the issue and to move forward expeditiously whenever a priest needed to be suspended or removed from ministry. Brunett's meeting with the secretary of the Congregation on Education was an entirely different matter. Archbishop Miller quizzed him in an inquisitional manner about Seattle University, just as Georgetown regularly experienced. But when Brunett told Miller that he met annually with all the Catholic theologians each year to discuss some vital theological issue, Miller was impressed. Apparently, it was the first he had heard of such initiative and wanted to know more about it. So later that night Brunett got ahold of me and asked me to write up our three-point relationship, which I had inaugurated when I became dean of the School of Theology and Ministry in 2000 and almost immediately had to deal with the *mandatum* controversy arising out of the promulgation of the Vatican document on Catholic universities *Ex Corde Ecclesiae*. The *mandatum* required any professor teaching Catholic theology to receive a mandate from the local bishop, an acknowledgement that the professor was accurately representing Catholic teaching and Catholic doctrine. I had recommended to Brunett that rather than dwelling on the neuralgic juridical points of *Ex Corde Ecclesiae* we move forthrightly and in good faith towards implementing the highly positive elements of the document. Brunett still had reservations about the arrangement, but after his encounter with Miller, he was purring with pride about how we were proceeding.

I'll close this chapter with one final vignette. In the millennial year 2000, I was on sabbatical. I stopped in Rome for a week prior to leaving for Tantur Ecumenical Institute in Jerusalem where I would be a scholar-in-residence for three months. So on New Year's Eve, Fr. Frank Case and I were in St. Peter's Square, enjoying the incredibly varied talents of a Harlem women's choir, an Italian boys' choir, and many others from around the world. Huge screens projected the performances to every location. Pope John Paul II, dubbed the "rock star," knew how to put on a big show. He had also exerted major pressure on Rome and the Italian government to clean up the city and repair aging buildings. In addition, much of the traffic was barred and rerouted away from the historic center. Ancient buildings looked stunningly new, often painted in soft pastels, rather than simply ocher and russet. He truly was a reincarnation of the Renaissance pope. But I read the complaint of a columnist in *Il Messaggero*, "Who is this foreigner to be telling us how to run our city?"

That night on the cusp of the third millennium in the Piazza di San Pietro, all was well. It was a joyous evening. As the evening wore on, it was getting cold, I suggested to Frank that we go back to the Jesuit Curia, get something soothingly hot, and then view the anticipated fireworks from the Curia rooftop, which has a panoramic vista of Rome and looks directly down on the Vatican. So by 11:45 I was up on the rooftop with about thirty other Jesuits, and I happened to be standing right next to Peter-Hans Kolvenbach. In his wry sense of humor, he said to me, "Now you watch. At five minutes to midnight, a magic carpet will come flying out the papal window. A few minutes later the pope will give his blessing to all the world. No carpet, no blessing!" And sure enough, the magic carpet flew out and the triumphant pope gave his blessing. Immediately, fireworks started exploding all around us, and soon some of the debris came raining down upon us. A long ways off, we could also see the fireworks soaring heavenward on the Quirinale where the Roman Symphony had just finished playing Beethoven's majestic Ninth Symphony. Indeed, it was a joyous occasion. The crowds leaving St. Peter's Square were so large that they jammed the streets for five hours afterwards. This memorable encounter marked my last time with Kolvenbach. I am exceedingly grateful for his astute and kindly leadership for over twenty-five years, marked by turbulence and high drama for the Society of Jesus. He died in November 2016 in Beirut.

12

The High Point of My Life
as a Jesuit—GC 34

I WAS ELECTED AS a delegate from the Oregon Province to attend General Congregation 34, which met in 1995. The saying that every man has fifteen minutes allotted to him on the world stage may be true for an extraordinarily small percentage of the world population. But the three months of the General Congregation were my fifteen minutes. It was the highlight of my life as a Jesuit, and it was a unique opportunity to be at the heart of the Society of Jesus, to take the pulse of our mission, to help with some reforms and updating.

Four years before I had been elected as the province relator, a new role envisioned by GC 31 in 1966 when the provincials would be called to meet in session with Father General. I thought that that first election by my Jesuit peers would be the end of it. As relator, I visited the province and made an independent report about the State of the Province to Father Kolvenbach. At forty-seven pages it was tediously long. I suppose I was trying to write the province classic. Kolvenbach himself was notoriously terse. So he probably winced when he held my report.

OPENING OF GC 34

Though it's hard to fathom now, email was still not available to us in Rome when the 34th General Congregation convened in January 1995.

Fax was the mainstay. We resided at Domus Pacis, a huge conference center run by Italian laity, across from the enormous Doria Pamphylia Park. It had a cantankerous fax machine that took considerable finesse to run. Somehow I mastered it, and I spent an hour each evening helping other delegates to send out their messages to their friends or home province. It was a good way to meet them. I sent my own weekly report to our province, so fortuitously I have a substantial record of my engagement with the Congregation. Ironically, after the Congregation finished, I discovered much more about what had happened than I was even aware of while I was in the midst of it all.

After arriving at the Domus Pacis, I sized up my room with its cold tile floors and totally inadequate lighting for any reading, I immediately went shopping to buy a small carpet and a desk lamp, which provided invaluable comfort.

A few days later I wrote my first letter back to the province: "Delegates are arriving from all over the world. I have already met Jesuits from Hong Kong, Madras, Colombia, Poland, Zimbabwe, Zaire, and it goes on and on. Six of us who studied together at the Gregorian University 25 years ago are also here. One of the Indians (Jerry Rosario) walks around barefoot and in a short-sleeve shirt, despite temperatures in the 30s and 40s. English is certainly the major language, but I am finding Italian 'molto utile' for talking with the cooks and communicating with the many Jesuit who have studied in Rome, just as I did. I did not expect to be drawn into bouncing around in my halting French so soon. Dress is informal, except among the Eastern Europeans who generally wear clerics."

During the first week we began with three days of prayer, invoking the Holy Spirit and praying for guidance in our discernment. We had reflection groups according to languages. I was placed in one of the two English/Italian groups, which meant everyone had at least a passive comprehension of whatever the second language was. I even plunged into offering a reflection in Italian. We soon proceeded to the election of officers. Fr. Adolfo Nicolás, a genial, prudent Jesuit originally from Spain and the current provincial of Japan, was the overwhelming favorite, who was elected as General Secretary to preside over all the meetings. We Americans were relieved when he announced in English, "I will use the language of our Asian Assistancy." Had he opted for Spanish, we would have tired much more quickly trying to track the translations through headphones.

Outside the general sessions, we met by language groups or by as-sistancies (geographical regions of the Society). Some of us elected del-egates were considerably taken aback when we saw the fracture among the American provincials. Several policy issues had regularly divided them, but at the Congregation, the division broke out around the role of communal discernment. A couple of provincials disdainfully dismissed its importance. Steve Sundborg, our Oregon provincial, strongly, but courteously, took them on. Soon it became quite clear that the same two provincials found all the procedures of the Congregation immensely bor-ing, taxing, and somewhat irrelevant. They were disgruntled with being there. For personal relief, one of them set out each evening, announcing humorously, that he was out "to discover whether there was a bad restau-rant in Rome." At the end of the Congregation, he declared failure! Apart from the Congregation, he was a great guy.

One of the early interventions in the Aula (the large conference room with everyone present) was an eloquent plea by Fr. Gerry O'Hanlon, a delegate from Ireland, urging that we construct a document about the role of women in civil and ecclesial society. By slightly over 50 percent, the Congregation gave it a modest boost. Immediately afterwards, I went up to Gerry saying I was keenly interested in being on any commission that might result and that our own province was one of the six which had requested this consideration about women. As it turned out, my brief conversation with Gerry paved the way for my most important role in the Congregation.

At the end of the first month, I wrote this summary: "Beginning tonight (Friday) we have a two-day weekend for the first time since our arrival. The work ethic is alive and well at the highest levels of the Society. In fact, Kolvenbach sets a torrid pace, even as he appears to amble grace-fully through the day. In addition to all the Congregation meetings, each day he hears the manifestations of three provincials for an hour each. Eighty of the troops are going to Naples for the break, but since I've been there several times, I'm enjoying 'Il dolce far niente,' delicious idleness in Rome. Our Congregation has set a slow but steady pace. Today, however, we voted 200 to 22 to close off any new postulates (agenda items) by February 21. The alternative was March 1. You can see how some few would like to be here forever. We have churned out about 30 presentation papers, despite our resolve to be brief. Jesuits taking the pledge to be brief works about as well as a drunkard in a bar taking the vow to swear off liquor."

"I have been directly involved," I continued, "in drafting two papers: one about the role of women in ecclesial and civil society, which examines the abuse of women, the sex trade, and the oppression within a patriarchal system, without getting into the controverted issue of ordination. The other 'Our Way of Proceeding,' echoing Arrupe's exhortations about discernment, seeks to speed implementation of the GC 34 decrees by identifying some key Jesuit characteristics." Later Kolvenbach would tell Peter Schineller, the drafter of "Our Way of Proceeding" that it was his favorite document. Not surprising, it was practical—Kolvenbach was always looking for ways to get the lead out of the Society and get things moving.

After four weeks, the Congregation seemed bogged down. The Americans nominated Fr. Howard Gray to talk with Father Kolvenbach about it. Kolvenbach's response was, "You Americans value efficiency, but relationships are more important." Somewhat chastened, after Howard reported back to us, we lumbered on. But a week later, the Congregation had arrived at a virtual stalemate, at the point where almost all realized we needed to fish or cut bait. We had piles of documents with good material on lay collaboration, the brothers, Jesuits and the role of women, chastity, ecumenism, and commitment to justice, but they were lumpy. They had no guiding focus. A discernment committee or steering committee was appointed, which became known in various languages as the "fire brigade" to put out the flaming, runaway documents or more brutally in Italian "La Macelleria," the butcher shop, to chop out all the bloody excess. The Indian Jesuits told us Americans, "We were waiting for you to intervene and speed things up!" Our reputation for blunt efficacy was intact.

Despite the fire brigade operating for two weeks, our river of documents was still hitting a logjam. We were about to deep-six some of the pieces and turn them over to ordinary governance. At that point John Padberg from St. Louis suggested to me somewhat crudely in Italian that more likely the documents would be dismembered, rather than neutered: *forse smembrato* (perhaps dismembered), *forse decapitato* (perhaps beheaded), but *non castrato*. Once a document came to the floor, we were seldom able to bury it.

On March 2, I wrote to the province: "The Aula's discussion on the document about chastity yesterday gave rise to a host of double entendre's. We reached a new high of metaphorical excess when a Spanish speaker, commenting on sexuality, said, 'A quantum of Eros must fertilize our Agape.' I guess he meant that erotic sexuality must be united with the highest love. Perhaps it sounded better in the original language?"

Decree Three "Our Mission and Justice," became very contentious during the debate in the Aula. The primary drafter of the document, who was from the British Province, had privately disclosed his intent on blunting the force of what he contended was the Society's single-minded commitment to social justice, which he held had had many negative effects. In his draft he gave much attention to the risen Christ in glory and the fullness of redemption—the kingdom of God at peace. One of the delegates from El Salvador passionately proclaimed, "By diminishing the role of the Crucified Christ, you are taking away our martyrs." He lamented, "The enduring sacrifice and the blood of the martyrs for justice were vastly neglected." A vigorous debate followed on all sides. My fellow Oregon delegate Teddy Kestler reveled in the debate, saying later, "The Christological debate was the best heard anywhere since the fourth century when the faithful were arguing about the role of Christ and the Trinity on the streets of Alexandria!" Teddy had a way of dramatizing theology. The document was sent back for major revision, and in the next round it had a rich association of the risen Christ and crucified Christ, one and the same, once and for all. The delegates resoundingly approved it.

In early March, springtime hit Rome. Mosquitoes pestered me in my room for a couple of nights. The swallows—*i rondini*—came sweeping in from Africa, but they could not obliterate the pesky mosquitoes. After the heavy rains, fat cockroaches scampered for shelter on the first floor of our building. Fortunately, I was on the second floor. Gerry Fagin from New Orleans said, "These little fellows are nothing compared to their cousins in the South."

By then, to our relief, we had a tentative calendar to finish by March 22 with a concluding Mass of thanksgiving at the Gesú. I would need to scramble to depart by March 23 in order to gear up for spring quarter classes, which started March 27.

Some highlights and one low point marked my time at the Congregation.

We achieved a significant breakthrough by expanding the Jesuit mission to include culture and interreligious dialogue, as well as justice. GC 32 had sent down a taproot into the heart of our mission as a service of faith that necessarily included the promotion of justice. But now after twenty years of experience, we needed to refine and strengthen the mission. The core social justice commitment gave way to a more complex root, an interlocking matrix brilliantly summarized in *The Servants of Christ's Mission #19*:

> No service of faith without
>> promotion of justice
>> entry into cultures
>> openness to other religious experiences
>
> No promotion of justice without
>> communicating faith
>> transforming cultures
>> collaboration with other traditions
>
> No inculturation without
>> communicating faith with others
>> dialogue with other traditions
>> commitment to justice
>
> No dialogue without
>> sharing faith with others
>> evaluating cultures
>> concern for justice.[1]

Dialogue became the watchword for the mission of the Society: dialogue with other faiths, dialogue with culture, dialogue with women, and so forth. All this augured well for a robust future, as we proclaimed ourselves "servants of Christ's mission." It was a justice-based mission geared to the times, coupled with understanding diverse cultures and other faiths. It was grounded in poverty. It collaborated with and supported the laity. It listened to and learned from women. We were discerning our way as pilgrims as we linked arms with Christ in his mission today. Tom Fox, the editor of *The National Catholic Reporter*, enthusiastically proclaimed our productive work as the "first Catholic documents for the Church of the 21st century."

As we finished our work, we were advancing the inspiration of the Council by freshly assuming its sources of inspiration. We were a pilgrim people on a continuing journey. The GC 34 documents reasserted a solid faith founded in a justice mission that engaged cultures throughout the world and welcomed interreligious dialogue. It was surprising

---

1. See #19 of the document for the full explication of the matrix. *Documents of the Thirty-Fourth General Congregation of the Society of Jesus*, 37.

that Vatican officialdom and John Paul II allowed them to go forward, considering the pope's much more pessimistic, defensive posture for the Church. Central authority continued to adhere to an institutional model of Church adamantly held together by the pope with all headed in one direction. The Church emitted the one reliable beacon of light in a stormy sea to give direction and solace to the faithful. In the mindset of John Paul, uncertainty was a sign of weakness. A pilgrim church discerning its way could suggest a dangerous erosion of faith. The papal prescription was simple: stay vigilant and obedient to Rome, especially in moral theology and doctrine.

By all accounts Kolvenbach had led us masterfully out of the relational snarl with the Vatican twelve years earlier. He steered us forward, but kept a low profile. He had an acute understanding of the needs of the worldwide Church and a realistic understanding of being able to meet those needs. During GC 34 he had also quietly assigned Giuseppe Pittau, SJ, a favorite of the Vatican court, to be the liaison between the Society and the Vatican in order to keep key officials informed of the proceedings of the Congregation. In the royal court, no surprises were the order of the day.

In another highly diplomatic, but also significant, moment, Kolvenbach invited Cardinal Paolo Dezza to address the Congregation. Yes, John Paul II had named him a cardinal in "gratitude for his services to the church." By now Dezza was ninety. He lived in the Jesuit Curia, attended by a nurse's aide. Kolvenbach invited him to tell stories about the popes he had personally known. Kolvenbach graciously escorted him up to the dais. Remarkably, Dezza had been a member of every General Congregation from 1938 up to 1983, from GC 28 until GC 33. At the latter, he turned the governance of the Society back over to the elected Superior General Kolvenbach. Dezza began with recollections of Pius XI in 1938 when he was attending GC 28 as a delegate from the Veneto (Venice) province. He was especially fond of Pius XII whose reign (1939–1958) coincided with Dezza's time as rector of the Gregorian University. And then he dwelt at great length on Paul VI, who was clearly his favorite. He didn't say much about John Paul II. The moment, orchestrated by Kolvenbach, was a way for the Society to thank Dezza for steering us through the rocky shoals threatened by a few warrior cardinals, who would just as soon have dismantled the Society. We were all aware that Dezza had quickly gained the confidence of the pope, as well as his peers in the Jesuit

Curia, by pushing forward with the same Jesuit mission Arrupe had advanced, but with much better communication with the Vatican.

Paolo Dezza died four years later at the age of ninety-four.

The most important documents of GC 34 were the triptych of three Mission documents introduced by Servants of the Mission of Christ. The latter provided the opening doors for the three mission documents on justice, culture, and interreligious dialogue. I became directly involved with the Servants document because my friend Howard Gray had drafted it. When Howard's first draft came to the floor, some outspoken delegates savaged it. A former provincial bellowed, "It's neither brief, nor is it introductory." The oldest American delegate also skewered it. The critics would probably have been more diplomatic had they known who had written it.

That night when Howard and I escaped Domus Pacis and walked down Via Julia to a delightful trattoria for dinner, Howard was still smarting. Over dinner I made three or four suggestions to him, which he later generously said gave him the breakthrough he needed when he rose early the next morning to redraft the piece. When it was presented again a few days later, the delegates quickly accepted it, practically by acclamation.

My dinner with Howard was memorable for another reason. I had been in a frenzied state for four days. I needed some spiritual advice and guidance in discernment. Greg Lucey, the president of the Jesuit Conference, had asked me to accept an assignment as the Spiritual Director of the North American College in Rome. It would have meant overseeing the spiritual direction of 120 seminarians, being the actual director for forty of them, and coordinating a team of the other directors. Initially, I was open to the idea. I liked Rome. I spoke Italian. I knew the North American from my days in Rome, and I had done a lot of spiritual direction.

I talked it through with my provincial Steve Sundborg, over a delicious pranzo in Trastevere. At one point in our conversation, Steve said, "Well, Pat, I see no reason for you not to accept it." From that point onward whenever I thought about it, my anxiety levels knew no bounds. Unnamed fears raced through me. The ambitious clerical atmosphere of the College, where many of the seminarians mounted the fast track towards becoming a bishop, was certainly one of my fears, but my anxiety seemed totally out of proportion to whatever the reality might be.

So that evening when I talked it through with Howard, about the importance of the position and about my desire to be available for mission, he sagely said, "Well, Pat, just because the Society should be there, doesn't mean that YOU should be there." Immediately, my wild anxieties subsided. We spent the rest of the evening in delightful conversation. The next day I explained to Greg Lucey that I needed to decline.

One of the most satisfying portions of the Congregation was my work on the document on women. Gerry O'Hanlon had brought a preliminary draft with him from Ireland, and eventually, three of us worked out the decree, along with a couple of others: Gerry, Bill Uren of Australia, and I. Often enough the three of us would finish the day and then escape to a nearby pizzeria. We also invited some women from the Philippines, Australia, and Ireland, among others, to read our draft and give us some feedback. The document went through multiple iterations and had three presentations in the Aula where it steadily gained support. It escaped the butcher shop, *la macelleria*.

After the first hearing, a Jesuit from India told me, "In India the woman is a goddess in the temple, and a slave in the home. So this document is vital for our mission. I hope you can thank women religious for how they make our mission possible. They are the ones who live with the people in the villages. They are nurses, counselors, catechists, and the people love them. The priest may come into the village only once a month." So I inserted a key paragraph of gratitude. I also urged that we not close the door on the ordination of women, but leave the door open for future, more profound understandings—which we did with a high degree of subtlety. Once our drafting was finished, I lobbied for its success by explaining to one of my Slovenian Jesuit friends in Italian the important justice issues for women that we were addressing. Happily, the next day he spoke in vigorous support of it in the general session, though his Italian was so garbled that no one quite knew what he had said, only that he was for it.

Early one morning Gerry caught me to say that the Holy See liked our document, and they wanted Gerry to draft a working paper for the Vatican for the forthcoming conference on women in Beijing. "Darn," I said, spontaneously. "We could have gotten more in there." Gerry explained that Giuseppe Pittau, the liaison informally appointed by Kolvenbach, had taken our document to the appropriate Congregation, and they saw it as a way forward for the Holy See to advance a much more positive agenda than they had a few years previously at the women's conference in Cairo. At that conference, the Holy See's nearly misogynist position had been lumped with the Arab countries and other fundamentalist religions. They wanted to avoid another imbroglio. We were clearly making a lasting contribution.

In the closing days a delegate from Venezuela and the future general of the Society, Arturo Sosa, said he wanted to thank those who had argued for the document on women in the church. He said that he had voted against the topic when it first came up. But as time moved on, he said he saw it as extremely valuable, second in importance only to the mission documents.

I had one confrontational incident during the Congregation, which undid me for a few days. In the document "On Having a Proper Attitude of Service in the Church," I thought one paragraph was fuzzy and waffled on the role of obedience. So I submitted an amendment, which was voted on and accepted in the general session. One of the Americans was furious, and wrote a scathing letter to me about my incompetence and how I had wrecked their document. Some of the other members of the Commission were upset, but nothing like this one. I tried to talk with him, but he would have nothing to do with me.

The offending paragraph was number seventeen. My version read: "Therefore, if there is a time for speaking out, there may also be a time for silence, chosen by discernment or even imposed by obedience. For if there is a time for representation, there is also a time for abnegation of our intellect and will to become for us a new way of seeing through the clouds of suffering and uncertainty to a higher truth and wisdom, that of the Cross."[2] I believe it echoed what Ignatius would have said, but my outraged critic thought I had infantilized obedience by suggesting the "abnegation of intellect and will" in certain (rare) circumstances.

A few days later Bert Thelen, the Wisconsin provincial who was later to leave the Society at age eighty, invited me to join him and a scholastic from the Gesú for a weekend in Assisi. We took the train. The serenity and quiet of Assisi was just the restorative I needed. We had simple quarters above a grocery store in the heart of Assisi. The next morning—Sunday—I woke to hear the bells tolling. They were enchanting, a taste of heaven in the Umbrian hills. A spring shower had cleansed the streets and now everything glistened in the sunlight. We hiked up to the hermitage of St. Francis on a road flanked by orchards. *I contadini,* the

2. "On Having a Proper Attitude of Service in the Church," *Documents of the 34th General Congregation*, no. 17, 148.

farmers, were burning the prunings from the trees, and the light smoke wafted round fruit trees just starting to burst with greenish-yellow leaves. Late afternoon we were treated to *pranzo al Americano*, including lemon pie, by some Franciscan Sisters from Lacrosse, Wisconsin. That evening I reluctantly turned back to Rome—thinking of how Ignatius in 1537 had God's promise that he would be propitious to him in Rome. But after the early companions arrived in Rome, the plague broke out a year later. Ignatius and his companions exhausted themselves caring for the sick. In addition, they were accused of Lutheranism, a heresy that could have brought judgment and death by the Inquisition. They were exonerated, but I have always been a bit skittish of God's promise of being propitious to me in Rome.

A few days later I received another boost. Robert Heyer, editor of Sheed and Ward, sent me a fax saying that they had accepted my book *A Spiritguide through Times of Darkness*. Pure joy! The title of my book felt relevant for the darkness I felt the previous week.

But that was not the end of it. At the end of the Congregation, we had a three-day waiting period, praying for confirmation of our discerned decisions. During that time anyone can bring up an objection to an already approved document. Without discussion, it then takes a 50 percent positive vote to bring it up on the floor for consideration. Sure enough, members of the Commission, "On Having a Proper Attitude of Service in the Church," called for a reconsideration of my paragraph. And with one or two votes over 50 percent, it was approved for reconsideration. After that, everything became surrealistic. The objections were made, but then others chimed in to support what I had written. At one point one of the Belgians, waxing poetic, talked about the sweet odor, the perfume, of obedience. At that point, my friend Teddy Kestler looked around to me beaming, as if to say, "Can you believe that you ever got into this?" No, I could not. One of the American objectors took it upon himself to speak for me, saying that he understood that now "even the author didn't agree with it." Which, of course, was not true. At that point I pushed my buzzer, and Kolvenbach himself caught my motion to speak, so Father Nicolás recognized me. I said something to the effect, "The problem remains with the original statement. I'm sure that what I wrote could be better nuanced, but my amendment is better than the original." At that point discussion closed. A vote was taken. And the objection was voted down by the slightest of margins. My amendment prevailed. There was no triumph. I was drained.

The most moving moment of the Congregation, I suspect for all of us, was a special presentation in the Aula. The provincial of Australia called upon the provincial of Congo/Rwanda to step forward. And then Ian Cribb, a Jesuit brother, explained that some months earlier an Australian journalist knocked on the provincial's office. The journalist said he had been in Rwanda shortly after the devastating genocide, and he had gone to the Jesuit Christus Center, a retreat house on the edge of Kigali. There, a short time earlier, the Jesuits had tried to protect some of the beleaguered Tutsis. But shortly, Hutu terrorists murdered the Tutsis as well as three of the Jesuits who had given them refuge. The journalist found a wooden, bloodstained crucifix in one of the Jesuit's bedroom. He didn't want to just leave it there to be ravaged further, so he rescued it. Then Ian said something along these lines to the provincial of Congo/Rwanda, "On behalf of the whole Society, we want to present this Cross from the Christus Center to you as a sign of our solidarity with you as companions in our Jesuit mission of the faith that does justice, whatever the cost." I know that I was not the only one in tears.

That same week we had a Mass of Remembrance honoring the thirty-seven Jesuits who had been assassinated since GC 32 because of their work on behalf of the Jesuit mission of the faith that does justice.[3] Even at the time in 1975 when the mission document on faith and justice was approved, Arrupe had prophetically said, "There will be many martyrs that come from this (decision)." I had met one of them in France, André Masse. Later in 1985 André took over as the director of the south Lebanon branch of St. Joseph University in east Beirut. His goal was to provide quality education to both Muslims and Christians in order to break down religious barriers between the two groups, and he was a mediator between the factions. On September 24, 1987, unidentified assassins carrying pistols with silencers smashed down the door of his office and shot him five times. He died instantly. André was only forty-seven.

In its final days, the atmosphere of the Congregation lightened considerably. An air of exhilaration pervaded the delegates, partly because we anticipated returning home, but more deeply because we sensed accomplishment and gratitude. We had solidified the Society's commitment to justice on behalf of the poor, but now we articulated its complexity as an interwoven matrix of faith, justice, culture, and interreligious dialogue. It was clear as well that the Congregation had given a resounding

3. William O'Malley, SJ, *The Voice of Blood,* has an excellent account of several of these Jesuit martyrs.

affirmation to the astute, diplomatic leadership of Kolvenbach over the previous twelve years.

While we continued to wait for the confirmation of the discernment we had made in writing the documents, we had an open mike. During this time Vinnie O'Keefe gave a speech in Latin, simply to note that no Congregation should be complete unless Latin was spoken on the floor at least once. His humorous little piece was the only time Latin was used. All the previous Congregations either mandated Latin, or it was the only vehicle of communication possible for some, such as the Chinese Jesuits. During this time, John Padberg, notable historian, released a cavalcade of statistics that he had tracked during all the proceedings. The Congregation lasted seventy-seven days. The languages spoken in the Aula included (roughly, as I recall): English 47 percent; Spanish 27 percent; French 15 percent; Italian 10 percent; and German 1 percent. Padberg also gave the total number of votes and several other interesting factoids. When I tried to verify these with him twenty years later, John was astounded that I recalled them at all and said that his note filing was not that diligent, so he had no record of it.

And finally, on the last night after a Mass of Thanksgiving, we had a variety show at Domus Pacis, emceed by the inimitable Vinnie O'Keefe, who alternated between English and Italian rendering jokes and awards. A top award was for the "best dressed Jesuits." By acclamation they were Fr. Kolvenbach, who never wore anything but a rumpled cassock, and Fr. Jerry Rosario of India, who in the middle of the Roman winter wore only a light shirt, slacks, and no shoes! Another popular choice was "the most conservative" and "the most liberal." A Polish Jesuit was the most liberal and an El Salvadoran Jesuit was the most conservative—just the reverse of the reality. The poor traditionalist Polish Jesuit was beaming with delight and bewilderment. He didn't seem to get the joke. The music and laughter went on into the night; it was a picaresque evening of the Society at its best. I had to leave in the middle of the party because I had an early morning flight to catch in order to return to Seattle to teach my courses in the spring quarter. Once I landed in Seattle, I had only two days before I was back in the harness, back to regular order, but with my heart and imagination and dreams filled with the wonderful encounters and contributions we had made during those three intense months of discernment and decisions on our Jesuit mission.

13

Mental Illness and the Jesuits

QUITE EARLY IN MY Jesuit life, I was struck by how many mental breakdowns there were among the Jesuits. Individual cases were talked about, but the pattern of recurrent breakdowns was not.

One curiosity I discovered in the Oregon province catalogue when I was a novice was that a Jesuit scholastic by the name of Mr. Stephen Crowley, SJ, age sixty-three, was residing at Eastern Washington Psychiatric Hospital at Medical Lake. No one seemed to know anything about him, or if they did, they were not inclined to talk about it. When he died four years later in 1966 at age sixty-seven at Western Psychiatric Hospital in Steilacoom, Washington, after fifty years as a Jesuit without ever being ordained, no one seemed to know his history or what had happened. He was the invisible, forgotten Jesuit.

I was aware of at least two of the men who had a breakdown while I was in the novitiate. We heard the screams of one of them in the infirmary. Someone said, "He went berserk." They tried to treat him right there in the infirmary, where for certain no one had psychiatric skills. Not long after, he left the novitiate. Joe Hauer, one of my best friends from college, entered the novitiate a year after me. He became more and more intense as each week went by. The Long Retreat, the thirty days of a silent Ignatian retreat, began for him and all the first-year men in October. One day—about twelve days later—Joe was simply gone. I found out later that the kindly rector of the house, Fr. Mike McHugh, had intervened. He talked at length with Joe, and drove him to nearby McMinnville where Joe caught a bus for home. My friend Ed Haasl a couple of years later related that Joe had still not recovered. He had taken up sculpturing and pottery, perhaps his family was supporting him, but he wasn't able to harness his degree in mathematics. He had no income.

Yet another classmate from Gonzaga, who had entered the Jesuits at the same time as Joe, had a breakdown a few years later during his studies in philosophy at Mount St. Michael's in Spokane. He left the Jesuits, but lost his self-confidence during the ordeal. Eventually, he was happily married and lived a productive life. Progressive psychiatric treatment or a timely intervention seemed to be missing in these cases.

An even more dire case that I encountered was Father Vic, who taught algebra at Gonzaga Prep when I was principal. He was a strong, gentle man. I knew a few bits and pieces of his story—namely that he had had a breakdown in 1952, a short time after he was ordained. One day he shared with me what had happened. They had sent him to an inpatient psychiatric care center run by the Alexian Brothers in St. Louis. Jesuit superiors and medical personnel were certain that the break was so severe that he would never recover. Vic described to me how in the middle of that anguish, he struggled and with great willpower came out of the storm. Somehow he emerged. He couldn't explain it much more than that. I suspect that his own formidable spirituality and God's provident Spirit lifted him out of the depths. It was an unrecorded miracle. Even so in the years after, he was fragile psychically. The kids loved him in class, but ran him ragged. He was a highly skilled craftsman, who made intricate inlaid wooden boxes, a tabernacle, and other objects of art. Though his hands were always shaking, he had remarkable powers to inlay the wood—with dexterous art and beauty. To my knowledge he had no further psychiatric care after he left St. Louis.

One of the genuine shocks to the province was when Peter Gaskell, a young scholastic, committed suicide in Spokane in 1974. Father Pat O'Leary, his rector at St. Michael's, gave one of the most moving, profound homilies I have ever heard.[1] He used St. Paul's text, "The knowledge that I have now is imperfect, but I shall know as fully as I am known" (1 Cor 13:13). Pat O'Leary said, "We experience in the midst of the joy

---

1. JOPA [Jesuit Oregon Province Archives], "Homily given by Patrick B. O'Leary, S.J." The Oregon Province archivist David Kingma was an invaluable aid for tracking down all the material related to this topic.

that comes from the power and presence of God's creative love the suffering and pain of being on the way to fullness, seeing only dimly, not face to face. . . . The ecstasy of light, the glory of Tabor, has its corresponding agony of darkness, the humiliation of Calvary. We gather together around the table of the Lord . . . in our pain at the death of one whom we have loved, Peter Gaskell. There was so much light and love in Peter, and this is what he always tried to share with us. He was indeed patient and kind; not one who might be jealous, boastful or conceited. We remember him as gentle, sensitive, a bit shy with a ready wit and a quick smile. In Peter, like all of us, there was darkness too; and the pain of it he chose to bear alone."

As Pat concluded the homily, he said, "Peter's death remains for us an experience where light is wrapped in shadow, a seeing of a dim reflection in a mirror that gives rise again and again to that longing to be taken up into that full presence of God where we will see face to face and in knowing God know ourselves and others as we are known by Him." And then Pat read this remarkable, untitled sonnet by Peter that gave us his own glimpse of that darkness and still presence of God:

SONNET

A splendid quietude for thoughts giving
Free reign to their expressions. How the night
Exudes that mystic power; that mysterious quiet
Which invites the soul to reflect on its purpose for living.
How many nights like this have been spent in seeing
Only an empty gloominess of nightfall;
The loneliness of dark that is felt by all
Who've never let another touch their being.
I have seen through that dark and ever deceptive shroud
Of night that colors the world with a hue of despair,
That reveals only an emptiness of being.
For night now breathes to me that peaceful air
Of the Divine; so full of life in seeing
That night is naught but the soothing mantle of God.

In that dark night, Peter had felt the "soothing mantle of God."

These are a few of the cases of mental breakdown of Jesuits I knew. Other cases were handled discreetly, quietly, and without any public awareness.

So imagine my shock when I had a mental breakdown myself and landed in the Province Medical Center psychiatric ward in Portland. At the time I was thirty-five. In my first year as principal, we had had an outbreak of severe accidents. A sophomore had been electrocuted as he climbed an electrical pole. Miraculously, he survived, but was damaged. A freshman had broken an arm in football practice, and the coaches sent him up to the property room with a student trainer who pulled his jersey off over his head. I was enraged at the coaches for their cavalier carelessness. Another student had been hit by a car as one of the mothers drove into the parking lot. The student was slightly grazed, but I comforted the mother who was absolutely shaken and distraught. And a fourteen-year-old student, with a history of heart disease, died in my arms in the principal's office. These were the more obvious stresses and tragedies.

These were also the years when the turmoil that characterized the universities had seeped on down to the high schools. Authority was up for grabs, and the school had to adjust rapidly to untamable, changing circumstances. Though I was the principal, I was too young and too green to flow with the tide, to rely on others for help, and to make key adjustments as we went along.

Another key factor was that my own psycho-spiritual-sexual development was arrested. I was achievement oriented and worked long hours to complete the multitudinous tasks that arose each day. I was good at it, but my efforts never seemed enough. And I didn't consult or delegate sufficiently in order to develop a coordinated team approach to the complex issues arising. Later when I was principal at Gonzaga Prep, I had a much better self-awareness of my limitations and gifts and where I needed to tap into the resources of others to make it all work for us and for the students.

Some years after my recovery, I had a revealing conversation with my psychiatrist Dr. Bill Zieverink about what might have happened. I provide an excerpt here. The full transcript is available in my first book.[2] Dr. Z begins, "You have a good balance in your biography. It's emotionally rich because it is personal. This combination is rather unusual. Usually these biographies are very dry or else soupy confessions. The question remains: 'How come?' Why did you have a psychotic break? It remains an unanswered question."

"We never did finger the precise reason."

2. Howell, *Reducing the Storm to a Whisper.*

"I don't think anyone can answer that question," Dr. Z. continued. "You came into this setting with conflicts and anxieties, but nothing stands out as *the* reason."

"Is that somewhat typical of a psychotic break?"

"Yes. Most people would like to put their finger on some cause. But people are too complicated. I mean, it's multi-causal."

"I do point to the trauma I had on the island of Molokai and to some tensions at Jesuit High."

"Yes, that's fine. You had all that going on. But why should that add up to a psychosis? I think there is a confluence of life events, and then some biological event is present at the age of 35 that was not there, say, at the age of 32, or at 40. Biologically you continuously change."

After some further conversation, we continued:

"I don't know what it is about you Jesuits," Dr. Z. injected, "but every one of you is hung up on the problem of evil."

"I allude to that by the quotation from Job."

"What does Job say?"

"It's a mystery. You don't knock your head against a mystery trying to solve it. You accept it, reverence it and go on living. Job responds to God, 'Behold, I am insignificant; what can I reply to You? I lay my hand on my mouth. Once I have spoken, and I will not answer; even twice, and I will add nothing more.'" (Job 40:4–5)

Dr. Z. exclaimed, "Boy, if anyone agrees with that it's me! But an awful lot of religious people are utterly beset with the paradox of how a good God could let this happen."

"It is how we deal with evil, death, depression, misery, and hunger."

"Exactly."

"I don't think there is a very good way of dealing with all that in a normal rational system. Living with it comes down to a sense of compassion and acceptance and going on from there. As you used to say so often: 'Things just aren't fair.'"

"Right. Who said it was fair? But where were you 10 years ago on all these things?"

"I accepted it rationally, but not emotionally. Ideas were there, but they didn't have a gut basis."

"Why? This event of the breakdown flooded you with emotion, and you were overwhelmed, and then you came back together again. You got a better understanding through psychotherapy, and you've gone on from there. So that you're a lot better off today than even before the breakdown. It is a real good outcome. It is not the common outcome. The pathway of tightness in your chest and continuing anxiety could have just gotten narrower and narrower. Your life could have become more and more restricted and defensive. Then it is an ever-increasing job just to maintain control."

"I was liberated by this event."

"But that's not the usual outcome. It can be very frightening. Why was it that you tended to rely so heavily on intellectualization and the rational? I mean, I don't know. We haven't talked much about that."

"I was successful in studies. Certainly in high school I could bury myself in my books, and at the same time I didn't really gain much reward for emotional expression."

"Do you think in your home, growing up, that's an accurate statement? Sex and aggression are the two things most people have a great deal of trouble with. They are the unresolved conflicts of adolescence often enough. . . . Every profession has a certain self-selection process. How many of your colleagues in the Society of Jesus have these same handicaps."

"Is that a rhetorical question too?"

He laughed, "I am sort of baiting the audience here! One would suspect, certainly in the Jesuits with their high degree of intelligence, a self-selection of those traits or styles, which would be rewarded. Certainly when I was at a Jesuit high school at St. Xavier's, Cincinnati, and at the Jesuit college at Holy Cross, the intellectual, the bright, smart and witty were way up there. But emotional and social skills were secondary."

"James Joyce had some devastating caricatures of Jesuits who were all mind and intellect and had sterile souls. The intellectual life and wittiness of Jesuits certainly appealed to me."

"O.K. That means a lot of your colleagues risk psychosomatic symptoms—tight chest, ulcers, headaches."

"Heart attacks at an early age and alcoholism."

"But how do you reconcile this intellectualization with what you described as an affective prayer life? And I suspect they have a lot of trouble because they sense their prayer life is somewhat sterile, and ideally their prayer life should be the most vibrant part of their life. What do they do?"

"Well, there's a close relationship between your prayer life and your other affective relationships. One feeds the other. So if you are a bastard in community, you are probably a bastard in prayer!"

He absorbed this hyperbole. Later in the conversation, he said, "The Society has had a lot of difficulty providing precisely this intellectual and emotional integration. It is a tragedy, because the Society has an enormous collection of talent that is hobbled emotionally."

FURTHER REFLECTIONS

One of the remarkable graces in my life has been that I had this mental breakdown, though I do not recommend it to anyone! It opened up doors I would never have imagined. Over the years I have been intimately involved with helping people with mental illness and supporting their families. For ten years a United Church of Christ minister and I hosted an annual conference at Seattle University entitled "Soul, Psyche, and Society," which delved into mental illness, both chronic and acute, and sought to educate the public and support families.

But my initial engagement was slow and incremental. It began in the psych ward itself. In the second of my four weeks at the hospital, after I was substantially stabilized, the attending psychiatrist asked if I would be willing to speak about my experience to a group of Portland police officers that he was helping to recognize mental illness and develop emergency assistance. I reluctantly agreed. It went all right. During the coffee break none of them chose to interact with me. I felt alone. But it was at that moment, I decided that I would not hide what had happened to me. That I would not accept the stigma regularly attached to people with mental illness. My decision came as a surprise and as a grace. So for forty years I have given talks on "Mental Illness and Spirituality," "On Overcoming Stigma—from a Biblical Perspective," "A Journey into the Heart of Mystery," and so forth. The titles change, but the stories and content only shift and slide around to make the point and to encourage people to face into the darkness. Denial or avoidance only exacerbates the underlying causes of the illness and breakdown. As I said before, in these talks I offer a liberal dose of my psyche ward spirituality. Stigma remains one of society's major blind spots. It still has a stubborn grip on people's imaginations. But just as Jesus broke down barriers, biases, and stigmatizations, we in our time need to work and pray for a similar metanoia or conversion.

My own experience and that nagging, untold story about Mr. Stephen Crowley, SJ, dying at a psychiatric hospital, led me to gain permission from the provincial in 2016 to examine some of the early Jesuit records. I wanted to discover what happened to Jesuits who had a severe breakdown in the era before the discovery of psychotropic drugs in France (1952), after which psychiatric care was transformed. Mr. Stephen Crowley, I found, had had an irrecoverable breakdown. As early as May, 1925, when Crowley was twenty-six, Father Paul Sauer, the province treasurer, had a record of "money paid for Mr. Crowley at St. Vincent's in St. Louis. Later there was a month spent at "The Chiropractic Psychopatic Sanitorium [sic], located in Davenport, Iowa."[3] His name then appeared regularly, according to Father Sauer, on accounts with Eastern State Hospital from January 1, 1929, onward. The records for Mr. Crowley are extraordinarily thin. Most often, all that remains are the financial records of the minimal amount required by the state, which was diligently paid out for his care year by year. A few exceptions occur in the record. When Fr. Leo Martin was rector at Mount St. Michael's, he used to visit him and made it a point to hear his confession. In fact, ensuring that the man received the sacraments, ideally, in a Catholic hospital, was the most enduring aspect of these reports. Another exception in Mr. Crowley's file came during the early days of Fr. Leo Robinson, SJ, as provincial when someone who knew Mr. Crowley offered to pay the expenses of a private sanatorium. So "Robbie" made inquiries on October 25, 1944, of Dr. H. A. Perry, superintendent at Eastern State. The doctor explained at length, "He manifests a number of bizarre mannerisms, has a habit of seizing chairs that he passes, raising them from the floor and slamming them back, occasionally hard enough to produce breakage. . . . He is often observed apparently responding to hallucinatory phenomena, though he denies the occurrence of such when questioned directly."[4] The correspondence also notes that Crowley has an aptitude for running away when he gains a chance. Dr. Perry concludes, "Mentally, the case is one of Schizophrenia for which there are presently both catatonic and hebephrenic features, together with moderately advanced deterioration. . . . Because of the duration of his illness, the ultimate prognosis would appear hopeless. It is my opinion that a transfer offers no added hope of ultimate cure, that he is receiving every needed attention here, and that he is as happy

3. JOPA "Letter of Charls Chapman, SJ, secretary to the provincial, to Rev. Joseph Logan, SJ, rector of Bellarmine Prep."

4. JOPA, "Letter of H. A. Perry, M.D., superintendent of Eastern State Hospital."

and content as one could expect."[5] That was the way that Mr. Crowley endured for another twenty-two years.

Through this research I discovered that I may very well have met Stephen Crowley. When I was a sophomore at Gonzaga, I got to know Fr. Leo Robinson, the former provincial, who by then was crippled by Parkinson's disease. "I walk with a cane," he humorously observed, "so people don't think I'm drunk." He visited Medical Lake every week. I suspect that my friend Ed Haasl arranged for a few of us to join Father "Robbie" on one of his visits to the psychiatric hospital. Ed was always involving me in fresh new ventures that I would never have undertaken on my own. My only recollection of the visit was that many of the patients were passive, heavily sedated. I am sure that, in the company of Father "Robbie," we have would looked in on Mr. Crowley. So at last after all these years and in my reconstructed memories, I met Mr. Stephen Crowley.

While in the province archives, I came across the records of others as well. Most of these showed up through the financial records that Fr. Sauer assiduously kept. At times there were surprises. The provincial Henry Schultheis wrote in 1960, "We have an inquiry about a lay brother Thomas G. Callaghan, who died in the Province in 1940. Apparently there is question of his inheriting some money." Schultheis narrates that the information they have includes that Brother Callaghan was born in 1877, entered the Society in 1909, and died on August 5, 1940 "in the Eastern State Hospital for the insane at Medical Lake." "Apparently he was in the hospital from 1923 until his death."[6] Brother Callahan had served at Holy Cross Mission in Alaska, at Seattle College, and at Gonzaga University. But his only assignment at Gonzaga, according to the Latin record, was "curat valetudinem," that is, he is taking care of his health.[7]

I ran across the records of other Jesuits who had been permanently hospitalized in St. Louis, Davenport, Islip, New York, or other institutions. They included a few personal notes, minimal psychiatric or medical reports, concern by Jesuit superiors for the man's spiritual welfare, and were largely traceable only through the financial records. Not much more.

Some years ago Father Charles Shelton, SJ, a clinical psychologist at Regis University in Denver, wrote an extensive article on the mental

5. Ibid.

6. JOPA "Letter of Henry J. Schultheis, S.J. to Father Monahan."

7. JOPA, "Letter of Father Schultheis to Mr. J. Eugene McMahan, Buffalo, N.Y."

health of Jesuits.[8] Charlie asserted, "the single greatest challenge facing the United States Assistancy today is the prevalence of mental-health issues (in all their degrees) in the lives of individual Jesuits."[9] He was including mental illness, as well as numerous manifestations of idiosyncratic behaviors that were emotionally problematic, and inferring that the crippling effects of psychological problems inhibited a free response to the apostolic availability, which Ignatius envisioned for his men. I would not entirely agree with Father Shelton on this dire assessment or at least I would say that the situation has vastly improved since he wrote this article twenty-five years ago. Several factors have brought about this improvement.

First and foremost, the very nature and model of Jesuit formation has radically changed. No longer is it regimented and predictable. Rather it seeks to elicit the talents and gifts of each individual man, something which was always the goal. But now with a deeper psycho-spiritual-sexual integration, young Jesuits are encouraged to deal with, name, and integrate their sexuality, rather than just bury it. The Jesuit hallmark of contemplatives in action has eclipsed the monastic formation that dominated in the 150 years after the Restoration of the Society in 1814.

A second factor is that alcoholism has been faced head on, rather than ignored or glossed over. In my early days as a Jesuit, every community with which I was familiar had two or three active alcoholics. They could suck the juice out of a community, creating a pall over all of us. No longer. Now men are regularly sent for treatment or enlisted in Alcoholics Anonymous or both. Those in recovery are remarkable exemplars of facing into and accepting and growing through their own demons. Their spiritual depth reveals itself in their homilies and their spontaneous compassionate care for others.

A third factor has been the practically universal abandonment of tobacco. Our recreation rooms, TV rooms, and hallways are no longer saturated by the stale odors of the chain smokers. Yet another factor is that meals are healthier—at least there's always a healthy choice. Younger men especially adhere to a regular schedule of exercise, including the running of marathons. Through these years the average life expectancy of Jesuits in my province has gone from sixty-two (in a 1965 study) to an average of eighty-four today, six years beyond the national average for men.

8. Charles M. Shelton, SJ, "Reflections on the Mental Health of Jesuits."
9. Ibid., 3.

Of course, excellent medical care is another big factor. But also greater joy and satisfaction in ministry. Mental illness still occurs, of course, but the men are no longer sent off to some asylum as permanent residents. With medication and psychiatric care almost everyone can be healthily grounded so that they are functioning, productive, and even happy.

The strength of Sheldon's article lies in naming the addictive behaviors that can beset a community. He lists some of the endless variations: "Tom is hard to live with because he is always cynical and incessantly criticizes the rector (year after year, no matter who the rector is)." "John is addicted to alcohol, finding his home in the bottle." "Tim is obese, Paul is hooked on television—doesn't matter much what the program is, and Michael is a compulsive workaholic, often absent from the community." Often enough, these men "have not addressed the fears, rage, the unmet needs that may accompany addictive behaviors."[10] Of course, healthy emotional integration exists as an ideal to which we aspire.

In the closing pages of my book *A Spiritguide through Times of Darkness*,[11] I developed several guidelines for what might constitute a healthy, well-integrated life. Over the years these have become commonplace for Jesuits. Briefly they include these features: personal prayer as an avenue to intimacy with God; cultivating a few friends and intimates with whom one can speak freely about one's interior life and struggles; a sense of humor, which is a mark of affection and playfulness; meaningful work and a sense of achievement; physical and mental exercise—recreation is crucial.

All these factors can lead to *increasing self-knowledge* accompanied by mature friendships, healthy community environments, a strong faith life, steady investment in work and meaningful volunteering, and experiments in risking new ventures.

Mental illness, of course, is a much wider societal challenge. The stigma attached to mental illness is still a major obstruction for healing, that is, for acceptance and reintegration into society. It's one of the reasons I have been so committed these last thirty years to helping families and faith communities become more knowledgeable, more accepting, more bold in reaching out compassionately to individuals with mental illness.

Twenty-five years after Vatican II and after Jesuit reforms had been initiated, the historian and raconteur of Jesuit lore, John Padberg, SJ,

10. Ibid., 4.

11. Patrick J. Howell, SJ, *A Spiritguide through Times of Darkness*, 189–209.

wrote a fine piece on all the changes that had occurred in Jesuit community life from the perspective of his own community at St. Louis University. He observed, "There is less feeling of being bound by minutiae, more a sense of individual responsibility; less a day regulated by rule, more a day structured by responsible choice; less a Jesuit community as an extension of a Jesuit apostolate, more a Jesuit community participating collaboratively in both a Jesuit university and other apostolates; less a religious house set apart and symbolized by cloister, more a religious house set in the midst of and symbolized by city streets at the front door."[12]

During all these years an issue, which went underground, even more tragically than mental illness, was the sexual abuse of minors and the abuse of students, parishioners, or people seeking pastoral care from a Jesuit. Much of the pattern of repression, ignorance, and maturation fixation, which I have reported above, certainly underlay the playing out of sexual proclivities during this period. The lack of sexual integration, the arrested maturity development, the playing out of adolescent fantasies years later as an adult were, at least in part, attributable to the rigid external norms and practices before and even for some years after the Second Vatican Council.

Within the diocesan structures many candidates for priesthood entered minor seminary at age fourteen; Jesuit candidates most often entered the novitiate at age eighteen, often after attending an all-boys Jesuit high school. Screening of candidates for issues, especially psychosexual development, was minimal. "Keep the rule and the rule will keep you" was the adage which, in retrospect, highlights how external and tangential were the psycho-sexual-social dimensions.

In this regard, the precipitous decline in vocations to the priesthood had a highly positive side effect because it has allowed for greater personal attention to the maturation of each individual candidate and an early intervention if deemed necessary.

The sexual abuse scandal had simmered below the surface for some time and broke wide open with the extensive, investigative reporting of the *Boston Globe* in 2002. The fact that Cardinal Bernard Law knew about the priest abusers and kept shuffling them around from parish to parish was the even bigger scandal with which the church is still reckoning. So let us now turn to this painful next chapter.

12. John Padberg, SJ, "How We Live Where We Live," 27.

14

The Sexual Abuse Scandal

THIS CHAPTER IS CRUCIAL for understanding what has happened to the Catholic Church and the Society of Jesus over the last twenty years. It underscores Pope Francis's call for the Church to be the face of God's mercy, and it urges forward the Society's commitment to reconciliation made in 1975 as a key component of justice. It relates a painful, excruciating story that's potentially a spur towards redemption.

On January 6, 2002, the *Boston Globe* broke the story of the sexual abuse of young boys and teenagers by priests. More importantly, the *Globe*'s reporters tracked down how the abuse was aided and abetted by the hierarchy. Multiple times Cardinal Bernard Law and some of his auxiliary bishops had moved abusing priests from one parish to the next. The bishops were more concerned about the reputation of the Church and the welfare of the priests than they were about children. It was a shocking scandal. And subsequent, in-depth reporting by the *Globe* over the next year brought home day after day how extensive the damage caused by the abuse had been.

Finally, over a year later, Cardinal Law submitted his resignation to Pope John Paul II, and the pope, it seems reluctantly, agreed. Not long after, he made Cardinal Law the archpriest of the Basilica of Santa Maria Maggiore, one of the four most prestigious churches in Rome. From the Roman perspective, it was a modest honorific, but from the American perspective, it was a further scandal and it underscored the complicity and blindness of the Church at the highest levels. More damning was that

Law was allowed to keep his powerful position, as one of three Americans in the Congregation of Bishops until he reached the age of eighty in 2011.

All the gruesome facts of the decades-long scandal are now only too well known. But the long-term damage to the Church will be unfolding for years to come. I am no expert on all these factors, nor was I intimately acquainted with any of the internal workings and confidential agreements arrived at during these turbulent times. But no Catholic, and certainly no priest, was left unaffected. The humiliation of the Church was universal. During the months after the *Globe*'s story, I felt that I was in the spotlight whenever I wore clerics in public. And some of my priest friends were publicly insulted, cast as perpetrators themselves. For instance, one of them, wearing clerics as he traveled, was deliberately delayed, questioned, accused, insulted by a TSA employee, such that he lost his flight. Of course, whatever we priests underwent was infinitesimal compared to the lifetime damage suffered by those who were abused.

Soon after the *Globe* exposé broke, I participated in some of the local meetings in Seattle of Voice of the Faithful (VOTF), founded under the effective leadership of James Post of Boston. VOTF had a clear, straightforward mission statement: "To provide a prayerful voice, attentive to the Spirit, through which the Faithful can actively participate in the governance and guidance of the Catholic Church."

It articulated three goals:

1. To support victims of clergy sexual abuse;

2. To support priests of integrity; and

3. To shape structural change within the Catholic Church.[1]

VOTF began when some parishioners in Boston met in their church basement to pray and reflect on what had happened to their children and their faith community. The organization rapidly grew to over 30,000 members nationwide. For the first time, VOTF gave a forum for those who had been victimized to tell their painful stories and to be received. When I heard their stories, I felt I was witnessing a living death—years and years of depression, alcoholism, even attempted suicide, by some of these men who had been abused as children or teenagers.

When the sexual abuse scandal broke in 2002, I was dean of our School of Theology and Ministry. I believed that as the Catholic university in Seattle, we needed to address the scandal head on. So I assembled

1. http://www.votf.org/whoweare/mission-statement/98.

two pastoral counselors and a leading theologian from our faculty, and we held a public conference on campus. The university lawyers were on tenterhooks about such an occasion because a very significant, well-known Jesuit who had taught at Seattle University from about 1950 to 1973 (until he died) was already the subject of a lawsuit. So lawyers meticulously briefed me about how to handle whatever came up during the open forum. I moderated the event and fielded the questions. All were respectful, inquiring, and eventually grateful for the forum. We probably should have held more of these, but it was a start.

ON CARRYING A SCANDAL BIBLICALLY

Later I noticed that one of our popular summer faculty members Fr. Ron Rolheiser, OMI, had given a talk in Canada entitled "Carrying a Scandal Biblically." So I managed to book him into Seattle University, and we had an overflow talk for his conference. I also invited Archbishop Alex Brunett of the Archdiocese of Seattle to introduce the talk. Simply by his presence, the archbishop endorsed the event. The archbishop said that for the past fifteen years, the Archdiocese of Seattle had attempted to provide programs of healing and reconciliation for those subjected to abuse. He said, "As archbishop I have endeavored to meet personally with victims of clergy sexual abuse and provide them with understanding and an offer of pastoral care and healing as long as their need exists."[2]

Rolheiser broke his talk into three parts: the crisis for the Church, especially the American Church; information about the disease of pedophilia; and finally what it means to carry a scandal biblically.[3] He emphasized that this scandal was the first crisis ever in the American Catholic Church. The previous major upheavals for the Catholic Church had been the Enlightenment and the French Revolution in the eighteenth century, which occurred well before the American Catholic Church had taken shape.

In his second point, Rolheiser explained how the psychiatric/psychological profession had believed that pedophilia was, in many cases, curable. And that the church, as well as other organizations, had relied on this professional perspective. But after 1985, it became eminently clear that the disease was not curable, it had to be contained. That is, the

2. Alex J. Brunett, "Introduction to Ron Rolheiser, O.M.I.," 96–97.
3. Ron Rolheiser, OMI, "On Carrying a Scandal Biblically."

person needed to be quarantined from having unsupervised contact with any children or adolescents.

But for us Catholics gathered that evening to ponder the depth of the abuse and the tragedy impacting so many young people, Rolheiser's third point was the most important. He gave us a spiritual, biblical perspective to strengthen our journey and to attempt to allow healing, reconciliation, and even redemption from this crucifying time. For his third point Rolheiser laid out several interlocking points about how to carry a scandal biblically. These are important enough even now to spend time pondering them:

1. Name the moment. Not everything can be fixed or cured, but it needs to be named properly. Jesus called this "reading the signs of the times." This scandal is a moment of humiliation, a moment of pruning. We need to name it and not try to escape the humiliation and what that calls us to.

2. Our faith is biblical, so we need to radiate the compassion of Christ. To carry something biblically means to reground ourselves in the non-negotiables of Christian compassion—respect, tolerance, patience, and graciousness. Wild anger and bitterness will not help carry this to any meaningful closure. And our compassion must, first of all, go out to the victim.

3. Healing is not self-protection or grasping for security. We need to always remember the faces of those subjected to abuse. Our primary preoccupation is to protect the innocent and to bring about healing and reconciliation. Everything else (worries about security, lawsuits, financial collapse) must come afterwards.

4. Carrying the crisis now is our primary ministry and not a distraction to our ministry. The church exists for the sake of the world, and we must keep that in mind as we face this crisis. Right now priests represent less than 1 percent of the overall problem of sexual abuse, but the issue is focused on us. Psychologically this is painful, but biblically this is not a bad thing. If priests' being scapegoated helps society to bring the issue of sexual abuse and its devastation of the human soul more out into the open, then we are precisely offering ourselves as "food for the life of the world." We, like Jesus in his crucifixion, are helping to "take away the sins of the world." This is not a distraction. It is the life of the church.

5. Painful humiliation is a graced opportunity. Humiliation leads to humility. This is a moment of purification for the church. We are being brought back to where we are supposed to be.

This scandal is putting the clergy and the church where we belong: with the excluded ones. When Jesus died on the cross, he was crucified between two thieves. Jesus was painted with the same brush as the others. We are church—all of us—and we need to carry this, all of us.

Eventually, this will pass. There will be resurrection, even from this. God is still God. Crucifixions do not end life; they lead to new, enriched life.

"This is a dark night of the soul," Rolheiser proclaimed, "by which is meant, like every dark night of the soul, to stretch the heart. The pain won't go away until we learn the lesson that it is meant to teach us." And we the church are being asked to be like Christ, namely to have our flesh be food for the life of the world so that this wound might be opened to healing.[4]

After his lecture, Ron told me that he was fortunate that he became provincial of the oblates in Canada in the 1990s, that is, after there was widespread knowledge that treatment for pedophilia was a chimera and that anyone beset by this disease needed to be removed from ministry and from any unsupervised contact with children or adolescents. "If I had been provincial earlier," he admitted, "I'm sure I would have reacted very much like my predecessors did."

When the *Boston Globe* broke the story, I was shocked at its depth and extent. I was further shocked at the gross violence towards young people. And yet a further scandal was the widespread, consistent cover-up which had occurred—at least up until 1985, much longer in certain dioceses, such as Boston. Certain serial perpetrators there, such as Rev. John Geoghan and Rev. James Porter, were so egregious that even if one wasn't aware of all the complex factors of the disease, it's clear they should have been laicized immediately and sequestered from any contact with children. Others may have been more marginal, but their destructiveness to given individuals was no less.

Some might ask how is it that you as a priest didn't know what was going on? Over a period of thirty years, I had some inkling of a problem in two circumstances. One was a priest at Jesuit High School in Portland,

4. This section extensively draws from Rolheiser, "On Carrying a Scandal Biblically."

and we forbade him to go near the athletic property room to hand out towels and help with athletic equipment. Voyeurism, rather than any overt sexual act, was at the heart of his behavior. In another case, Fr. Jack Leary, SJ, one of my esteemed mentors at Gonzaga University, had been removed as president because of accusations brought against him. At the time I thought it was a single incident. Years later, I understood that it had occurred over a period of time. Otherwise, he remained a priest "in good standing." That's about as much as I knew.

Still later I heard word that a diocesan priest, who had been welcomed into the Gonzaga Jesuit community for some kind of sabbatical, had suddenly been removed and sent home to Louisiana. He was Fr. Lane Fontenot. His notoriety became widespread as early as 1986. In that year the *Times Acadiana* unearthed charges against seven priests in the small diocese of Lafayette, Louisiana.[5] It was a thorough, extensive, shocking exposé. The *Acadiana* reported:

> The bishop and vicar general have engaged in a cover-up; however it has been a strange one, wedded to a monarchical concept of power, divorced from democratic principles. In refusing to extend the pastoral hand to victims' families—and deal candidly with the laity and clergy alike—[Bishop] Frey and [Father] Larroque have let insurance lawyers dictate their silence. And in a cruelly ironic twist, blunders by those lawyers have deepened the stain of scandal about the diocese. In real dollar terms, the cover-up has been a disaster.

The great irony, even tragedy, is that the Lafayette scandal of which Lane Fonetenot was a part created so little stir outside the confines of that Louisiana diocese. It's clear in retrospect that 1985 was the pivotal moment in the sexual abuse crisis when the Church had the opportunity to finally act responsibly and justly. But in too many places, clericalism, the abuse of power, and the cover-ups continued.

At the bishops' national meeting in 1985, the canon lawyer Fr. Tom Doyle, OP, who worked in the Vatican Embassy in Washington, DC, briefed all the bishops about the extent of the sexual abuse of minors by clergy and explained that traditional counseling and psychiatric care of the abuser were no remedy. Along with others he produced "The Manual," which told bishops what needed to be done. Some acted on it immediately. One of those, once again, was the remarkable Archbishop

5. "The Anatomy of a Cover-Up," *The Times Acadiana*.

Raymond Hunthausen. He came home from the bishops' meeting and told the priests' personnel office—Fr. Jack Walmsley and Sister Carol Ann McMullen, SNJM—exactly what they needed to do. And Jack and Carol Ann immediately set about putting the policies in place, which included notifying the police about any such cases of abuse. Within months the first such case became public when a young priest, Father Paul, who had been ordained less than a year, was accused and subsequently convicted. He spent two and a half years in the Monroe State Penitentiary. If all the bishops had acted responsibly at this point, the crisis would have been a great deal less, and many vulnerable young boys and adolescents would have been spared.

Here's what Fr. Tom Doyle had recommended in 1985, which he summarized on PBS *Frontline* years later:

> We prioritized dealing with the victims. That was number one. We said at the time: "Don't send clerics in there to the family. Send someone other than clerics. Send a kindly sister, a nun, somebody who can go in and not be identified with the clerical world." We told them to be totally open with the media, report it to the police and so on. The second part of our proposal [was] the creation of a commission by the bishops or a committee that would study this issue, every angle of it, and get the most up-to-date information on all angles. That meant getting involved in the secular world—psychological, legal liability, the whole thing.[6]

It was a lost opportunity. Not only that, but Fr. Tom Doyle became a pariah and, though his own Dominican order fully supported him, bishops largely ostracized him. He became an Air Force chaplain for the next twenty years, though he still remained highly active as an expert witness and canonist in addressing the sexual abuse crisis. In the same *Frontline* interview Fr. Doyle reviewed these last thirty years and said,

> I can say that there is little doubt that the achievements that have been made in recognizing the horror of sexual violation, the causal role of the institutional churches and other institutions in enabling it and the high priority now given to the protection of children and vulnerable adults would never have happened were it not for the courage, the persistence, the patience, the dedication and even the anger of the victims and the survivors. We have changed history!

6. Jason M. Breslow, "Tom Doyle."

During all those years, the sexual abuse by clergy and then the defensive protectiveness by bishops, still ingrained in a clerical cultural, severely tested the credibility of the Church and its leadership. The Dallas Charter for the Protection of Children and Young People (2002), by which the bishops sought to build a firewall against further abuse, effectively suspended some of the traditional, canonical protections for priests accused of malfeasance, but it gave the bishops a solid fortress from which to rebut its critics. It also has caused an unresolved fracture between the local bishop and many of his priests. The considerable success of the Charter, however, was that it brought accountability home to each diocese, put in place multiple safeguards for the protection of minors, established training programs for every priest to recognize abuse, and set up well-publicized reporting-of-abuse mechanisms.

Once the *Boston Globe* broke the story, a cascade of cases and lawsuits opened up across the United States, both in dioceses and in men's religious congregations. The first diocese to declare bankruptcy was the Archdiocese of Portland, which had multiple cases, especially by a few highly notorious, serial abusers. Archbishop John Vlazny explained that the major insurers of the archdiocese had abandoned them and the bankruptcy was the best way to keep the parishes and schools operating while still paying claims.[7] For a medium-sized diocese Portland faced an unusually large number of abuse claims. They included more than fifty against Fr. Maurice Grammond, who had died two years before at age eighty-two, and more than twenty against Thomas Laughlin, who had been laicized.

I had passingly known both of them when I was a young priest in Portland. Grammond had been the pastor of two parishes on the Oregon Coast where I had celebrated Sunday Masses a couple of times. And Tom Laughlin was a gregarious, hail-fellow-well-met priest who showed up at all the major social occasions, including our Jesuit High auction to raise money for scholarships. A mother had reported Father Laughlin to the bishop after her two sons had been abused as altar boys. She had been assured by the Archbishop Vlazny's predecessor that it would be taken care of, but then Father Laughlin was appointed to the prestigious St. Thomas More parish in the West Hills—at which point the parents realized they had been deceived and angrily and justly opened a lawsuit against the archdiocese.

7. Alan Cooperman, "Archdiocese of Portland, Ore. Declares Bankruptcy."

Despite the suits filed against multiple dioceses, I had not expected the sexual abuse scandal to land as a bombshell in the middle of my own Jesuit province. But that's what happened. Already, Fr. Steve Sundborg, when he was provincial from 1990 to 1996, said that one-third of his time was spent dealing with the sexual abuse crisis, most of all, in listening to stories of the victims who had been abused as far back as 1921, or to accounts by a sibling of a brother who had been psychologically destroyed by earlier clerical abuse. And then, after several years spent by two provincials, Sundborg, John Whitney, and the relatively new provincial Pat Lee announced on February 17, 2009, that the Oregon Province was filing for Chapter 11 bankruptcy. The province was facing hundreds of claims of sexual abuse by Jesuits over a sixty-year period. According to the province spokesperson, most of the alleged abuse occurred "forty, fifty, and even sixty years ago." And nearly all of these claims were in Alaska villages or Native American reservations in Washington, Idaho, and Montana. The province spokesperson added, "Of nearly 3,000 Jesuits who have served in the Oregon Province since 1950, less than one percent has credible allegations of misconduct made against them." Most of those accused were either dead or elderly and ill.

The provincial Pat Lee said in a prepared statement, "Our decision to file Chapter 11 was not an easy one, but with approximately 200 additional claims pending or threatened, it is the only way we believe that all claimants can be offered a fair financial settlement within the limited resources of the Province." He underlined our ultimate goal: "We continue to pray for all those who have been hurt by the actions of a few men, so that they can receive the healing and reconciliation that they deserve."

The province had already settled more than 200 claims since 2001 and had paid in excess of $25 million from its own resources. Insurance covered a good deal more. Since so many of the accusations of abuse came from Alaskan native peoples, plaintiffs' lawyers charged that the Jesuits had used Alaska as a dumping ground for problem priests. I always found this claim to be utterly gratuitous since, often enough, some of our very best, most dedicated men had volunteered to be missioned to Alaska. In fact, it was such a difficult mission that most of the time a Jesuit was not sent there unless he had specifically volunteered to do so.

With the filing of the bankruptcy, all our assets were frozen, and a bankruptcy judge had to oversee and approve all the budgets of any Jesuit community. I was superior of the Seattle University Jesuits, so this freeze created the need for highly detailed reporting. It meant we had to squeeze every available drop out of our budget so that the province as a whole could be kept solvent. It meant curtailing maintenance, foregoing the replacement of aging cars, chopping personal budgets and other essentials. The men took the stringency in good stride. We were supposed to be men of poverty. We had just never expected lawyers to enforce it.

Knowing that the bankruptcy was about to be announced, I had prepared an eight-week "retreat in everyday life" for any Jesuit who wished to make this time of trial a central part of his Lenten observance. Ash Wednesday that year was February 25, so we began our darkening journey in the midst of the solemn events of forty days of fasting and penitence in preparation for Easter. I prepared a twenty-five-page prayer guide for any Jesuit wishing to join in this pilgrimage of faith, while we were undergoing the humiliation of public accusations, sometimes vilified in the press. At the same time we wished to join hands and hearts with our brothers and sisters who were abused by priests during a time when they were young, tender, and vulnerable. By way of example, for the fourth week of the eight, I offered this prayer:

Grace Being Sought
We pray for a deep-felt awareness of the freedom we
need, as a province of Jesuits in companionship with
others, to be able to work together and to accept our lives
and capabilities with humble realism.

At my urging, the provincial Pat Lee also made a quick round of the Jesuit communities in Tacoma, Portland, Spokane, and Seattle to announce the forthcoming bankruptcy and to lead us in prayer and reflection. Pat was the perfect provincial at the time since he had profound sensitivity and was so knowledgeable about Jesuit spirituality. He took us to a deep place of peace, humility, reconciliation, and a stance of forgiveness.

Once the province bankruptcy started to unfold, the plaintiffs' attorneys claimed that the Jesuits owned much more extensive assets than was the actuality. They asserted that the Jesuits "owned Gonzaga University, the University of Seattle (sic) and Seattle Preparatory School, all within the province." But all of these educational institutions were incorporated separately as far back as the 1890s. The federal judge, who oversaw the bankruptcy, quickly ruled out this spurious claim of the plaintiff attorneys. She said words to the effect, "Don't quote canon law to me about influence, sponsorship or ownership. This is a civil court. We are focused only on civil law."

We endured three miserable years of litigation. Massive amounts of province files had to be copied and sent to the plaintiffs. The underlying tragedy of the courtroom maneuvers was that they did not do a whole lot to mitigate and heal the pain and scars of those who had been abused, though it provided a palliative.

At times the province teetered on the edge of complete bankruptcy and the prospect of closing out the entity known as the Oregon Province. Pat Lee again deserves credit for not only challenging some of the plaintiff attorneys for some of their excesses, but also for holding us all together as a province and a community of men dedicated to serving the poor, marginalized, and those most in need of our help.

No one can deny the awful harm wreaked upon innocent youth by Catholic priests. However, high-profile contingency lawyer John C. Manly, centered out of Los Angeles, repeatedly voiced outrageous statements and wild falsehoods about the Catholic faith. Manly's venom against the Catholic Church cannot be overstated. Some concluded that his mean-spiritedness and dishonesty could only be categorized as vile.[8] Over the years Manly reportedly amassed a fortune of over half a billion dollars from attorneys' fees for his aggressive role in prosecuting cases against the Catholic Church.

After three years of discovery, allegations in the press, a few stage shows orchestrated by Manly, and widespread publicity, the Northwest Jesuits and their insurers agreed to pay $166.1 million in a bankruptcy settlement aimed at compensating nearly 500 people with active claims of sexual abuse by priests. Creditors included about 460 people with sexual abuse claims against priests and another fifteen or twenty with physical abuse claims. Under terms of the global settlement, the Northwest Jesuits paid $48.1 million and the insurer Safeco paid $118 million. About $6 million from the settlement went into a pool for future claims from those who had not come forward by the original deadlines. About 40 percent of the settlement went to lawyers' fee. And a huge additional amount covered their expenses. The median payout to victims was to be $300,000, according to John Manly, the lead plaintiff attorney.

The rawness of all these events still rankles when I return to them. But we have moved on. It's a new time. Our hope is that the victims of

8. http://www.themediareport.com/. The same source relates how a judge censured Manly for some of his statements.

abuse have experienced healing and some vindication for their years of suffering. By civil law we were barred from any contact with those who were abused once they brought suit. So we have minimal knowledge of what has happened with them during the ordeal and in subsequent years. Our prayers continue to go out to them. And we are grateful that because of their courage, we are better Jesuits, better priests, and a better Church. In addition, strong safeguards and care are in place to protect children now and into the future. Their sacrifice has not been in vain.

15

The Ultimate Surprise:
Francis, the First Jesuit Pope

THE RELATIONSHIP OF THE Jesuits with the papacy took a remarkable turn in the last decade and a half. Surprisingly, it began with Pope Benedict XVI and then culminated with Pope Francis. Over the last fifty-some years, we Jesuits have ridden a remarkable roller coaster: from the warm affirmations of Pope Paul VI through the suspicions of John Paul II to the mixed response of Benedict, who was both affirming and retrenching, to the new light of day in Pope Francis, who embodies the originating spirit of Pope John XXIII, who had launched Vatican II.

Sixteen years ago, in a remarkable lecture given at Seattle University when I hosted a conference on the fortieth anniversary of the opening of Vatican II, Dominican John Markey affirmed that Vatican II was indeed a Copernican revolution in the life of the church and created the most fundamental shift in 1,500 years in its basic self-understanding. "The Second Vatican Council," Markey said, "was clearly a revolution in that it fundamentally and irreversibly altered the historical development of a massive social and cultural institution" in ways that no one could have predicted.[1] Markey made several insightful analogies of the very nature of a revolution and two likely trajectories which might result. He based his analysis on the classic study *The Anatomy of a Revolution* by Crane

1. John J. Markey, OP, "George Washington, Napoleon, John Paul II and the Future of the Vatican II Revolution," 15.

Brinton.[2] Revolutions, once they are underway, Brinton had observed, tend to have their own organic and inevitable course that governments and individuals can only tinker with but never fully overpower.[3] Markey then summarized four basic, ecclesial insights:

First, only at Vatican II did the Roman Church begin to exist as a world church as such. Before that it was essentially a European church exported to the world. The Church suddenly realized that it lived in hundreds, and even thousands, of different cultures throughout the world. So questions of authentic unity inevitably arise.

The second revolutionary insight was that the grace of God was much wider and more pervasive in human life than Neo-Scholastic manuals had envisioned and far more than most pastors believed. At Vatican II the Roman Catholic Church recovered the fullness of grace as a gift, as God's radical presence in the world. It realized it did not have a monopoly on grace. It also rejected the trickle-down theory of grace whereby God "gives grace to the pope and then he passes it on to the bishops and they give it to the priests, and so forth."[4] This great recovery in the understanding of grace helped the Church radically reinterpret the liturgy, the sacraments, and its relationship with other Christian denominations, the Jewish people, the Muslims, and all people of faith.

Third, Markey said, the recognition of the primacy of baptism and the call to holiness of all the people of God foundationally altered the internal life of the Church. The laity has its own unique mission and is not subservient to the clergy.

The fourth revolutionary event that permeated the entire Council, according to Markey, was the remarkable rediscovery of the Holy Spirit's profound role in the life of the church and in our salvation. Before the Council the Holy Spirit had been generally neutralized and limited to the discussion of certain sacraments or the teaching authority of the magisterium. The action of the Spirit cannot be contained within any one place or time or people.[5] Yves Congar in his classic study on the church was amazed to discover that almost everywhere that he might have expected to find reference to the Holy Spirit in Church documents, there were instead references to the popes or to Mary.

2. Crane Brinton, *The Anatomy of a Revolution*, 265–71.

3. Ibid.

4. Markey, "Revolution," 17.

5. Ibid., 18.

After delineating the four revolutionary breakthroughs, Markey said, "At some point in the revolutionary process a reaction sets in and there is an attempt to stop, slow down, or reverse the revolution."[6] Inevitably, there is a "return to normalcy," which does not completely reverse the revolution, but tries to stop it from progressing further under the banner that it has gone too far. During this cooling down, certain changes are halted or reversed, others are consolidated and institutionalized. Drawing on the work of Brinton on the history of revolutions, Markey offered two different examples of this stage of the revolution: George Washington and Napoleon Bonaparte. Washington brought political stability to the struggling new Republic by offering a firm, direct model of leadership that ended a decade of instability and disunity among the colonies. Washington and his allies cut off further debate on a number of issues that were divisive: slavery, the rights of women, and the inter-relationship of the states with the federal government. In effect he put off critical issues for resolution later. Though Markey did not allude to it, Pope Paul VI similarly arrested the revolution by withdrawing birth control, married clergy, and reform of the Roman Curia from the Council's agenda. And not surprisingly, these are still major divisive points more than fifty years later.

Napoleon, in contrast to Washington, established a dictatorship that mirrored the monarchy that the revolution had sought to replace. But Napoleon and his successors could never fully extinguish the ideals and underlying values of the revolution. Critical dimensions of the revolution would not be lost mainly because of the establishment of the Napoleonic code of law.

Markey postulated in that same symposium in 2002 that John Paul II represents neither the Napoleon nor the Washington model, but a third model—in between the two of them because John Paul II managed simultaneously to both advance the revolution and to suppress it. With regards to the internal life of the Church, John Paul II represented both a reaction and restoration model; he maintained the centralized power in the hands of the ordained, particularly the bishops and Roman Curia. But John Paul II also seized on the vision of the Council for relationships to the wider Christian and non-Christian world. He spoke out strongly, consistently, and persuasively on human rights and social justice issues. Markey concluded this section by saying John Paul II represents the first

6. Ibid., 19.

great pope of the post-Vatican II Church, but he hoped John Paul would be the last great pope of the pre-Vatican II Church. When Markey spoke, Pope Benedict XVI was not yet on the horizon, and so we had yet another pope that straddled both the pre-Vatican and post-Vatican II church.

Markey commented that the administration of John Paul II had no positive, forward-looking message; rather it relied almost exclusively on the personal popularity of the pope as its only positive feature, and John Paul substituted his own message for the foundational theology and mission of Vatican II. Markey then speculated what the next stage of the revolution would inevitably bring. He commented—rather bleakly—that it often took fifty or sixty years before the revolution became assimilated and recognized as the benchmark from which everything subsequently flows.

Markey's lecture was compelling, and, in fact, prescient because it gave us a glimmer of how the papacy of Pope Francis might eventually emerge from the bleak, repressive days of John Paul and give the Church a renewed hope in authentically living the gospel in our own day.

When Cardinal Josef Ratzinger was elected pope on the fifth ballot in 2005, many Jesuits, myself included, and certainly liberal Catholics, shuddered. Our hopes for some abatement in the doldrums of the Church seemed stymied. The fresh winds of the Council had seemingly been brought to a standstill. Ratzinger, of course, was known as the watchdog of orthodoxy in the Church, and certainly his liturgical sensibilities represented a Restorationist point of view. As head of the Congregation for the Doctrine of the Faith, he had taken multiple steps to brake the impulses of the Second Vatican Council even as he affirmed its central importance to the Church. If truth be told, I was aghast when Ratzinger was elected because he represented so much of the negativity which had swirled through the Church with one repressive papal intervention after another. But, in the end, I was surprised.

In a pivotal address to the Roman Curia cardinals in December of 2005 in his first year as pope, Benedict gave a long, theological discourse to the cardinals, some of whom no doubt were nodding off or anticipating the grog at their Christmas party. Now as pope, Ratzinger's tone was more irenic than it had been when he headed up the Congregation for the Doctrine of the Faith. He put forth a hermeneutic of reform, which acknowledged both the continuous teaching of the Church, but also its marvelous breakthroughs and fresh understandings of the gospel—some clear discontinuity with what had gone before. Relations with the Jewish people and rejecting the anti-Semitism, which had pervaded the Church for so long, and had infected many a pope as well, would be one among several unmistakable signs of a radical change in Church belief and practice, he noted.

Despite such tentative positive steps, Benedict continued to stifle spirit-filled initiatives arising from local churches. For instance, he undermined the ecclesial authority of National Conferences of Bishops. In his lofty view they had no teaching authority unless they had 100 percent unity on any given issue. The most painful result of this *disprezzo* (Italian for disdain) was the promulgation of the new, so-called English translation of the Roman Missal. Earlier the American bishops and the English-speaking had approved a graceful, modern translation, but the Vatican Curia rejected this highly literate, accessible text. The substitute Vatican-imposed text was Latinate, pedantic, laden with semi-Pelagian slants, and out of the mainstream of normal English usage. Its obscurity supposedly suggested transcendence, one of the goals of centralized authority. The Oxford scholar Nicolas King, SJ, famously demonstrated how the Vatican-instigated text was not even faithful to the original Latin, but inserted tendentious reactionary theology.

My good friend Father Mike Ryan, pastor of the Cathedral parish in Seattle, led an international effort to suspend its implementation, "why not just wait," with a website that sparked an international uprising, but to no avail.

The laity noticed such unusual words as *consubstantial, conciliation, ineffable, beseech thee, oblation* (lots of oblations), and *feigned* creeping into the texts. Wobbly adverbs—*humbly, rightly, greatly, graciously, kindly*—dotted the landscape. I personally didn't have much problem with a traditional word like *consubstantial,* because it was a technical, theological term used in the original Nicene Creed. My main stumbling block was the syntactical labyrinth that I had to grope my way through as a priest when I offered the prayers. I found myself wandering in the semi-darkness groping for a noun, a verb, for something that made sense. The Vatican II Constitution on the Sacred Liturgy had mandated, "The rites should be distinguished by a noble simplicity, they should be short, clear—and they should be within the people's powers of comprehension and normally should not require much explanation" (paragraph 34). The New Missal fails in almost every way. Its texts are ungrammatical, unintelligible, and un-proclaimable. Certainly a far cry from prayer.[7]

7. See Bishop Donald Trautman, "The New Missal Has Failed."

A large factor, which led to a much healthier, cordial relationship between the Jesuits and Pope Benedict, was that Father Peter-Hans Kolvenbach, after his election as superior general in 1983, had cultivated multiple relationships with key cardinals in the Curia, not least of whom was Cardinal Ratzinger. The two of them by all reports had a warm, understanding relationship. Soon after Ratzinger was elected pope, Kolvenbach, who had already served as superior general for twenty-two years, asked the new pope for his approval to tender his resignation to a Jesuit General Congregation. Benedict approved in principle, but said in a jocular mood, "Let's wait a bit. It would not look good for the 'white pope' to have the 'black pope' resign just a few months after being in office." The reference, of course, as we saw earlier with the befuddled Tennessee Williams, was that the pope himself wears a white cassock and the Jesuit general, who also has an unlimited term of office, wears a black cassock.

Soon it came about. Two years later Kolvenbach was able to call a general congregation in order to offer his resignation. So in 2008 at GC 35 the delegates accepted Kolvenbach's resignation and expressed the Society's immense gratitude for leading the Society during such an arduous, delicate time. After the customary *murmuratio* or murmuring consultation among the delegates, they elected Adolfo Nicolás from the Japanese province on the first ballot. Later when Benedict addressed the delegates in the Aula Clementina, his scholarly background shone forth and provided the rich backdrop for his warm, affectionate affirmation of the Society of Jesus. He was perhaps the most scholarly pope we have ever had.

Benedict declared, "The Church needs you, relies on you and continues to turn to you in trust, particularly to reach those physical and spiritual places which others do not reach."[8] And then echoing Pope Paul VI, he continued, "Wherever in the Church, even in the most difficult and extreme fields, at the crossroads of ideologies, in the social trenches, there has been and there is confrontation between the burning exigencies of man and the perennial message of the Gospel, here also there have been, and there are, Jesuits."[9]

He had done his homework. Benedict then went out to praise three outstanding, historical achievements of the Society. "It suffices," he said, "to think of Matteo Ricci in China, Roberto De Nobili in India, or of the

---

8. Benedict XVI, "Address of His Holiness Benedict XVI to the Fathers of the General Congregation of the Society of Jesus," 822.

9. Paul VI, "Address to the 32nd General Congregation of the Jesuits."

'Reductions' in Latin America. And you are rightly proud of them." What was most surprising about Benedict's laudatory reference was that popes in the eighteenth century had scuttled, even condemned, these creative pastoral initiatives. Benedict offered the first-ever papal affirmation of all these pioneering Jesuit efforts to provide a bridge between cultures. He said that in its history the Society of Jesus had initiated extraordinary encounters between the gospel and world cultures. He then urged us to "set out once again in the tracks of your predecessors" to "build bridges of understanding and dialogue" with those who do not belong to the visible church—and, at the same time, to remain faithful and loyal to the church, to the Word of God, and to the Magisterium's task of preserving the integral message of Jesus the Christ. In a word, he was once more missioning us to "the frontiers," just as Pope Paul III had done in the 1540s when Ignatius and companions had first founded the Society. Benedict clearly affirmed that great risks had to be taken. It was an extraordinary affirmation of the Society and the journey we had set out upon over forty years before under the leadership of Pedro Arrupe.

Benedict's address was consoling because he so thoroughly understood our historic mission in the Church. He rightly cast our Jesuit mission as bridge building between the frontier and the center; out on the margins, but linked with the core teaching preserved by the Magisterium. In my own life as a Jesuit I have frequently found myself in this role as a bridge. I have reached out to people with mental illness and their families. I have been a bridge between our Jesuit university and the local church, especially the bishops who could be highly critical of the university for not being Catholic enough. I was an ecumenical bridge within the Catholic and Protestant worlds of our School of Theology and Ministry, which included ten different Protestant traditions. At times I stood in the tension of opposing views—buffeted by critics, but articulating the reality as best as I could.

The most stunning part of Benedict's papacy was his resignation. It was the surprise of surprises. On February 11, 2013, he announced that he would resign as pope, effective February 28. That a pope would resign was unheard of in modern times. In fact, the last one to resign had been Pope Gregory XII, who did so under pressure in 1415 in order to end the Great Schism. I was also aware because of my reading of Dante's *Inferno* that Pope Celestine V, a pious old monk dragooned into the papacy, had resigned in 1294 after only five months as pope, paving the way for Boniface VIII to be elected. Since Boniface was the archenemy of Dante and had caused his exile from Florence, Dante placed poor old Celestine in hell as a cowardly fence-sitter. Interestingly, Benedict had earlier visited the tomb of Celestine in a remote part of Italy not just once, but twice, each time placing his stole over the tomb and praying as he did so.

During that same February of the pope's resignation, my deadline for writing my religion column for the *Seattle Times* came due, so I wrote an explanation of what to expect in the papal conclave called to elect a new pope. I explained to the general public that Benedict had humbly assessed his own physical capacities and decided the time had come. He was aware of how chaotic the Vatican governance had been during the last years of his predecessor John Paul II. As Pope John Paul II diminished in his last years, rival cardinals jockeyed for position and influence. During that time Cardinal Ratzinger himself provided stability and sanity while others elbowed for position. So now, as pope, he undoubtedly did not want to see this unseemly chaos occurring again.

I could understand his assessment because I had a firsthand encounter with how incapacitated John Paul was when I had visited him with Archbishop Alex Brunett the summer before he died. The poor man, haunted by disease, was propped up like a piece of cardboard. Clearly, we had a crippled papacy. In fact, a Jesuit friend of mine at the Curia had told me that Ratzinger was one of the three cardinals actually running the church, but that they were often at odds among themselves. Now eight years later Benedict wisely sought to avoid a repetition of such chaotic, headless leadership.

Perhaps the most disappointing aspect of Benedict's legacy, at least among moderate Catholics, was his continued appointment of bishops of men who hewed to a narrow party line. But on the more positive side, Pope Benedict strove to rekindle the faith in Europe through a more dynamic, more evangelical preaching of the gospel. He was a kind and holy pastor, as well as an influential theologian. I predict he will be seen as continuing the legacy of John Paul II, although in a more subdued, more scholarly, less superstar way. The summer before he resigned, one of my knowledgeable Jesuit friends at the Gregorian University told me that Benedict had given up on governing the Church. "He is devoting all his remaining time to his scholarship. He believes that that will be his lasting contribution to the church." A rather amazing abdication.

In the conclusion to my *Seattle Times* column about the forthcoming election, I wrote, "I have no special insight about whoever the next pope might be. But I will venture out on a limb and go with the cardinal from

Argentina, who is fluent in Italian." I came close, but I picked Cardinal Leonardo Sandri, sixty-eight, who was in the Vatican as the Prefect of the Congregation for Eastern Churches. He had been the Vatican "sostituto" or chief of staff for five years and seemed to be a capable manager. As an Argentinian with Italian ancestry, I surmised that he could be seen as the "best of both worlds." Well, I was close! I just had the wrong Argentinian cardinal with an Italian background. I had automatically ruled out Jorge Bergoglio, the other cardinal from Argentina, because, at age seventy-six he was too old, but more importantly, he was a Jesuit. In the 450 years of the existence of the Society of Jesus, no Jesuit had ever become pope.

On the day of the papal election I was having lunch with one of my college classmates. The white smoke had gone up, but a long delay ensued. Then finally, the new pope came out on the balcony. When his name was announced, I'm afraid that I said, "Oh, no." I had heard through the Colombian Jesuits that Bergoglio was known to be authoritarian, distant from the Jesuits. He reportedly was charismatic, but apparently in a somewhat self-centered way. I quickly stifled my dismay. And then I was amazed, as most everyone was, at the new pope's modest demeanor and humility. When he asked us all to pray for him, I surely did. And I was doubly encouraged by his choice of the name Francis for Francis of Assisi, the saint renowned for care for the poor, for his mystic vision of the unity of all creation, and for his challenge to the extravagance of the institutional church in his time.

Francis inaugurated a fresh, new time in the church. In fact, my friend Father Mike Ryan said to me, "Pat, I hadn't realized how dark the cloud was over the whole church for the last thirty-six years until Francis was elected." And now these nearly six years with Papa Jorge Mario Bergoglio have been an amazing journey for the Church and for me personally. I have been caught up in the new hope-filled wave in unexpected ways.

The first phase was six months after his election. I was working as an associate editor at *America* magazine in Manhattan, as a part of my sabbatical. When I arrived a few days after Labor Day, I found that a top-secret project was underway: Fr. Antonio Spadero, SJ, the Jesuit editor of *Civiltá Cattolica* in Rome, had conducted an exclusive interview with the pope, which *America* editor Matt Malone, SJ, had instigated the previous spring at a meeting of editors of Jesuit journals in Lisbon, Portugal. Surprisingly, Pope Francis agreed and *America* had first right of publication for the English version. *America* had commissioned the Italian theologian

Massimo Faggioli to translate the original Italian of Father Spadero into English. The translation was accurate, but stilted and uncharacteristic of English-language rhythms. As it happened, I was the only one on the *America* staff who spoke and understood Italian! So for three days and nights I assiduously labored over the text, comparing the Italian and the English, back and forth, back and forth. In the end, I made fifty different amendments, aiming for a translation of dynamic equivalence, rather than a slavishly literal one. It was a strange experience, murmuring to myself as I worked on the text, "Well, this is what the pope really means," and then putting it into accessible English. It was one of the most graced experiences I have ever had. It allowed me from the beginning to enter into the mind and heart of this remarkable pope.[10]

Later I spent May 2014 in Rome and attended one of the pope's regular weekly audiences out in St. Peter's Square—along with 50,000 other people. I found a marked difference between him and Pope Benedict. Francis gave an eight- or ten-minute reflection, and then he moved around through the crowds, hugging more children and babies than anyone else in the history of religious or political life. Benedict, by contrast, would give a fifty-minute theological discourse and then formally greet distinguished visitors who had a special ticket for access to the pope.

Once I returned to Seattle University that fall, I was booked into several Catholic parishes and other venues to give talks on Pope Francis, his early background, his Jesuit spirituality, and especially how I interpreted his leadership as pope.[11] Protestants and Jews were equally upbeat and interested. I had to keep updating my PowerPoint, because Pope Francis was on the move. Fresh, groundbreaking events were happening week by week. Finally, I simply called my presentation: "Pope Francis: What's He Up to Now?" All in all, it was an amazingly refreshing time. Almost all of the attendees at my talks were older, mostly fifty to seventy-five years old—those who had welcomed the changes and lived through them. Rarely was anyone under thirty in attendance. Younger Catholics might be attracted to Francis, but the majority of them were not going to invest their time, energy, and devotion learning more.

10. See my account in Patrick J. Howell, SJ, "Sabbatical Turns into Quite an Event."

11. Austen Ivereigh, *The Great Reformer*—probably the best informed and knowledgeable account about Bergoglio in the context of the multiple political, ecclesial, and social conflicts in Argentina.

In my "pope talks" about Francis, I noted these three features, among many others:[12]

First, Francis has brought an end to the monarchical style of the papacy. From the moment of his election he has simplified the papal dress, the manner of speech, and his mode of travel, and he has enlarged the Church's engagement with all people. He has not just advocated the preferential option for the poor, he admirably lives it. He has frequently critiqued the clericalism, insularity, and narcissism endemic to the Church.

Francis believes in subsidiarity. Early on, Pope Francis announced that far too many issues are routinely referred to Rome for a decision. Many of these, he said, are more appropriately handled at the local level. In a word, he does not argue about dismantling centralization, he simply does it. He assumes the diversity of a world Church, he believes in appropriate subsidiarity, and he urges that many decisions be made locally in accord with local custom, local language, and local context. He has also appointed cardinals from the far-off reaches of Tonga, the Ivory Coast, Burkina Faso, Myanmar, Cape Verde, Bangladesh, and Mauritius, repeatedly skipping over traditional sees such as Turin and Venice, Philadelphia and Los Angeles. Francis assumes that all the local churches have significant contributions to make to the universal church. He is shifting the center of the Church from Rome out to the periphery, to the frontier—to the whole world.

Francis uses a consultative, discerning style of authority typical of the Jesuit order. The whole Church needs to enter into a period of discernment, of deep listening, he says, so that the sense of the faithful (*sensus fidelium*)—that is, how the Holy Spirit is acting in and through the whole Church—might be determined. He adds that by virtue of their baptism, the people of God carry within them an instinct of faith "which helps them to discern what is truly of God." Pope Francis's model of discernment constitutes a much different model of leadership from what the American bishops and faithful had grown accustomed to under Pope John Paul II and Pope Benedict XVI, both of whom were at home with a strong, centralized authority. Most bishops, one assumes, would welcome the new shift; it gives them more authority for their own pastoral instincts. Of course, not everyone is exactly pleased with the innovations of Pope Francis. Cardinal Raymond Burke, his most outspoken critic,

12. Patrick J. Howell, SJ, "Pope Francis Meets the American Church."

said that the church under Francis "is like a ship without a rudder" and "many in the church are feeling seasick!"

Francis removed Burke from powerful positions in the Curia and appointed Burke as cardinal patron of the Order of Malta, an ancient equestrian order that arose out of the time of the Crusaders. We need more equestrian orders to saddle them with such bishops so that they can ride off into the sunset! Though the great majority of laity are delighted with Francis, some of the clergy range from cautious, to wait and see, to can we survive this papacy.

Francis is the first pope formed as a priest and ordained (in 1969) after the Second Vatican Council had concluded. So Francis takes the Council for granted. He signals that the battle for meaning over the Council is done. He does not enter into the disputes on interpretation of the Council that occupied Pope Benedict. The interpretive lens of Francis is gospel centered: "Is the Church becoming a Church of and for the poor?" "Are we binding up the wounds of those who are hurting?" "Have we broken out of a self-centered clericalism and narcissism?" And, most of all, "Have we embraced God's mercy and manifested God's divine mercy to others?" The mission of the Church is not to itself. Rather the Church needs to be a "field hospital," to go out to where the people are hurting. And in a field hospital the first thing you ask is not, "What is your cholesterol count?" It's rather "Where do you hurt?" and "How can I help you?" I wish pastors, deacons, and lay ministers would do the same for young couples seeking to get married or to wade through the still tortuous process of an annulment. The first question should not be, "Are you registered in the parish?" It should be, "How can I help?"

Even before Bergoglio was elected, he told the cardinals assembled before the election that the Church was too narcissistic, too concerned about itself, too clerical. And he concluded with this stunning metaphor: "Christ is knocking on the door, but he's knocking on the door of the church to get out."

Francis has shifted the mission of the Church. He is not caught up in the American cultural wars, but has returned to the gospel as his primary text. And there, not surprisingly, he finds that the care for the poor, for the oppressed and the marginalized is paramount. As a humorous spirituality author wrote, if one doesn't care for the poor, not Jesus, not the Buddha, not Allah, not even God himself can save you. The American bishops have had a different agenda. They have expended great amounts of political capital trying to stem what they identify as the erosion of religious liberty in a world of rampant secularism. And, therein, the war against abortion is the major battle. Without neglecting their importance, Francis has significantly shifted the focus away from hot-button topics such as abortion, marriage between only a man and a woman, and the ordination of women to the abundant compassion and mercy of God, continually poured out to sinners and to the neglected, with a special regard for the poor.

LOOK TO CHICAGO FOR A CLEAR SIGNAL OF CHANGE

Earlier, in the 1970s, when Archbishop Jean Jadot was the apostolic delegate, Pope Paul VI appointed a series of American bishops known for their reforming attitudes and a strong concern for social justice. Cardinal Joseph Bernardin of Chicago most clearly typified this cadre of bishops. But from 1978 onward, Pope John Paul II appointed a series of bishops devoted to a strong defense of Catholic tradition and teaching, committed to fending off the secular culture. Cardinal Francis George, Bernardin's successor in Chicago, was often seen as one of the hierarchy's sharpest minds and most outspoken advocates for orthodoxy on issues such as abortion, contraception, and the Catholic liturgy. Now that Pope Francis has appointed Blase Cupich as the new archbishop of Chicago and advanced him to cardinal, the Church can expect that Cupich may be representative of a new generation of bishops—those who mix with the people, listen to their joys and sorrows, and are enthusiastically committed to a Church known most of all for its mercy and compassion.

The American bishops appointed by John XXIII and Paul VI flourished in the 1970s and early 1980s. They were pastors. Many of these bishops had experienced the transforming effect of the Council and were schooled in the latest theology, scriptural exegesis, and pastoral leadership because during the Council they mixed daily with the leading theologians at the time. Raymond Hunthausen, bishop of Helena (1962–75) and then archbishop of Seattle (1975–91) was a revered example of this generation who brought back the spirit and impact of the Council to the people.

Over the last three decades well-educated Catholics have become increasingly disaffected by some of the leadership in the Church. Some have left. People have wearied of simplistic homilies, of scolding by priests from the pulpit, and of inappropriate homilies, such as condemning abortion and birth control during a wedding. Perhaps the biggest pastoral failure has been with young people, especially those seeking to get married in the Church or to be granted an exception, such as for a wedding outdoors. Young adults do not "fit" the rules. But little or no accommodation is made, and what could be a marvelous pastoral opportunity becomes a big turnoff. Laws were made for the people, not for the convenience of the clergy and pastoral associates.

A shift in the American bishops may, however, be occurring. They are clearly supportive of Francis' encyclical "Laudato Si," the bold papal initiative for the care of the planet with special regard for the poor. The noted theologian and incidentally one of my mentors at Catholic University, Elizabeth Johnson, has called it the most important encyclical ever written.[13] Another significant landmark was the pope's appointment of three cardinals among the American hierarchy who were much more in synch with his pastoral approach. By 2018, Francis had appointed fifty-nine of the 125 cardinals who would be among those eventually choosing his successor.

The cardinals in conclave picked Francis in March 2013 to accomplish reforms of a curia and a clerical culture that had become so distorted that some leaders brazenly betrayed the faithful and the gospel. Crises ranged from the horrors of sexual abuse of children to more prosaic financial scandals. But the cardinals got more than they bargained for. Francis has shaken up the curia, begun extensive reforms of the Vatican financial system—not just the notorious Vatican Bank, but through subordinates, has begun audits of all the budgets of the Vatican bureaucracy overseen by various cardinals. He has removed incompetent officials and started to appoint new and younger men to drag certain church institutions into the twenty-first century. The appointment of clearly pastoral bishops as cardinals further signals a sea change. But even further, Francis has changed the conversation, he has brought hope to those who had given up, he has revived interfaith and ecumenical interests. He portrays the beaming face of Christ, the God of mercy and compassion. One of my overly enthusiastic friends said, "When you put a Jesuit in charge, nothing is ever the same again!" Interestingly, Pope Francis and the former Jesuit General Adolfo Nicolás were in frequent conversation, and the pope apparently conferred with him on various issues until Father Nicolás retired.

13. Elizabeth Johnson, CSJ, "A Theologian Looks at 'Laudato Si.'"

CLOSING—WHEN THE DARKNESS FALLS
ON MY FINAL DAYS

In 2016 the Jesuits meeting in GC 36 received the resignation of the high-ly esteemed Adolfo Nicolás, SJ, and elected Arturo Sosa, SJ, of Venezuela as the new superior general. Prior to the election, Fr. Bruno Cadoré, the Master General of the Dominicans, gave the homily at the Mass of the Holy Spirit. He gave a stunning confirmation of the journey we have been on ever since Arrupe declared "great risks had to be taken." Though he didn't cite Arrupe, Father Cadoré challenged the delegates to once again "dare to risk the audacity of the impossible." In effect, he said, "Keep it up." He joined Pope Paul VI and Benedict XVI in his challenge to the Jesuits to go to the peripheries, go to the lonely outposts and bring the Word of God to those who would otherwise not hear it.

The delegates had another surprise in store for them. Historically, it was customary for all the delegates to troop over to the Aula Clementina in the Vatican to be greeted and sometimes admonished by the pope. But Pope Francis, predictably pastoral, drove over to the Jesuit Curia in a little Volkswagen to greet Father Sosa and all the delegates. Then he delivered a reflection on how the Society of Jesus can best serve God, the church, and the world, after which he took questions from the delegates.[14] Our provincial Scott Santarosa and elected delegate Mark Ravizza were clearly moved by the candor, the freshness, and warmth of their brother Jesuit. They said Francis underscored the centrality of discernment; it's our Jesu-it way of proceeding. He explained that journeying with Christ, requires three dimensions: 1) asking God insistently for consolation; 2) allowing oneself to be moved by Jesus crucified, and 3) being led by the Holy Spirt in tandem with thinking with the Church. Francis continues the legacy of Vatican II, which "set the Church on a path of reform and unprecedented engagement with the modern world: one where condemnation was re-placed with listening and where those who fall short of Church teaching are offered the 'medicine of mercy.'"[15]

So the incredible journey continues. The characters in the drama have aged and changed. A fresh, vitalized generation of Jesuits now car-ries forward the spirit of St. Ignatius and Pedro Arrupe in keeping with the vision of the Second Vatican Council to go back to the sources and to

14. Carol Glatz, "Pope Tells Jesuits to Walk to Peripheries, Be Open to the Future."
15. Christopher Lamb, "A Shepherd Clearly Steering the Flock," 4.

update all things in the light of the contemporary world.[16] The Society of Jesus faithfully did that. By reason of entering the Society at age twenty-one in 1961, I was present at the beginning. And I have relished and been graced by these many years at the heart of the Society.

The close of the 36th Congregation happened to coincide with the last days of the Oregon Province, which divided from California on February 2, 1932, and now eighty-five years later merged with the California province to form a new province in a radically new time, with new visions and mandates from the universal church. The consolidation obviously occurred because American Jesuits have diminished from over 8,600 in the early 1960s to 2,229 in 2017, but it also facilitates regional and global ministries. Oregon Jesuits had a reputation for being rough and ready, for a "holy uncouthness," as one Jesuit famously put it. We've been blessed with excellent superiors, committed to thoughtful, well-discerned decisions. Inevitably, the two provinces come from different cultures, different histories, different ways of exercising authority. The road ahead will be a little rocky. But we are brothers in Christ, companions on the journey, discerning together how the Spirit is impelling us into the future. Our new Jesuit West province stretches from Nogales on the border of Mexico, ministering to immigrants, to the Yukon Delta, ministering to the Yupik people—certainly symbolic of the peripheries to which we are called.

A few year ago when I turned seventy-four, a good friend asked me, "Pat, what would you do if you had your life to live over again." I responded immediately, "I wouldn't. I have had a great life. I have loved every minute of it." But moments later I added, "I would have liked about fifteen more years of prime time—that time of life when all the gears are clicking and the challenges are great enough to animate all your talents, energies and devotion."[17] I am far from chanting my "Nunc dimittis," the prayer of Simeon holding the Christ Child: "Now, O Lord, you may dismiss your servant in peace." My health is good, my energy strong, and I look forward to the ongoing graces flowing from our collective discern-

---

16. And this continuing vitalization is clearly happening with the next generation of Jesuits. See János Lukács, SJ, "Next Generation of Questions for Ignatian Spirituality."

17. What I did not expect was another run at leadership. During the years 2017 to 2018 while I was seeking publication for this book, I became executive director of the Loyola Institute for Spirituality in Orange, California, a marvelous, innovative center to deliver "spirituality on wheels" in both English and Spanish to people who would not otherwise have had access to the Spiritual Exercises of St. Ignatius.

ment for a Church and the Society of Jesus ever more faithful to our call-ing. Even so, the last words of Georges Bernanos's novel *The Diary of a Country Priest* come to mind: *Tout le grâce*. All is grace. Every Jesuit yearns for this realization that in the end all is grace, and prays with Ig-natius the *Suscipe,* the prayer of surrender—which is sung at every Jesuit celebration of first vows to final vows, from ordination to one's fiftieth jubilee as a priest.

> Take my heart, O Lord, take my hopes and dreams.
> Take my mind with all its plans and schemes.
> *Give me nothing more than your love and grace*
> *These alone, O God, are enough for me.*
> "*These Alone Are Enough,*" Dan Schutte

Bibliography

"The Anatomy of a Cover Up." *The Times Acadiana,* January 30, 1986.

Appleyard, J. A., SJ, and Howard Gray, SJ. "Tracking the Mission and Identity Question: Three Decades of Inquiry and Three Models of Interpretation." *Conversations on Jesuit Higher Education* 18 (Fall 2000) 4–15.

Arrupe, Pedro, SJ. "World Justice." In *A Planet to Heal,* 33–73. Rome: Ignatian Center of Spirituality, 1975.

———. Letter to Jesuits in Jesuit Relief Services, August 6, 1981.

———. "On Marxist Analysis." December 8, 1980. Letter.

Asselin, David T., SJ. "Notes on Adapting the Exercises of St. Ignatius." *Review for Religious* 28 (1969, reprint 1983) 292–301.

Balleis, Peter, SJ. *In the Footsteps of Pedro Arrupe: Ignatian Spirituality Lived in the Service of Refugees. Jesuit Refuge Service,* November 1, 2007.

Becker, Joseph M., SJ. "Changes in U.S. Jesuit Membership, 1958–1975." *Studies in the Spirituality of Jesuits* (January and March, 1977) 1–106.

Benedict XVI, Pope. "Address of His Holiness Benedict XVI to the Fathers of the General Congregation of the Society of Jesus." February 21, 2008.

Breslow, Jason M. "Tom Doyle: Vatican Is the World's Last Absolute Monarchy." *Frontline,* February 25, 2014.

Brinton, Crane. *The Anatomy of a Revolution.* New York: Random House, 1965.

Brunett, Alex J. "Introduction to Ron Rolheiser, O.M.I." In *Seattle Theology and Ministry Review* Vol. 3, edited by Patrick Howell, SJ, 2003, 96–97.

Buckley, Michael J., SJ. *The Catholic University as Promise and Project.* Washington, DC: Georgetown University Press, 1998.

Burke, Kevin, SJ. "Introduction." In *Pedro Arrupe: Essential Writings,* 15–38. Maryknoll, NY: Orbis, 2004.

Burke, Kevin, SJ, ed. *Pedro Arrupe: Essential Writings.* Maryknoll, NY: Orbis, 2004.

Carroll, L. Patrick. "The Spiritual Exercises in Everyday Life." *Studies in the Spirituality of Jesuits* 22.1 (January 1990) 1–48.

Carroll, L. Patrick, SJ, and Katherine Dyckman, SNJM. *Inviting the Mystic, Supporting the Prophet: An Introduction to Spiritual Direction.* New York: Paulist, 1981.

Clancy, Thomas H., SJ. *An Introduction to Jesuit Life: The Constitutions and History through 435 Years.* St. Louis: Institute of Jesuit Sources, 1976.

Clifford, John W., SJ. *In the Presence of My Enemies.* New York: W. W. Norton, 1963.

The Constitution on the Sacred Liturgy (Sacrosanctum Concilium), no. 14. In *The Basic Sixteen Documents of Vatican Council II,* Austin Flannery, OP, gen. ed., 117–61. Northport, NY: Costello, 1996.

Coday, Dennis. "Charles Curran to Retire from Full-time Teaching." *National Catholic Reporter* (May 15, 2014).

Conwell, Joseph F., SJ. *Contemplation in Action: A Study in Ignatian Prayer.* Spokane, WA: Gonzaga University Press, 1957.

———. *Darkness in Light.* Unpublished manuscript on the Rules for Discernment of Spirits in Jesuit Oregon Province Archives (JOPA).

———. *Impelling Spirit: Revisiting a Founding Experience, 1539.* Chicago: Loyola, 1997.

———. *Walking in the Spirit: A Reflection on Jeronimo Nadal's Phrase "Contemplative Likewise in Action."* St. Louis: Institute for Jesuit Sources, 2003.

Cooperman, Alan. "Archdiocese of Portland, Ore. Declares Bankruptcy." *Washington Post* (July 7, 2004).

Crowley, Walt. "To the Brink and Back." In *Seattle University: A Century of Jesuit Education,* 87–95. Seattle: Seattle University Press, 1991.

Currie, Charles, SJ. "Pursuing Jesuit, Catholic Identity and Mission at U.S. Jesuit Colleges and Universities." *Catholic Education* (March 2011) 346–59.

Documents of the 31st and 32nd General Congregations of the Society of Jesus. St. Louis: The Institute of Jesuit Sources, 1977.

Documents of the Thirty-Fourth General Congregation of the Society of Jesus. St. Louis: Institute of Jesuit Sources, 1995.

Donahue, John, SJ. "Catholic Biblical Scholarship 50 Years after *Divino Afflante Spiritu.*" *America* (September 18, 1993) 6–11.

Dyckman, Katherine, Mary Garvin, and Elizabeth Liebert. *The Spiritual Exercises Reclaimed: Uncovering Liberating Possibilities for Women.* New York: Paulist, 2001.

English, John, SJ. *Spiritual Freedom: From an Experience of the Ignatian Exercises to the Art of Spiritual Direction.* 2d ed. Chicago: Loyola Press, 1973, 1995.

Fahey, Joseph J. "The Making of a Catholic Labor Leader: The Story of John J. Sweeney." *America* (August 28, 2006) 16–18.

Fitzgerald, Paul A. *The Governance of Jesuit Colleges in the United States, 1920–1970.* Notre Dame, IN: University of Notre Dame Press, 1984.

Flannery, Austin, OP, general ed. *The Basic Sixteen Documents of Vatican Council II.* Northport, NY: Costello, 1996.

Franck, Frederick. *Exploding Church.* New York: Delacorte, 1968.

Glatz, Carol. "Pope Tells Jesuits to Walk to Peripheries, Be Open to the Future." Catholic News Service, October 25, 2016.

Gray, Howard, SJ. "An Experience in Ignatian Government: Letters to a New Rector." *Studies in the Spirituality of Jesuits XIV* (September, 1982) 12–32.

Häring, Bernard, CSSR. *The Law of Christ.* Vols. 1 & 2. Translated by Edwin G. Kaiser, CPPS. Westminster, MD: The Newman Press, 1961, 1963.

———. *The Law of Christ.* Vol. 3. Translated by Edwin G. Kaiser, CPPS, Missionary Society of St. Paul the Apostle in the State of New York. Westminster, MD: The Newman Press, 1966.

———. *My Witness for the Church.* New York: Paulist, 1992.

Hebblethwaite, Peter. "Don Pedro in History." *America* (February 16, 1991) 156–88.

———. *Pope John XXIII: Shepherd of the Modern World.* New York: Doubleday, 1985.

Henriot, Peter J., Edward P. DeBerri, and Michael J. Schultheis. *Catholic Social Teaching: Our Best Kept Secret*. Rev. ed. Maryknoll, NY: Orbis and the Center of Concern, 1987.

Hoffman, Paul. "Pope Paul Compares Defecting Priests to Judas." *New York Times* (April 9, 1971).

Howell, Patrick J., SJ, and Gary Chamberlain. *Empowering Authority: The Charisms of Episcopacy and Primacy in the Church Today*. Kansas City: Sheed and Ward, 1990.

Howell, Patrick J., SJ. "The 'New' Jesuits: The Response of the Society of Jesus to Vatican II, 1962–2012: Some Alacrity, Some Resistance." *Conversations on Jesuit Higher Education*, vol. 42, issue 4 (Fall 2012).

———. "Pope Francis Meets the American Church." *America* (September 15, 2015). http://papalvisit.americamedia.org/2015/09/15/pope-francis-encounters-the-american-catholic-church/.

———. *Reducing the Storm to a Whisper: The Story of a Breakdown*. Kansas City: Sheed & Ward, 1985; later reprinted by Ulyssian, 2000.

———. "Sabbatical Turns into Quite an Event." *Seattle Times*, Faith & Values (September 26, 2013).

———. *A Spiritguide through Times of Darkness*. Kansas City: Sheed & Ward, 1996.

Hunthausen, Raymond G. "We Need a Miracle—Expect One: Reminiscences on Vatican II and My Life as a Bishop." *Seattle Theology and Ministry Review*, ed. Patrick J. Howell, SJ. Vol. 3. Seattle University (2003) 6–14.

Ivereigh, Austen. *The Great Reformer: Francis and the Making of a Radical Pope*. New York: Henry Holt, 2014.

"Jesuits Today." Decree 2, no. 1 in *Documents of the 31st and 32nd General Congregations of the Society of Jesus*, 291. St. Louis: The Institute of Jesuit Sources, 1977.

Johnson, Elizabeth, CSJ. "A Theologian Looks at 'Laudato Si.'" *Conversations* 50 (Fall 2016) 36–39.

Johnson, Lyndon B. "Voting Rights Act Address." Washington, DC, March 15, 1965.

JOPA [Jesuit Oregon Province Archives]. "Emergency Meeting: Seattle University Crisis (October 10, 1970), Chinook Hotel, Yakima," Provincial Records for Fr. Ken Galbraith.

JOPA [Jesuit Oregon Province Archives]. "Homily given by Patrick B. O'Leary, S.J." (August 2, 1974) "Personal Papers of Mr. Peter Gaskell, S.J.," Box 1, File 2, Obituaries and Memorials.

JOPA. "Letter of Charls Chapman, SJ, secretary to the provincial, to Rev. Joseph Logan, SJ, rector of Bellarmine Prep," from "Personal Papers of Stephen Crowley," Box 1, File 1, Personal History.

JOPA. "Letter of Father Schultheis to Mr. J. Eugene McMahan, Buffalo, N.Y." (April 8, 1960) "Personal Papers of Br. Thomas Callahan," Box 1, File 1, Personal History.

JOPA. "Letter of Henry J. Schultheis, S.J. to Father Monahan," (April 16, 1960), "Personal Papers of Br. Thomas Callahan, Box 1, File 1, Personal History.

JOPA. "Letter of H. A. Perry, M.D., superintendent of Eastern State Hospital," to Rev. Leo J. Robinson, SJ, (October 27, 1944). "Personal Papers of Stephen Crowley," Box 1, File 1, Personal History.

Kertzer, David I. *The Pope and Mussolini: The Secret History of Pius XI and the Rise of Fascism in Europe*. New York: Random House, 2014.

Kovaleski, Serge. "Obama's Organizing Years, Serving Others and Finding Himself." *New York Times* (July 7, 2008).

Lakeland, Paul. *The Liberation of the Laity: In Search of an Accountable Church.* New York: Continuum, 2003.

Lamb, Christopher. "A Shepherd Clearly Steering the Flock." *The Tablet* (December 10, 2016) 4–5.

Ledóchowski, Wlodomir. "An Instruction on the Use of the Radio." In *Selected Writing of Father Ledóchowski,* 432–34. Chicago: Loyola University Press, 1945.

Lukács, János, SJ. "Next Generation of Questions for Ignatian Spirituality." *Ignatiana* 17 (2014) 171–87.

Markey, John J., OP. "George Washington, Napoleon, John Paul II and the Future of the Vatican II Revolution," *Seattle Theology and Ministry Review* 3 (2003) 14–25. Address delivered at "Fanning the Flame: Symposium Celebrating the 40th Anniversary of Vatican II," October 12, 2002.

McCoy, John. *A Still and Quiet Conscience: The Archbishop Who Challenged a Pope, a President, and a Church.* Maryknoll, NY: Orbis, 2015.

McDermott, James, SJ. "Let Us Look Together in Christ." An Interview with Peter-Hans Kolvenbach. *America* (November 26, 2007) 9–12, 14.

McDonough, Peter, and Eugene C. Bianchi. *Passionate Uncertainty: Inside the American Jesuits.* Berkeley, CA: University of California Press, 2002.

O'Keefe, J. M., ed. *Catholic Education at the Turn of the New Century.* New York: Garland, 1997.

O'Malley, John W., SJ. *The Jesuits & the Popes: A Historical Sketch of Their Relationship.* Philadelphia: St Joseph's University Press, 2016.

———. "Reform, Historical Consciousness, and Vatican II *Aggiornamento.*" *Theological Studies* (1971) 573–601.

———. *What Happened at Vatican II?* Cambridge, MA: Harvard University Press, 2008.

O'Malley, William, SJ. *The Voice of Blood: Five Christian Martyrs of Our Time.* Maryknoll, NY: Orbis, 1980.

"Our Mission Today." In *Documents of the 31st and 32nd General Congregations of the Society of Jesus,* Decree 4, 298. St. Louis: The Institute of Jesuit Sources, 1977.

"On Having a Proper Attitude of Service in the Church." In *Documents of the 34th General Congregation* (1975) no. 17, 148.

Orsy, Ladislas. "Towards a Theological Evaluation of Communal Discernment." *Studies in the Spirituality of Jesuits* no. 5 (October 1973) vi, 139–88.

Padberg, John, SJ, ed. *Jesuit Life & Mission Today: The Decrees & Accompanying Documents of the 31st–35th General Congregations of the Society of Jesus.* St. Louis: Institute of Jesuit Sources, 2009.

Padberg, John, SJ. "How We Live Where We Live." *Studies in the Spirituality of Jesuits* 20.2 (March 1988) 1–37.

Padberg, John W., SJ, Martin D. O'Keefe, SJ, and John L. McCarthy, SJ, eds. *For Matters of Greater Moment: the First Thirty Jesuit Congregations: A Brief History and Translation of the Decrees.* St. Louis: Institute of Jesuit Sources, 1994.

Paul VI, Pope. "Address to the 32nd General Congregation of the Jesuits." In *Documents of the 31st and 32nd General Congregations of the Society of Jesus,* edited by John Padberg. St. Louis: Institute of Jesuit Sources, 1977.

———. "The Up-to-Date Renewal of Religious Life." *Perfectae Caritatis,* no. 2. In *The Basic Sixteen Documents of Vatican Council II,* Austin Flannery, OP, gen. ed., 385–401. Northport, NY: Costello, 1996.

Ratzinger, Josef, and Karl Rahner, SJ. *Episcopate and Primacy*. London: Burns & Oates, 1962.

Reed, Roy. "Alabama Police Use Gas and Clubs to Rout Negroes." *New York Times* (March 8, 1965).

Rolheiser, Ron, OMI. "On Carrying a Scandal Biblically." In *Seattle Theology and Ministry Review* 3 (2003) 97–106.

Rynne, Xavier. "Letter from Vatican City." *The New Yorker* (November 30, 1963) 144.

Schonberg, Wilfrid P., SJ. "Jesuits in Oregon." Sheridan, OR: St. Francis Xavier's Novitiate, 1930.

Shelley, Thomas J. "The Ellis Essay: 40 Years Later." *America* (June 3, 1995) 23–24.

Shelton, Charles M., SJ. "Reflections on the Mental Health of Jesuits." *Studies in the Spirituality of Jesuits* (September, 1991) 1–47.

Spadero, Antonio, SJ. "A Big Heart Open to God." *America* (September 20, 2003) 15–38.

Staunton, Brendan. "Fifty Years a Jesuit." *Interfuse* 158 (Winter 2014) 22–27.

Toner, Jules, SJ. *A Commentary on Saint Ignatius' Rules for the Discernment of Spirit*. St. Louis: Institute for Jesuit Sources, 1982.

Trautman, Donald, Bishop. "The New Missal Has Failed." *The Tablet*, blog (March 2015). https://www.thetablet.co.uk/blogs/1/603/the-new-missal-has-failed.

Tylenda, Joseph, SJ. "Commentary." In *A Pilgrim's Journey: the Autobiography of Ignatius of Loyola*, 113. Collegeville, MN: Liturgical, 1985.

USA 2017: Catalog of the Provinces of the United States. Washington, DC: Jesuit Conference, 2017.

Van Hollebeke, Monda. *Jebbie: A Life of John P. Leary, S.J.* Seattle, WA: Tekelectric, 1987.

Wills, Garry. *Bare Ruined Choirs*. Garden City, NY: Doubleday, 1971.

Index